SLOW TRA

New Forest

Local, characterful guides to Britain's special places

Emily Laurence Baker

EDITION 2

Bradt Guides Ltd, UK
The Globe Pequot Press Inc, USA

Second edition published July 2023
First published April 2013
Bradt Guides Ltd
31a High Street, Chesham, Buckinghamshire, HP5 1BW, England
www.bradtguides.com
Print edition published in the USA by The Globe Pequot Press Inc,
PO Box 480, Guilford, Connecticut 06437-0480

Text copyright © 2023 Bradt Guides Ltd
Maps copyright © 2023 Bradt Guides Ltd; includes map data © OpenStreetMap contributors
Photographs copyright © 2023 Individual photographers (see below)
Project Manager: Emma Gibbs
Cover research: Pepi Bluck, Perfect Picture

The author and publisher have made every effort to ensure the accuracy of the information
in this book at the time of going to press. However, they cannot accept any responsibility
for any loss, injury or inconvenience resulting from the use of information contained in this
guide. All rights reserved. No part of this publication may be reproduced, stored in a retrieval
system, or transmitted in any form or by any means, electronic, mechanical, photocopying,
recording or otherwise without the prior consent of the publisher.

ISBN: 9781804690482

British Library Cataloguing in Publication Data
A catalogue record for this book is available from the British Library

Photographs
Individual photographers credited beside images & also those from picture libraries credited
as follows: Alamy.com (A); Dreamstime.com (DT); Shutterstock.com (S)

Front cover New Forest moorland and ponies (Adam Burton/A)
Back cover Buckler's Hard (Beataaldridge/DT)
Title page Autumn colours at Highland Water Inclosure (Go New Forest)

Maps David McCutcheon FBCart.S

Typeset by Ian Spick
Production managed by Zenith Media; printed in the UK
Digital conversion by www.dataworks.co.in

AUTHOR

American-born **Emily Laurence Baker** has lived in England for 32 years, dividing her time between London and the New Forest. Her articles on numerous topics have been published in *The New York Times*, *Financial Times*, *The Wall Street Journal Europe*, *The Washington Post*, *The Guardian*, the *Daily Telegraph*, *The Sunday Times*, and many other publications. She's also written the London edition of *City Walks with Kids* for Chronicle Books. In London, she is a qualified Blue Badge tourist guide, taking visitors and locals on literary and historic walks, as well as exploring royal palaces and London's grand churches. Her website is ⊘ emilylaurencebaker.com and she can be found on Instagram ⬚ emilylaurencebaker1.

AUTHOR'S STORY

I didn't love the Forest when I first moved here. I had hoped to live on the coast but couldn't find anything suitable. The house search gradually moved inland and my husband and I fell hopelessly in love with a cob cottage (which I later realised was akin to living in a sandcastle), where ponies poke their heads over the gate to see if there is anything better on our side and cows plod past on their way to the heath for a drink.

When I began to write this book I realised that I had been living on the Forest's periphery for many years – emotionally anyway. I rushed to work, rushed to children's activities, rush, rush, right on past the glories of this extraordinary landscape. As much as I enjoyed cycling and walking deep in the woods and out in the windy heaths, and the animals that stop traffic and meander down the high street, I didn't truly love the Forest until I understood its complexities.

I couldn't begin to love this land until I got to know the people who maintain it, those whose passion for the Forest and understanding of its origins help keep it as magical as when the earliest commoners grazed their animals here. Only when I understood the intricacies of this 'mosaic of habitats' as the professionals call it, could I fully appreciate how remarkable the diversity is within this relatively small area. You can still find yourself alone in the silence of woodland, heath or saltmarshes. I'm delighted to live in a place where I'm often forced to stop because a herd of cows has convened in the middle of the road.

ACKNOWLEDGEMENTS

I've been so impressed with the passion people feel for the Forest and I thank them for sharing their personal views with me. I hope I have conveyed their messages accurately. I dedicate this book to the inspiring people who in turn dedicate their lives to ensuring that the New Forest lives on. A few special acknowledgements to those who really made a difference with the writing of this book, beginning with my husband, Shu-Ming, for his endless patience and support and without whom I might have given up. And to Forest friends old and new: Andy Shore and Dave Dibden for showing me I live too fast; Richard Reeves for his warmth, humour and astounding knowledge; Ian and Tracy Thew for their warm hospitality; Sam Lewis for showing me another way; Marcus Ward and Russell Wynn for their tireless dedication to the Forest; Neil and Pauline McCulloch; Pete White; Tom Hordle for (still!) inspiring me; Jonathan Gerrelli; Erica Dovey; Andrew Parry-Norton; Dylan Everett; Sarah Oakley; Pete Durnell; Lawrence Shaw; Andy Page; Derek Tippetts; Brice Stratford; Henry Cole; Tom Baynham; Paul Girling; and Catherine Chatters. An extra big thank you to the inspirational James Aldred, whose perspective from the treetops helped me love the Forest even more. Thank you for finding the time to talk to me.

And to the incredibly warm, friendly and positive group at Bradt, for their hard work and professionalism. Thank you to Claire Strange for enabling me to tell the Forest story, and, most especially, enormous thank yous to the meticulous, and eternally positive, team of Anna Moores and Emma Gibbs, for their extreme patience, encouragement and for making my work better.

CONTENTS

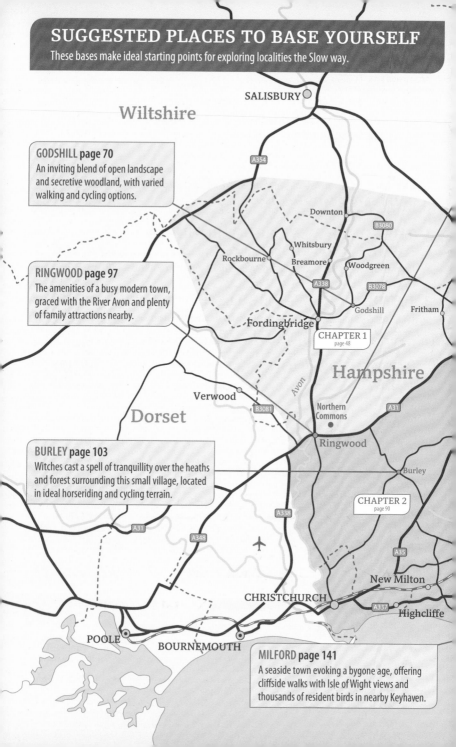

SUGGESTED PLACES TO BASE YOURSELF

These bases make ideal starting points for exploring localities the Slow way.

SALISBURY

Wiltshire

GODSHILL page 70
An inviting blend of open landscape and secretive woodland, with varied walking and cycling options.

RINGWOOD page 97
The amenities of a busy modern town, graced with the River Avon and plenty of family attractions nearby.

Downton

Whitsbury
Rockbourne   Breamore
Woodgreen

Godshill   Fritham

Fordingbridge

CHAPTER 1
page 48

Hampshire

Verwood

Dorset

Northern
Commons

Ringwood

BURLEY page 103
Witches cast a spell of tranquillity over the heaths and forest surrounding this small village, located in ideal horseriding and cycling terrain.

Burley

CHAPTER 2
page 90

New Milton

CHRISTCHURCH
Highcliffe

POOLE
BOURNEMOUTH

MILFORD page 141
A seaside town evoking a bygone age, offering cliffside walks with Isle of Wight views and thousands of resident birds in nearby Keyhaven.

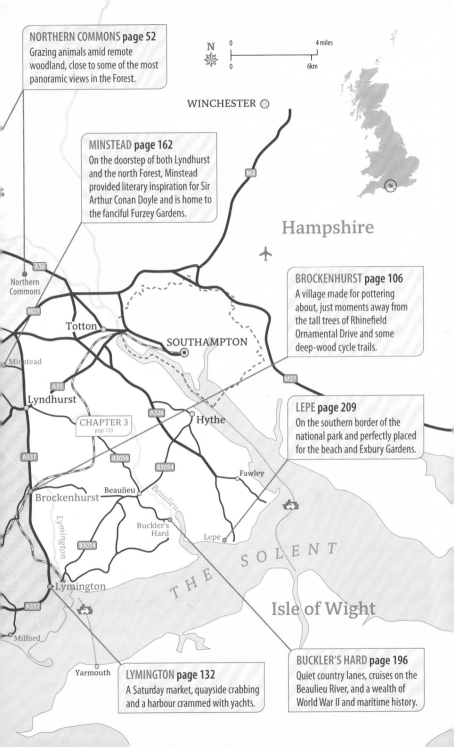

NORTHERN COMMONS page 52
Grazing animals amid remote woodland, close to some of the most panoramic views in the Forest.

N 0 — 4 miles
0 — 6km

WINCHESTER ○

MINSTEAD page 162
On the doorstep of both Lyndhurst and the north Forest, Minstead provided literary inspiration for Sir Arthur Conan Doyle and is home to the fanciful Furzey Gardens.

Hampshire

M3

✈

BROCKENHURST page 106
A village made for pottering about, just moments away from the tall trees of Rhinefield Ornamental Drive and some deep-wood cycle trails.

A36

Northern
Commons

M27

Totton

SOUTHAMPTON

Minstead

A35

Lyndhurst

CHAPTER 3
page 150

A326

Hythe

M27

LEPE page 209
On the southern border of the national park and perfectly placed for the beach and Exbury Gardens.

A337

B3056

B3054

Fawley

Brockenhurst — Beaulieu

Beaulieu

Lymington

Buckler's
Hard

Lepe

B3054

T H E   S O L E N T

Lymington

A337

Isle of Wight

Milford

Yarmouth

LYMINGTON page 132
A Saturday market, quayside crabbing and a harbour crammed with yachts.

BUCKLER'S HARD page 196
Quiet country lanes, cruises on the Beaulieu River, and a wealth of World War II and maritime history.

KONMAC/S

DEREK TIPPETTS

GOING SLOW IN
THE NEW FOREST

With the free-roaming animals often halting traffic on Forest roads, the New Forest is almost 'Slow' by definition. It's not a big area, and savouring it slowly is the best way to appreciate its many distinctive qualities. The main things to do in the Forest are Slow in character: walking, cycling, horseriding, birdwatching – at the risk of sounding trite, it's all about nature. Even most of the attractions highlighted here relate in some way to natural surroundings. It's an easy place to literally walk off the beaten path. There are so many trails throughout the Forest and it doesn't really matter if you veer off one and aren't quite sure where you are. My happiest hours have been when I don't know where I am and have discovered a new corner of the Forest that subsequently becomes a favourite spot.

That said, the Forest can be disorientating. Anyone doing serious walking should have an Ordnance Survey Explorer map OL22 and a good pair of waterproof boots. Dry ground in the New Forest can quickly become a sodden mass or thick mud; this is not the place to walk in sandals or delicate trainers.

Beware of using satnav. One of the great delights of the Forest from a Slow perspective is that your internet and data-dependent gadgets won't work in many parts of the Forest. And plugging in postcodes to guide you where you are going? Sometimes that takes you to an entirely different place than you intended. I have found the app what3words (a geocode system designed to find locations based on three fixed words) to be the most reliable for getting where I'm going.

As much as the book is designed to help newcomers enjoy the Forest, I hope its contents will inspire residents and regular visitors to

◀ 1 An old traditional pub in Lyndhurst. 2 Red stag bellowing during rut.

THE SLOW MINDSET

Hilary Bradt, Founder, Bradt Travel Guides

**We shall not cease from exploration
And the end of all our exploring
Will be to arrive where we started
And know the place for the first time.**
T S Eliot, 'Little Gidding', *Four Quartets*

This series evolved, slowly, from a Bradt editorial meeting when we started to explore ideas for guides to our favourite part of the world – Great Britain. We wanted to get away from the usual 'top sights' formula and encourage our authors to bring out the nuances and local differences that make up a sense of place – such things as food, building styles, nature, geology, or local people and what makes them tick. Our aim was to create a series that celebrates the present, focusing on sustainable tourism, rather than taking a nostalgic wallow in the past.

So without our realising it at the time, we had defined 'Slow Travel', or at least our concept of it. For the beauty of the Slow movement is that there is no fixed definition; we adapt the philosophy to fit our individual needs and aspirations. Thus Carl Honoré, author of *In Praise of Slow*, writes: 'The Slow Movement is a cultural revolution against the notion that faster is always better. It's not about doing everything at a snail's pace, it's about seeking to do everything at the right speed. Savouring the hours and minutes rather than just counting them. Doing everything as well as possible, instead of as fast as possible. It's about quality over quantity in everything from work to food to parenting.' And travel.

So take time to explore. Don't rush it, get to know an area – and the people who live there – and you'll be as delighted as the authors by what you find.

look beneath the surface of this remarkable location. It wasn't until I started writing this book that I began to take guided walks offered by organisations and individuals and realised how much I'd been missing and how little I really knew about the Forest.

Specialised walks can make the perfect introduction to the Forest. I am not a birdwatcher and was intimidated by my first birdwatching foray when everyone turned up in khaki gear with binoculars strapped to their belts. But in the Slow sense, there is no better way to see the Forest than standing quietly in hopes of spotting a rare winged creature. 'Most of us don't have time to walk this slowly through the Forest, and you wouldn't do it if you weren't here for this purpose,' said a fellow participant on a bird walk. Instead of stomping across heathland, I learned to look from the ground up by examining tiny flowers on the edge of paths or gently lifting bracken to be rewarded with a bright pink wild orchid. A walk on one topic will lead to you learning a surprising amount about all aspects of the Forest – because everything is interdependent.

I was fortunate to spend time with many people whose families have been here for generations. They are at one with the Forest, partly because it is almost in their blood but also because they pass through slowly. Andy Shore, the Forest keeper at Bolderwood, said it best: 'As soon as you move fast, you miss things. If you're in a car, you see less than if you're on a bike. If you're on a bike, you see less than if you walk.' I suspect that he would add that you ought to just stand still every so often: stand still and listen to the Forest around you.

THE NEW FOREST NATIONAL PARK

As an area, the New Forest encompasses about 92,000 acres. The national park, however, is slightly larger. The Forest itself and some of its surrounding area was designated a national park in 2005 after months of public inquiry and hearings to determine the exact boundaries; the park now encompass some 220 square miles, stretching from the edge of the Wiltshire chalk downs in the north to the Solent coast in the south, the Avon Valley in the west and across to Southampton Water in the east. This is Britain's smallest national park but also the most densely populated. Some 38,000 people live within its borders. Towns are within its confines, as are remote heathland and woodland. This book doesn't stick to the park exclusively but strays a few miles beyond it where appropriate.

One day as I walked across the windswept expanse of Beaulieu Heath, located well within the New Forest border, a group of walkers stopped me and asked where the New Forest was. I was, of course, puzzled – until I realised that they expected to find a giant woodland and their definition of 'forest' didn't include the great swatches of grassy lawn, heath and bog from which they had just extricated themselves.

'New Forest' is a misnomer in modern terms. There are, of course, woodlands – both ancient and ornamental – comprising oak, beech, and holly, as well as conifer inclosures planted largely for timber harvesting. The term 'forest', however, dates from a time when the word meant

USEFUL WEBSITES

Forestry England ⊘ forestry.gov.uk/newforest. All-encompassing, with guided walks and visitor information, including campsites and history.

Go New Forest ⊘ thenewforest.co.uk. A community interest company that manages tourism for the national park. Commercially orientated, with current events and online accommodation booking.

Go New Forest Card ⊘ card.gonewforest.com. Offers discounts at hotels, restaurants and attractions in the New Forest National Park.

New Forest Commoners Defence Association ⊘ realnewforest.org. Volunteer organisation that defends commoners and their animals. Excellent resource for understanding commoners' work and lifestyle.

New Forest Knowledge ⊘ nfknowledge.org. Collaborative website from New Forest Heritage Centre and the National Park Authority (NPA) with historic and current information on people, places and processes within the Forest.

New Forest National Park Authority ⊘ newforestnpa.gov.uk. Excellent for general background and for walking routes on its app.

Real New Forest Guide ⊘ newforestguide.uk. An independent, well-researched website that offers excellent background, history and outdoor activities. Particularly good for info on conservation and wildlife.

Visit Hampshire ⊘ visit-hampshire.co.uk. Good for suggestions of attractions and activities, particularly if you are visiting other locations in Hampshire.

something else altogether. When William the Conqueror claimed this area for his private hunting ground in 1079 (his boundaries were in fact larger) the word 'forest' meant tracts of land reserved for the king and his barons to hunt rather than wooded land. 'New' is a relative description, but to William it was his personal 'Nova Foresta'.

What the Beaulieu Heath walkers didn't realise is that only about 23% of the Forest is woodland in the modern sense of the word. Nearly 50% of the Forest is termed 'open forest', meaning unenclosed woodland, bogs and wet heath; heathland and lawn. The co-existence of these very rare habitats is extremely unusual and fosters a huge diversity of species.

But the New Forest's distinction doesn't stop there. This is also one of the last places where pastoral management, meaning the exercising of 'common rights' of animal grazing to maintain the landscape, continues. The ponies and cattle that wander the land are more than just a pretty rural feature; they, and the commoners who own them, work to keep the open Forest as it is for the rest of us to enjoy. The grazing practices here ensure that a complex network of natural habitats thrives. Nothing like this exists on such a large scale anywhere else in western Europe.

Perhaps the most prized feature of the Forest is that the public is, by and large, free to wander. The roughly 130 car parks managed by Forestry England are, at the moment, free and convenient for the huge number of walking trails (beware that parking on verges or in front of gates is likely to result in a ticket). Minimal signage is deliberate in an effort to maintain the natural appearance of the area. But that 'hands-off' management style gives visitors extra responsibilities. The Forest is a working environment, for commoners tending their stock, animals grazing the land, conservationists protecting rare habitats of flora and fauna, and for harvesters of timber, all of whom need to be treated with respect.

This is becoming increasingly important as visitor numbers increase. It might sound odd to preface a book that encourages people to come to the Forest with a simultaneous warning about the harm they can cause. But it's critical to tread carefully and not view the New Forest as a giant playground for human recreational activity; we are beholden to the Forest and its intricate workings. The New Forest code (⬦ newforestnpa. gov.uk/visiting/help-care-for-the-forest/new-forest-code) should not be taken lightly: enjoy the animals from a distance, park only in car parks, drive slowly while looking out for animals, and don't leave anything behind.

The people of the Forest are as important as its natural wonders. My conversations with those who live and breathe this landscape are included in this book in the hope that readers' experiences will be enriched and that they will be inspired to protect and care for this extraordinary place.

A NEW FOREST MISCELLANY

Here I include a selection of Forest cameos to set the scene about what makes this area exceptional.

FURTHER READING

As a long-time resident of the New Forest, I have a substantial library of books on the region. The four listed below are those that I feel capture the essence of the Forest best.

Aldred, James, *Goshawk Summer: A New Forest Season Unlike Any Other* (Elliott & Thompson, 2021). Wildlife cameraman James Aldred was commissioned to film a family of goshawks in the New Forest when lockdown hit (see below). His observations from a treetop hideaway while the Forest was devoid of humans are magical, and his descriptions of the Forest adapting to the return of human are sobering. Excellent for instilling a Forest frame of mind.

Stratford, Brice, *New Forest Myths and Folklore* (The History Press Ltd., 2022). To understand the Forest as old-time residents do, you need to appreciate the myths and legends that have grown up among the landscape. Brice Stratford is passionate about these tales and communicates them well.

Sumner, Heywood, *Cuckoo Hill: The Book of Gorley* (J M Dent & Sons, 1987) In his mid 40s, the English Arts and Crafts painter, Heywood Sumner, bought land near Fordingbridge and built a house, known as Cuckoo Hill. In 1910 he published an account of his adjustment to rural life and descriptions of the local landscape. This splendid republication is illustrated with his watercolour paintings.

Wise, John R, *The New Forest: Its History and its Scenery* (Smith, Elder and Co., 1863; numerous reprinted editions). This is the classic book on history, folklore and general Forest heritage. It's surprising how relevant some of the descriptions are today.

VIEW FROM THE TREETOPS

James Aldred, an Emmy-winning natural history cameraman who specialises in filming from tree canopies in the rainforest and other remote wildernesses around the world, grew up in the New Forest. During the Covid lockdown of 2020, James witnessed life from a treetop deep in the Forest, while filming the documentary, *The New Forest: The Crown's Hunting Ground*. He watched and filmed a nest of goshawks from his tiny hide some 50ft above ground, and also witnessed lots of other wildlife, including humans, after lockdown lifted. His memoir, *Goshawk Summer*, provides an unusual look at what happens in the Forest when we are not there, plus a dramatic perspective on how the Forest copes with its abundance of visitors.

I was lucky enough to chat to James about his experiences, and asked him if anything surprised him about the Forest from his birds'-eye view.

'I'm always surprised, relieved and reassured by how little the Forest changes between my visits,' James told me. 'I think this is one of the truly unique things about it – that I can still sit on the same fallen tree trunks I sat on many years ago and still find badgers where I used to watch them as a child. It has a timeless quality that is especially unusual in these times of rapid change in other places.'

James's unique vantage point during Lockdown offered an unparalleled vision of how the Forest might be if there weren't so many human visitors and a sobering insight into our influence. 'I got the impression that the absence of people during lockdown became accepted by the natural world very quickly. There was a shifting base line of normality, largely due to the fact that lockdown happened during springtime, so there were a lot of newly fledged birds and young mammals that had no prior experiences of human beings. But this meant that there was a sense of naivety among the newborn animals and birds that could never last once lockdown was lifted. The panicked flight and desperate calls of ground-nesting curlew and lapwing disturbed and chased by unruly dogs and off-road cyclists, made for particularly poignant examples, as did dead fox cubs lying on the previously empty roads.'

In his book, James describes his fears of treating this landscape as 'domesticated parkland' and he told me that he feels we ask too much of our wild spaces, thus putting them under intense pressure. I asked him how people could get the most out of their visits to the Forest. 'A little respect for the needs of the wildlife that we share the Forest with goes a long way,' he said. 'All animals – including us – require space and time to be themselves away from obligation to others. I believe that time spent sitting quietly on one's own in natural environments, away from the distractions of modern living, helps maintain a vital sense of perspective and personal balance. I also believe it helps increase self-awareness, confidence and personal contentment, while also encouraging empathy for other beings, whether they be human or not.'

COMMONING

Commoners are landowners who hold ancient rights to the New Forest as common land and who collectively manage the terrain by grazing animals on the open Forest. This system of land management is as old as the Forest and the Rights of Common even pre-date William the Conqueror's afforestation.

Common rights were granted to a property, not a person. Certain homes within the Forest (and some outside) still hold these ancient rights. The most commonly practised one today is keeping animals, including ponies, cattle, donkeys, and in some cases, sheep and pigs, that roam freely on Forest land.

'The Forest would be inaccessible without commoners grazing animals,' explained Andrew Parry-Norton from his 1,500 acre farm near Cadnam. 'It helps maintain the landscape. Without commoners, someone would have to manually cut the grass, and many wildflowers wouldn't be able to grow.'

Commoning is as much about the cultural heritage of the Forest as it is about the animals. Many families have worked together for generations, as is the case with Andrew, who is a fourth-generation farmer at Storm's Farm, where, together with his wife, Sarah, he raises cows, pigs, chickens and ducks. He grew up on this land, as his father did before him.

Sadly, commoning today is rarely financially viable as a full-time living, with the exception of commoners like Andrew, who run very large farms. 'Commoning has changed dramatically in the last 30 to 40 years,' said Andrew. 'When I was a child, every farm in the area was a full-time proposition; many supported two to three families. Now it's more likely that commoners are part-time and have a day job to support themselves.'

"Without commoners, someone would have to manually cut the grass, and many wildflowers wouldn't be able to grow."

Most commoners – many of whom work for Forestry England as their main job – continue to graze animals to retain the tradition and social core of this very private community (and, of course, the Forest itself).

Outside forces threaten the practice of commoning, particularly the large number of visitors to the Forest and the rise in housing prices. When people buy homes with commoning rights and choose not to exercise them or keep grazing animals as pets, the traditional system begins to break down. Because non-commoners and visitors often perceive the Forest as place for recreation rather than a working environment, there is an inevitable clash in perspective on land usage.

'To graze animals on the Forest, a commoner must have enough back-up land for when stock needs to be removed from the Forest, such as when animals are ill or when there is a national incident like foot and mouth disease,' Andrew explained. 'Many farms have been bought up by people who didn't grow up in the Forest, and who use the land for stables and paddocks for riding ponies. This drives up land prices and makes it prohibitive for commoners to remove their animals from the Forest when necessary.'

Despite assurances from the National Park Authority to protect the commoning way of life, many commoners are gloomy about future prospects. But Andrew is optimistic. Although he laments the loss of the traditional commoning lifestyle, he is pragmatic about these deep-rooted changes that accelerated when the New Forest became a national park. 'Visitors are not going away,' he said. 'Commoners can no longer look back at how the Forest used to be but need to look forward and change with the times so that everyone can work together to maintain it. We have a huge responsibility to get things in place for future generations.'

Many people credit the stubbornness and tenacity that seems to be an integral personality trait of commoners for their survival. 'They don't like change and they'll fight to keep everything the way it has always been,' one senior Forest manager told me. 'But that's precisely the quality that keeps the system going.'

The Parry-Nortons deliver meat, eggs, chicken, burgers, game and even Sunday Roast boxes all around the Forest from their farm shop, The Commoners Larder (✆ 02380 813479; ⬧ thecommonerslarder. co.uk). They also welcome visitors to Storm's Farm.

RIGHTS OF COMMON PRACTISED TODAY

Some ancient privileges that are attached to certain properties in the Forest, like **marl**, which once allowed commoners to dig clay rich in fossil shells to improve soil, are no longer practised. The rights most likely to be exercised today are:

Estovers While this is technically the right to take firewood from the Forest, these days commoners with this right are provided with stacks of firewood from Forestry England timber plantations.

Pannage Also known as the right of mast, this is the right to turn pigs out on to the open Forest during the pannage season in autumn.

Pasture The right to graze livestock, usually ponies and cattle, on the open Forest. Some properties also have the right to graze pigs and/or sheep.

GUARDIANS OF THE FOREST: THE AGISTERS

'People visit the Forest and think that it's just here, on its own, existing all by itself. In fact there is a whole system at work with commoning at the core,' Jonathan Gerrelli, head Agister and foreman to a team of five, told me. 'One of the biggest misconceptions about the Forest is that the animals you see on the heaths and among gorse bushes are wild. They are in the sense that they graze the land, but they all belong to someone and are carefully looked after.'

It's easy to catch a glimpse of Agisters driving their Land Rovers on Forest roads or patrolling the Forest on horseback. Their job is to assist commoners (page 15) in looking after their 'stock': primarily ponies, cows and donkeys. Agisters are appointed and employed by Verderers, members of the ancient court that protect their rights and other groups who oversee the management of the Forest.

Agisters know the Forest intimately because their daily remit is to comb the land and look out for ponies and cattle that need assistance or to be moved because of changing land conditions. These officials are on-call all day, every day, which can mean being called out in the middle of the night for an emergency, usually a pony that has been hit by a car.

Born in the Forest, Jonathan keeps cattle and ponies, as do all Agisters. Like all commoners, he is concerned about the future. Rising land prices, a growing number of outsiders settling in the area, and increasingly diverse user interest groups in the Forest all threaten this ancient system of land management. As visitor numbers have steadily increased, much of Jonathan's job now is liaising with the public. His easy-going charm and ability to deal with all types of people makes him a good ambassador but you can't help but think that he's happiest out in the Forest working with animals and commoners.

One of the busiest times of year is autumn when stock is rounded up. Ponies are herded into pounds located around the Forest where Agisters check their health and worm them, and brand any foals that are to remain in the Forest. They also collect marking fees from commoners and cut the tails of ponies to indicate that fees have been paid. The procedure derives from a medieval custom when fees were collected from 'strangers' who wanted to graze animals but had no right to do so. Agisters also have the authority to ask a commoner to remove a pony that they feel at any time of year is unhealthy. The animal is then taken from the Forest until it is deemed well enough to return.

The romantic notion of the Agister riding around on his horse all day saving the Forest isn't completely true to life. There is a lot of paperwork involved and a number of unexpected surprises. 'Often I'll plan to go out on my horse and examine the stock and the land and then the phone goes with someone telling me there is a mare stuck in a ditch or someone needs help rounding up cattle,' said Jonathan. 'But that's one of the things I really like about my job – I never know exactly what the day holds.'

And when he does finally get out on his horse to make the rounds, the frustrations of the job balance out with the joys. 'When I'm riding out across the Forest and I see a bunch of ponies, that's when I think I'm lucky to get paid to do what I love.'

PONIES

Since medieval times, ponies have grazed the Forest, and still appear in certain villages today. Two things about the Forest's roughly 4,500 ponies need to be clarified. First of all, they aren't horses. And secondly, they aren't wild; all ponies are owned by commoners (page 15). When you see what seems to be a well-mowed grassy lawn, it's actually that way because ponies very helpfully tidy the grass and keep brush growth under control in the open Forest.

New Forest ponies are by nature sociable and mild-mannered. But sometimes their peaceful existence is threatened by humans, who mean well by stroking them or feeding them when in fact these actions can lead to their removal from the Forest.

'The worst thing a visitor can do is feed a pony and yet it happens all the time,' said Jonathan Gerrelli, head Agister. 'Ponies learn quickly that humans mean an easy source of food. So by the end of the summer, they may approach people and possibly become aggressive in pursuit of a snack. Then visitors complain and that pony may have to be removed from the Forest.' As tempting as it is to approach them, the kindest action is to leave them alone.

Some ponies wander and graze freely in the Forest for their whole lives. Others are used for breeding or sold at auction (page 172) to become family riding ponies. Efforts to 'improve' the breed were undertaken hundreds of years ago and continue today. Stallions are kept in paddocks for most of the year until spring when a select number are released on to the Forest for breeding. Verderers carefully choose and monitor the stallions from a stock of about 30; the number that are put out depends on the existing pony population.

After years serving as 'architects of the Forest,' ponies have adapted to their environment with rough tongues that enable them to eat a prickly winter diet of heather and gorse, a surefootedness to dance across mires and bogs, and a hardy constitution to stand out in wind, rain and cold without the blankets worn by their paddocked cousins.

AN UNEASY BALANCE: TOURISM & THE FOREST

There is a lot of disagreement within the New Forest about how land should be managed, how to control recreational users, and the implementation of environmental initiatives. But the one sentiment that is uniformly echoed among Forest leaders, conservationists and commoners is that the greatest threat to the Forest's survival is tourists.

'The huge number of people who come to enjoy the Forest may unwittingly destroy the very landscape they have come to see,' said Jonathan Gerrelli, head Agister. It is not just the roughly 15 million people who come here each year, which is maximum capacity now, but also the ways in which they interfere. 'Visitors don't realise how one seemingly innocent action can undermine the whole system at work. A commoner can spend three hours rounding up cattle and someone comes along with their dog which divides them, and there goes a whole half-day work. For those who do this in addition to a nine-to-five job, that's especially frustrating.'

"When you see what seems to be a well-mowed grassy lawn, it's actually that way because ponies very helpfully tidy the grass."

Jonathan and other Forest leaders worry that the Forest is not robust enough to cope with all the user interests that make demands on the landscape. 'One cyclist may not understand why it's a problem if they ride on unmarked trails, but they fail to consider that there are many more cyclists right behind them and the extreme numbers will ultimately damage the Forest irrevocably.'

It's not always tourists who don't understand Forest workings. Even some people who live here don't understand its intricate management system. 'It's all down to education,' Andrew Parry-Norton (page 16) told me. 'Commoners traditionally have been a reclusive group; it's almost as if they closed the drawbridge after themselves. But we need to engage and explain to people why walking their dog past a cow with a calf can be a dangerous idea because the cow might become aggressive.'

Andrew also believes that commoners need to engage with the tourism sector. 'Hotel and restaurant staff need to be educated too, so they can pass the message on to their customers. When people understand the intricacies of this working environment, they will treat the Forest with greater respect.'

There is no simple approach to tourist management and possible ideas range from charging in car parks to taxing campers or building in a voluntary donation to hotel bills. But any solutions to limiting visitor numbers are complicated by the fact that so many people live within National Park boundaries and require unlimited access – and some 16 million people live within a 90-minute drive of the Forest and visit regularly. At some point, certain areas may be designated for particular pursuits. 'Although it's wonderful to have so many people enjoying the Forest, visitors need to understand that this is a working forest and not just a playground,' said Jonathan.

WHO IS IN CHARGE

Anyone who has spent even a little bit of time in the Forest quickly realises that it can be a political hotbed. So many groups have a vested interest in this land that they often conflict and you'll hear a different perspective on the Forest depending on whom you talk to. It's very clear, however, that the many management groups all wish to preserve the Forest and the commoning system; the sticking points are usually in the details.

The National Park Authority (NPA) and Forestry England are the most visible organisations but neither owns any land. The NPA is an umbrella organisation that has authority for planning. Although initially many groups were opposed to the addition of another layer of management when the Forest became a national park in 2005, increased funding from having National Park status has benefited commoners and preservation efforts.

Forestry England manages 47% of Forest land on behalf of the Crown, which owns about 90% of the Forest. This traditionally meant overseeing commercial timber plantations but in more recent years the focus has turned to conservation. Forestry England manages most car parks and some campgrounds, employs rangers and conservationists, and has an impressive group of volunteer rangers who undergo a strict selection and training process. Other major organisations that own and/or manage land include the National Trust, Hampshire County Council and the Hampshire & Isle of Wight Wildlife Trust (HIWWT). The irony is that projects that benefit one part of the Forest or group sometimes inadvertently hurt another area or group interest. But you could also argue that the divergent voices are a positive, even if, frustrating, dynamic.

'There are lots of people who care about the Forest but come at it from different angles,' said Marcus Ward, co-director of Wild New Forest, a wildlife consultancy group that supports conservation in the New Forest. 'This is a positive time, though, because increasingly, all these specialist groups are working together better. People are realising we are much stronger together than we are separately.'

BUTTS, BOTTOMS & BALLS: A GLOSSARY

Sometimes it's hard to keep a straight face when reading a map of the New Forest. What follows is a brief guide to the meanings of some of the Forest's distinctive terms.

Agister Employed by the Verderers, the five Agisters are responsible for the welfare of New Forest ponies.

AONB Area of Outstanding Natural Beauty.

Balls Hills in the northwest of the Forest, such as in the holiday village of Sandy Balls, which is near an expanse of heathland called Burnt Balls. The term originated from sand and gravel outcrops during the reign of Henry VII.

Bog A type of mire that obtains most of its water from precipitation.

Bottom A valley. Examples are Longslade Bottom near Sway and (yes, really) Slap Bottom at Burley.

Butt A Bronze Age barrow (burial mound).

Commons Defined areas of land that are subject to Rights of Common.

Commoner A person exercising Rights of Common attached to property where they live.

Down Open heathland.

Furze An ancient term for an area of abundant gorse.

WAS THAT A PIG I SAW?

It can be odd enough to come to the New Forest for the first time and see ponies and donkeys at roadsides and in certain village streets, but there is nothing quite like the first time you encounter a pig snuffling around in the woods. Every year, for a short time in autumn, pigs are released in the Forest to munch on beech mast, chestnuts and, most importantly, acorns, all of which can be toxic to ponies and cattle. Pannage, as the practice is called, is one of the ancient Rights of Common (page 15) affiliated with certain Forest properties.

'Pigs are put out where there are a lot of oak trees because this is where ponies are in most danger,' explained Robert Maton, Agister for the Brockenhurst area. 'They can eat a lot of acorns, and that helps the ponies.'

Verderers determine when pannage will begin and end depending on how heavy the acorn crop is in any given year; according to ancient

---

Mire Wetland area dominated by peat-forming plants that arise from the incomplete decomposition of organic matter.

Hat A small area of woodland standing on its own, as in Little Standing Hat at Brockenhurst.

Purlieu Land on the edge of the Forest that was once included in the Royal Forest but later separated and is exempt from Forest law. Dibden Purlieu, once part of the ancient Forest, is now part of Hythe.

Rights of Common Ancient privileges that are attached to certain properties in and just outside the Forest; page 15.

Shade A place where animals rest but not, as the word suggests, in a sheltered spot. Usually refers to hilltops and open places relatively free of flies.

Verderer Any of ten officials who look after commoners' rights and Forest land use.

INCLOSURE VS ENCLOSURE

Even people who have spent their entire lives in the Forest argue over what these terms mean. Very simply, **inclosures** are places fenced off from grazing animals to protect trees for commercial timber harvesting. **Enclosures** result when private landowners have secured permission to close off land from commoning rights. The terms are increasingly used interchangeably.

law, it must be a minimum of 60 days. In years of heavy acorn fall, the pannage season is sometimes extended. The number of pigs put out ranges from 200 to 600 although that's a big decline from the 19th century when there would be as many as 5,000 or 6,000. The only place you see pigs all year round is near the Northern Commons (page 52), which were the original 'adjacent commons' of the New Forest and have slightly different guidelines.

When it comes time to rounding up pigs at the end of the season, it helps to know a bit about pig behaviour. 'Pigs don't rough it the way ponies do,' said Robert. 'After a day of foraging they like to find somewhere warm and cosy to sleep. If the owner lives on the Forest, the pigs often will go home to sleep and if not, they'll find an open barn or shelter.'

There have been stories in recent years about pigs behaving aggressively towards people. This is unlikely but not impossible. 'A sow with babies can be dangerous and very grumpy. Best just to treat them with respect and make a wide berth', said Robert.

And those trendy rings that the New Forest pigs wear in their snouts? Those are more than a fashion statement. They prevent pigs from digging deep into the ground and disrupting the Forest floor.

LIDAR: HIGH-TECH MOLE

As glorious and magical as the New Forest is above ground, there are remnants of a bygone world deep beneath our feet that reveal a lot about previous generations. In 2010, archaeologists began an enormous project to map archaeological features of the New Forest by using the revolutionary technology of Lidar (Light Detection and Ranging). The results have brought history to the surface by revealing Bronze Age burial mounds near Burley, an Iron Age fortified enclosure at Brockenhurst, and major World War II bombing targets and craters at Ashley Walk, among other findings.

'Lidar has revolutionised the way we look at how humans have shaped the landscape,' said Lawrence Shaw, Lead Historic Environment Adviser for Forestry England. 'Everyone talks about what a completely natural landscape the New Forest is but Lidar studies reveal that there is nothing natural at all. This land has been influenced by human decisions of land management – whether by grazing animals, quarrying or planting trees – from long before William the Conqueror made this his hunting ground.'

The researchers found evidence of Celtic Romano field systems across the Forest that show ancient people were trying to farm here, which would have been a difficult endeavour considering the naturally poor soil. 'From earliest times, the land here was less about agriculture and more of a resource for industrial uses like charcoal, clay and timber,' said Lawrence.

It's not all about archaeology though: researchers also have been able to identify ancient trees, old river systems, scrub growth and erosion. In this way, Lidar helps to ensure that ancient sites are not damaged during conservation work because ancient earthworks and veteran trees can be identified before any groundwork begins. 'Lidar was a huge help in water-course management in the New Forest,' said Lawrence. 'We were able to see the meandering courses of rivers before they were straightened for industrial purposes and this enabled us to restore them to how they originally were.'

The New Forest was the first national park in the UK to have its entire landscape surveyed by Lidar. The technology works by scanning a pulsed laser beam side to side from an aeroplane to map the ground below in three-dimensional high resolution. It can 'see through' all but the most dense vegetation like holly and conifer plantations to reveal the physical footprints on the ground surface that humans leave behind. 'There is an element of interpretation in understanding the mounds, cuts and bumps left by humans,' Lawrence told me. 'You are using shapes and formations to make an educated guess of how people lived.'

The findings aren't necessarily something the average person can go out and see on a walk, but the data certainly gives us something to muse on as we wander, and helps us to envision who might have been here before us. Lidar revealed a linear feature at Hampton Ridge that has been identified as a Roman road running from Cadnam to Fordingbridge. This ties in with evidence of Roman potteries that existed throughout the Forest, shards of which can still be found today.

Lidar also helps to visualise large tracts of land that would be difficult to comprehend without its aerial perspective. 'The scale of the World War II bombing targets at Ashley Walk is hard to comprehend on the ground but when you see the craters and mounds and targets from above, it all becomes clear,' said Lawrence.

The 3D maps are stored at the Historic Environment Records office in Winchester where they are available to the public. You can also

view laser maps of the Forest and wartime heritage sites online at
⊘ newforestnpa.gov.uk/heritagemapping.

CLIMATE CHANGE: NEW FOREST WINNERS & LOSERS

It is no secret that Britain's climate is warming faster than other parts of the world and the predictions of hotter, drier summers and warmer, wetter winters are already visible. 'Climate change is one of the biggest threats to the survival of the New Forest as we know it today,' said Professor Russell Wynn. Russell, who tracks numerous species of birds, mammals, insects and trees in his research work as co-director of Wild New Forest, a wildlife consultancy, said that there is a delicate balance of winners and losers within the New Forest as conditions change. 'The winners of climate change tend to be mobile species, those that can relocate,' he told me. 'So we are already seeing moths and insects here from southern Europe that you wouldn't traditionally see in the New Forest.'

Even if you are an insect-phobe, that's good news because moths play a huge role in supporting a diverse ecosystem by pollinating flowers and helping seed production, as well as serving as a barometer for the health of the environment.

Climate change losers tend to be those species that are immobile, for example the fantastic bearded tooth fungus, which already is extremely rare in the New Forest but which Russell fears might be extinct before too long. He also worries that beech trees, a hallmark of the Forest, may disappear completely as they struggle to cope with increased summer droughts that dry out their roots and then make them vulnerable during the increasingly high winds of winter. There has already been an increased number of fallen trees of all varieties in recent years.

'Of course we know that the climate is warming gradually overall but it's the extreme climate events that will make the New Forest suffer most, from drought to intense rainfall,' he explained.

Climate change is also affecting the birds we see in the Forest. Severe drops in populations of various types of warblers have made Russell concerned that these birds could be headed for extinction here. 'The

1 Foxglove flowers. 2 Avocet at Keyhaven Nature Reserve. 3 Pearl-bordered fritillary.
4 Male sand lizard. 5 Red fox. 6 Fungi: the New Forest is a haven for mycologists. ▶

ALLOUPHOTO/S

DEREK TIPPETTS

OLIS PICS/S

DEREK TIPPETTS

MICHAL NINGER/S

DEREK TIPPETTS

population of wood warblers has dropped by as much as 95% in just a decade,' said Russell. He speculates that this could be less about the environment in the New Forest and more about problems encountered on their migration route, perhaps extremely arid conditions in Spain.

On the brighter side, little egret are easy to spot in the New Forest now, as they have expanded their range, possibly due to warmer temperatures here. Spoonbills, which used to come to the Forest only for breeding, now spend the winter in places like Lymington-Keyhaven Nature Reserve.

All of these dramatic changes highlight the importance of the conservation work that takes place in the Forest. Russell and numerous other conservationists dedicate their lives to preserving this astounding landscape, not only so that we can enjoy it but so that it will live on and flourish. Supporting biodiversity is a catchphrase we hear everywhere but understanding its importance is easy to see within the relatively small, but spectacularly diverse, landscape of the New Forest.

ALIEN INVADERS

'Himalayan balsam was introduced to Britain in the 19th century as a decorative plant in the gardens of grand homes,' said Catherine Chatters, New Forest Non-Native Plants Officer at the Hampshire & Isle of Wight Wildlife Trust, as she bent down to pull out a sample. 'Now it has invaded rivers and other waters throughout the New Forest to the detriment of native species.'

I joined Catherine and her loyal band of volunteers for a day's session of balsam pulling in a damp woodland beside the Passford Water, a tributary of the Lymington River.

On that day, there were seven of us, all regulars except for me. The group, some of whom also volunteered for other Forest projects, were experienced and clearly devoted to Catherine and her mission to eliminate non-native species from the New Forest. 'Not only do non-native plants like balsam crowd out native ones but there can be economic issues down the line when plants invade structures. There can even sometimes be health issues, as with giant hogweed, which has a toxic sap that can cause burning blisters. So it's important we get them out.'

The New Forest Non-Native Plants Project began in 2009 to stop the spread of invasive non-native species in the New Forest area, particularly along river valleys and in wetland habitats. It is hosted by HIWWT and supported by many other organisations. And it's made tremendous progress. Since I met Catherine and her loyal army of volunteers on that day, Himalayan balsam has been successfully removed so that an array of native woodland flowers, including bluebells, now grow in its place.

The project initially focused on five invasive plants, including the balsam, giant hogweed and Japanese knotweed, but has since moved on to others, including parrot's feather, cotoneaster, and three-cornered garlic.

Not all foreign species were introduced in Victorian times – many are more recent takeovers. Harmful plants can be introduced carelessly by people who are clearing ponds or gardens and dump the waste in the Forest, where it takes root. Catherine emphasises the importance of disposing of garden waste in designated sites. Non-native plants can also appear in the Forest because birds have carried seeds or they have floated downriver from private ponds.

In 2021, Catherine was awarded a British Empire Medal for her services to biosecurity – but I'm guessing she is even more gratified by viewing the flourishing bluebells and red campion at the Cadnam River, where five years previously Himalyan balsam had towered.

RESTORING NATURAL HABITATS: MIRES & HEATHLAND

'They are the unsung heroes of the Forest,' said Sarah Oakley, an ecologist at Forestry England , as we surveyed an extensive stretch of mires at Denny Bog, near Beaulieu Road Station. 'Mires work like sponges and are critical to how water is stored and distributed throughout the Forest. But they are extremely fragile.'

The New Forest National Park has 75% of northwestern Europe's valley mires – areas of permanently waterlogged soil in shallow valley bottoms. In their natural state, water moves slowly through valley mires. Over hundreds and thousands of years, the accumulations of sphagnum mosses – that live there in permanently waterlogged conditions – gradually turn into peat. Drainage and development has caused mires to decline in other parts of England, making the New Forest one of the most important sites for this rare habitat. 'New Forest mires are among the most pristine in Europe but they too have shrunk,' said Sarah.

Many New Forest wetlands decreased in size with the progressive increase in drainage across the Forest. This ramped up in the 1850s and continued until the 1970s when ditches were dug to contain water in channels, speed up drainage and, in theory, improve or create better grazing for stock. 'Unfortunately, even when you dig a drain further down in the valley, the damage of headward erosion goes back up into the mire. The water table is progressively lowered through the whole system,' explained Sarah.

In the late 1990s, work began to restore New Forest wetlands that had been drained, aiming to improve the condition of streams and mires here, which are internationally protected habitats. The wetland restoration project is part of a larger, long-term plan to return the Forest to a more natural state in balance with nature. Sarah is also involved with restoring some conifer plantation areas to heathland, another key habitat that stores carbon and reduces the amount of carbon dioxide released into the atmosphere.

'The ground tells you what it wants to be,' said Sarah. 'As we clear the conifer plantations that were planted for timber, we can see heather emerging, which shows the land naturally wants to be heathland.'

The timing is right; as the effects of the climate crisis have intensified, the New Forest's lowland heathland, the most extensive heathland remaining in Europe, plays an even more important role in combatting climate change by storing carbon. 'People can find it confusing that we are removing trees at a time when the popular narrative is all about planting trees,' said Sarah. 'But as people realise the important role the New Forest can play as a carbon sink, the more they understand how essential this work is.'

Sarah is confident about the future. 'It's an exciting time for the Forest,' she said. 'People who work here have seen benefits of our conservation efforts and more people are joining together to restore the Forest.'

A SIGN OF LOCAL QUALITY: THE NEW FOREST MARQUE

'Local' has become such a buzzword that its meaning is often distorted but the New Forest Marque (newforestmarque.co.uk) is a genuine means of identifying local produce. It is a scheme supported by the National Park Authority to help local producers stand out in the marketplace.

In order to secure a marque, producers must meet stringent standards relevant to their specialty and their products must source at least 25% of their content or materials from the New Forest. Members include bakers and other food producers, craftspeople, butchers and farmers. Lodging and dining establishments also participate in the Marque scheme by buying and serving local produce from Marque members.

'The Marque scheme reassures the public of the provenance of their food,' said Andrew Parry-Norton (page 16) and member of the scheme. 'This educates consumers and tells the story behind the food they are eating, something that more and more people care about.' It also enables members to market their produce as a niche product and charge more for it. And that, in turn, benefits the Forest by keeping the ancient commoning practices alive.

WHEN FOREST FIRE IS A GOOD THING

It can be quite a shock to see fire spreading across heathland and disturbing to see the spindly black skeletons of gorse left behind, but controlled fires are a critical element of maintaining the New Forest. Every year between November and March, Forestry England burns about 2–3% of heathlands with about ten controlled burns each day.

'If we didn't practise controlled burning, heathland would revert to scrubby woodland and we'd lose the fragile habitat that we're trying to maintain,' said Dave Morris, Open Habitats Manager at Forestry England. Not only is burning essential for regenerating growth, it is also the main method of preventing birch and pine from taking hold.

"Now designated areas are burned on a roughly 25-year cycle, which actually invites greater diversity of species."

The lowland heath (characterized by gorse and heather) that is such a rare habitat globally and therefore so important to the New Forest, thrives in low-nutrient soil. Burning maintains that status. 'People get upset when they see the forest burning because they think we are destroying habitats haphazardly. But in fact there is a lengthy planning process that begins in the spring when we determine the next season's burning sites.' An area is deemed to be ready when emerging seedling trees of birch or pine appear, and when heather is getting to the end of its natural life cycle. The burning teams regularly assess ground conditions to ensure there is enough moisture so as not to damage peat and underlying layers. A fire break is made prior to the burning, using a cutting machine, to contain the fire.

Managed burning has been practised in the Forest for hundreds of years. It began as a means of clearing land but at some point commoners realised that regeneration was a by-product and produced a palatable food source for livestock. Now designated areas are burned on a roughly 25-year cycle, which actually invites greater diversity of species at different stages of regrowth.

Like most other aspects of Forest management, controlled burning has been influenced by environmental awareness. 'We select sites to burn based on when certain species inhabit a particular area. We burn about ten acres at a time whereas 60 years ago, before we understood about creating diverse habitats, as much as 120 acres were burned at one time,' explained Dave. The burning process is one of the best examples of integrated Forest management. For example, as gorse begins to regrow,

GHOSTS OF THE FOREST

If you ever find yourself alone in a dark, wooded corner of the New Forest, it's easy to imagine spooky beings crouched in the undergrowth of tall, ancient trees. Sometimes it feels as though the Forest has a life of its own, as if there is an entire world of supernatural beings flitting in and out of the spaces you can't quite see. Many Foresters believe wholeheartedly in pixies (page 33), so much so that they are an integral part of the Forest.

There are also many oft-repeated ghost stories and you can visit many of the associated places. One of the most famous stories concerns the murder of King William II, known as William Rufus (the Red King). The site is marked at the **Rufus Stone** (page 66) near Minstead. The less-well known aspect of this story is that after Rufus was shot, Sir Walter Tyrell washed his hands in nearby **Ocknell Pond** and fled to France. Some Foresters say that the pond turns red on 2 August each year, on the anniversary of William's death, and that Tyrell's dog appears as a death omen to the

unlucky few who glimpse it. Forest residents also claim that William's spirit haunts the trail taken by the cart that transported William's body to Winchester for burial.

There are some interior ghosts too. At the **Angel and Blue Pig pub** on Lymington High Street, guests in the bedroom next to the old ballroom swear to have heard enthusiastic piano music, while staff say they have seen the ghost of a former coachman who appears in the kitchen and awaits his free supper.

Not too far away, at **Hurst Castle** in Milford, the ghost of King Charles I supposedly wanders the grounds. He was imprisoned here before being sent to London for his beheading. And in the north Forest at **Braemore House**, there hangs a cursed painting. Two elderly sisters lived here during the 1600s, and the portrait of the elder one still hangs exactly where it did during their lifetimes, because the subject of the painting threatened to put a curse on anyone who moved it. In the 1950s, a cleaner did so and broke his leg in a fall later that day.

it provides ideal cover for the Dartford Warbler, one of Britain's smallest ground-nesting birds that is endangered.

NEW FOREST PIXIES

'When it comes to a surviving belief in pixies, Foresters remain apart,' said Brice Stratford, lifetime New Forest resident and author of *New Forest Myths and Folklore*. 'There is nowhere else in England where the traditions and lifestyle have carried on as unchanged as they have in the New Forest. That might be why the belief in pixies is as strong as it is here.'

New Forest pixies have a more agricultural leaning than those found further south in Devon and Cornwall, being strongly linked with old-time commoning families that have been working the land for many generations. Even today, Brice told me, belief in mischievous pixies who can cause harm is still strong in the Forest. 'Many people won't say outright that they believe in supernatural beings but then they exhibit behaviours that show they don't want to get on the wrong side of witches or pixies.' He mentioned a few pubs that leave a pint of beer outside the back door for nocturnal visitors, and commoners who pour beer around crops or bury biscuits to assuage restless pixies and assure a successful harvest.

Pixies are said to bestow blessings on those who court them. They can change their size and shape at will and generally appear in two forms in the New Forest: as a tiny old man with round ears, either naked or simply clad, or as a small, wild-looking pony, known as a colt pixie. Colt pixies are believed to lure ponies and livestock into woods and bogs, which is why you will sometimes see a ribbon braided into a mane or tail on a New Forest pony as protection.

New Forest pixies are also collectively known as pigsy or pugsy and some are revered with individual names. Gran Collin is a giant pixie known as king of the New Forest pixies, who has a twin brother called Tiddie Cole, who is only the size of a human thumb. The

"The best-known in Forest lore is undoubtedly Puck, a dark character who is believed to lead ponies astray."

best-known in Forest lore is undoubtedly Puck, a dark character who is believed to lead ponies astray – even to their death. Puck appears widely in English folklore but seems to have a kinder personality in other parts of the country. The quintessential New Forest pixie is Lazy Laurence, who is said to protect apples and cider.

There are many places today associated with pixies but the best known for sightings are Furzey Gardens (page 165), Puckpits Inclosure by Emery Down, Pikes Hill in Lyndhurst and Ragged Boys Hill (page 62). As for the colt pixies, there is no better place to look for them than Colt Pixie's Cave on Beaulieu Heath (Beaulieu Rd ♥ SU34990162), across from Hawkhill Car Park – a Bronze Age barrow where legend has it that mischievous colt pixies once lured children inside.

WATCH WHERE YOU STEP

The New Forest is one of the most important places in the UK for ground-nesting birds, many of which, including the nightjar, curlew and lapwing, are at risk of disappearing completely from the country. These birds return to the New Forest each year for its mix of wetlands, bogs and open heathlands; and of this, the New Forest is a designated Special Protection Area for birds.

Unfortunately, populations of these birds have been declining significantly in the past 40 to 50 years, both in the New Forest and around the world, with climate change, habitat loss and – particularly of relevance in the Forest – human encroachment largely to blame. Walking across a heath or wetland in spring where such birds are nesting in the grasses can cause parents to abandon their nest and expose chicks to predators.

Recognising the New Forest's worldwide importance in protecting these habitats, Forest leaders have established quiet zones from March to August, closing a few car parks and asking people to avoid those areas during nesting season. Orange-and-red signs are placed close to these areas and other key breeding grounds. Among car parks most likely to be affected are Hinchelsea, Ogdens, Ocknell Pond and Crockford. Forestry officials will also close car parks ad hoc if they recognise that an established pair is threatened by human activity. 'There is no firm data yet, but we can already see that these initiatives are helping more chicks to hatch,' said Marcus Ward, co-director of Wild New Forest, a wildlife consultancy group that supports conservation in the New Forest.

DEER: A COMPLICATED BALANCE

Deer are everywhere in the New Forest, although you may not always see these elusive and skittish creatures. This is somewhat surprising, considering that virtually every management organisation in the Forest agrees that there are currently too many. 'Although deer are important to the Forest's ecosystem,' Andy Page, Head of Wildlife Management for Forestry England South District, told me, 'they also cause a lot of damage to farm crops and woodland. They also trigger a large number of road accidents.' Overgrazing by deer also tends to create more uniform habitats, which squelches the opportunity for biodiversity.

When William the Conqueror claimed this land, it's likely that deer numbers were even higher than the current population. Records show that even in the 18th century, there were so many deer that hundreds starved to death during winter.

Today there are five deer species in the New Forest. Red and roe deer were in the area well before William arrived; the Normans then introduced fallow deer, now the most common species. Sika deer are largely found in the Beaulieu area, having originated here as a gift from King Edward VII to the second Baron Montague. They are kept separate from the red deer of the west Forest to avoid interbreeding. Montjac arrived in the UK from China in the late 1800s. They moved south and into the New Forest after an escape (or deliberate release) from Woburn Park in Bedfordshire in the early 1900s. These small, almost dog-sized deer eat *"Forest keepers are truly passionate about the deer they look after and work humanely and sensitively with them."* woodland voraciously and are a threat to native roe deer – the concern is that they could drive them out of the Forest in the same way that grey squirrels saw off red squirrels.

Deer always have been managed in the Forest, whether by early kings hunting or from the 19th century, by dogs known as the New Forest Buckhounds. When this practice ceased in 1997, New Forest keepers began culling deer under careful guidelines.

'Deer have no natural predators, so without management of numbers, they eat out their local environment,' Andy said. 'If we didn't cull them, they would eventually suffer starvation and sickness.' Keepers cull about 1,300 to 1,800 deer annually across ten regions, or 'beats' of the Forest. The culling process is far from shooting for sport – Forest keepers are truly passionate about the deer they look after and work humanely and sensitively with them, as part of an intricate management system. In April each year, a census is taken of the four main deer species in the Forest and from that a plan is designed for culling. Much research is conducted to analyse numbers, breeding patterns, and to assure the gene pool is kept strong. Venison from the deer culls is processed by Forestry England and sold to licensed game dealers.

Deer are naturally timid so if you want to see them in the Forest, the best advice is to venture out in early morning or dusk and try to stay downwind where they won't detect your smell. For an even better chance, head for the Deer Watch Trail at Bolderwood (page 106), where an elevated platform overlooks fields where fallow deer are frequently seen.

THE GENTLE ART OF FISHING

Most fishing waters in and around the New Forest are privately owned so you generally need to have a permit from a local organisation, such as Forestry England, in order to fish, in addition to a UK rod licence (*⊘* gov. uk/fishing-licences). There are about 20 species of fish represented in New Forest waterways and sea fishing is also possible on the Solent. 'But it's the chalk streams that make fishing in Hampshire so special,' said Ian Thew, a qualified fishing instructor. 'The purity of the water, the constant, year-round, water temperature and subsequent abundance of insect life encourage fish to breed and grow in abundance.'

Ian, who coaches both beginners and more experienced fishermen in game angling and fly-fishing, recommends receiving instruction in this gentle art. He suggests that beginners try **Holbury Lakes Trout Fishery** (*⊘* 01794 341619 *⊘* holburylakes.co.uk), just north of the New Forest, which has four well-stocked lakes and chalk stream fishing in the river Dun, or **Damerham Fisheries**

"The ultimate fishing day would be to hire a private guide, as they often have access to private waters."

(*⊘* 01725 518446 *⊘* damerhamfisheries.co.uk) a trout fishery three miles west of Fordingbridge on the Allen River with three well-stocked, spring-fed lakes. The ultimate fishing day would be to hire a private guide, as they often have access to private waters. Just east of Lepe in the New Forest National Park, **Cadland Fishery** (*⊘* 02380 893582 *⊘* cadland.co.uk) has four lakes for coarse fishing with day tickets available. **Orchard Lakes** (*⊘* 07790 915434 *⊘* orchardlakes.co.uk) near New Milton is one of the most prolific fisheries in the southern forest. The six lakes set within 56 acres of farmland are stocked with 12

SLOW FOREST FISHING: AN EXPERT'S VIEW

Ian Thew, qualified fly-fishing coach

The New Forest has many fishing opportunities, bound in the east and west by two celebrated rivers and in the south by the sea; few other areas of Great Britain offer the angler such variety. The Avon and the Test rivers begin life north of the Forest as crystal-clear chalk streams that rush headlong down the country in their haste to reach the sea. By the time they get to the Forest, they have matured to mighty rivers that now take their time and flow at a more leisurely pace to their journeys' end. These rivers, together with the smaller Beaulieu and Lymington, both of which rise within the Forest, provide excellent fishing opportunities for the game angler who seeks that king of fish, the salmon or their humbler cousins, the sea trout, brown trout and grayling. For the coarse-fishing enthusiast, these rivers abound with record-breaking pike, barbel, chub, perch and many other species.

Where there are rivers there will always be lakes and still-water fisheries. The New Forest is no exception. Day-ticket permits can be obtained from a variety of locations that will provide such quarry as fat, rainbow trout for the fly-fishing aficionado or monster carp for the coarse-fishing enthusiast. And then there are the sea and the tidal waterways where the fishing can be as diverse as hand-lining for crabs from Lymington quay, fly-fishing for bass on the mouth of the Lymington River or beach casting for whatever comes along at Hurst Spit.

No matter where you chose to fish in the Forest – in the dappled shadows of Forest trees, beside the lush water meadows of the Avon, on the banks of a picturesque lake or even on samphire-covered saltmarshes – you will enjoy a slow pastime in a distinct fishing region of Great Britain.

Ian offers private fishing and shooting coaching for individuals and groups of all abilities (℘ (01425 403735; ◈ burleyrailscottage.co.uk). He also is the author of *From a New Forest Inclosure*, musings on life from his home deep within the Forest.

different species of fish. A bit further west, outside Ringwood, **Moors Valley Country Park**, (℘ 01425 470721 ◈ moors-valley.co.uk) runs beginners' courses during the summer and school holidays and sells day tickets for its lake.

Sea fishing is somewhat simpler; no licence is required. Popular locations are at Hurst Spit (although tides and weeds can be tricky here) and local beaches where you can stand and enjoy the scenery with your fishing rod. You can go out with guided fishing boats from Milford, Keyhaven and Lymington. The national website for charter boats (◈ charterboats-uk.co.uk) lists a directory of local captains. If you arrange in advance, most boats will supply equipment.

HOW THIS BOOK IS ARRANGED

For the purposes of this book, there is no need to distinguish between the New Forest and the national park. Where 'forest' is capitalised, it refers to the New Forest. The three chapters split the New Forest directionally, roughly using the A31 and the A337 as divisions. Although I've divided the Forest into three basic regions, the overall Forest is small enough that you can reach all areas easily in a day. In summer, traffic can make that goal more difficult, especially around the Lyndhurst area.

All business establishments included here have been selected by me; no charges have been made for inclusion.

MAPS

Each chapter begins with a map with **numbered stopping points** that correspond to numbered headings in the text. Bear in mind that the New Forest is relatively small so a listing in one chapter may only be a couple of miles from one in another chapter. The featured walks have maps accompanying them.

The best OS map for the Forest is the double-sided 1:25,000 scale map Explorer OL22 (showing field and woodland boundaries, among other walker-friendly information). Rather annoyingly, you need four sheets of the smaller scale 1:50,000 Landranger series maps for the whole area: most of it, however, is on sheets 195 and 196, with the northernmost bits on sheets 184 and 185, but there's only a tiny bit on the latter.

ACCOMMODATION

Accommodation has been chosen with an eye to geography and because an outlet embodies the Slow philosophy, either in general atmosphere, because the proprietor is particularly helpful to guests, or because it embraces a 'green' ethos. The rise of Airbnb has tolled the death knell for standard B&Bs that were once prevalent here but I've included a few of the remaining stand-outs. In terms of rates, as with all things in the Forest, season matters. Off-season rates are obviously better and often negotiable, and many establishments offer package deals that make a holiday outside of summer worthwhile. In most cases, it's a good idea to contact the accommodation directly rather than booking through a third-party website. There are often last-minute opportunities for one-night stays even for establishments that claim a two-night minimum.

ℹ TOURIST INFORMATION

Fordingbridge Information Office Kings Yd, Salisbury St, Fordingbridge SP6 1AB
✆ 01425 654560 🖱 fordingbridge.gov.uk ⊙ Easter–Nov 10.00–16.00 Mon–Fri; Nov–Easter 10.00–16.00 Mon, Wed & Fri. Council office primarily for residents but has small selection of brochures and maps and helpful staff.

Milford on Sea Parish Council 22 High St, Milford SO41 0QD ✆ 01590 644410
🖱 milfordonseaparishcouncil.gov.uk ⊙ 10.00–15.30 daily. Parish office primarily for residents but with visitor information leaflets and friendly and knowledgeable staff.

New Forest Heritage Centre Main Car Park, Lyndhurst SO43 7NY ✆ 02380 283444
🖱 newforestheritage.org.uk ⊙ 10.00-16.00 daily. Not officially a tourist information centre but this is the closest you'll get to one in the New Forest. The museum has background on the Forest and the gift shop has the best selection in the Forest of books on the area. There is also a small section with maps and brochures of local attractions. An excellent starting point for any visit to the Forest.

St Barbe Museum New St, Lymington SO41 9BH 🖱 stbarbe-museum.org.uk. The desk at the entrance to the museum is staffed by locals who can answer questions. There are racks with leaflets, maps and books on the area.

Campsite rates can be deceptive in that each has different charges for what is considered 'extra'. Rates are often calculated on the basis of two people with additional charges for extra children and adults.

FOOD & DRINK

I've listed favourite pubs, tea rooms and places to eat, with a firm accent on places that serve local produce or are worth singling out for some other reason, such as intrinsic character. Opening hours are listed here for most venues but the New Forest is highly seasonal and hours often change at short notice; always check the website for current opening times.

GETTING AROUND

I'd like to encourage people to **visit without a car** but it can be difficult, particularly in the north Forest where public transport is virtually non-existent. Cycling, horseriding and walking are ideal methods of Slow travel.

Some lodging establishments offer discounts to guests who arrive without a car. Businesses that participate in the **Green Leaf Tourism** scheme that promotes eco-friendly tourism are listed on the website of New Forest District Council ($\oslash$ newforest.gov.uk).

TRAINS

South Western Railway run direct trains daily from London Waterloo to Brockenhurst, which takes 90 minutes and is the most direct route to the Forest. There are also trains from both London Waterloo and London Paddington to Ashurst, on the eastern edge of the Forest near Southampton. Another option is to take a train from London Paddington to Salisbury, from where you can take a Morebus X3 route to Fordingbridge in the north Forest, which takes about 40 minutes.

Options for getting around within the Forest by train are limited to services on the line between Bournemouth and Southampton. From Bournemouth the line goes through Hinton Admiral, New Milton and Sway, then cuts across the heart of the Forest through **Brockenhurst** (the main access point), **Beaulieu Road** (a good three miles northwest of Beaulieu, but well positioned for walks) and **Ashurst New Forest** (three miles northeast of Lyndhurst), before entering suburban Southampton and Totton.

Within the Forest, the Lymington to Brockenhurst Community Rail Partnership runs a local train from Brockenhurst to the Isle of Wight ferry landing in **Lymington**.

BUSES & COACHES

National Express coaches ($\mathscr{O}$ 08717 818181 $\oslash$ nationalexpress.com) from London Victoria (via Heathrow Airport) stop at Southampton and Ringwood.

Three major bus companies provide travel to and around the south and west New Forest. **Bluestar** ($\mathscr{O}$ 02380 618233 $\oslash$ bluestarbus.co.uk) operates services from Southampton to Lyndhurst, Brockenhurst and Lymington, as well as buses to Hythe, where you can catch service 9 to Calshot, at the mouth of Southampton Water. **More** ($\mathscr{O}$ 01202 338

---

1 Aquatic fun at New Forest Water Park. **2** Cycling. **3** Kayaking. **4** Horseriding through the forest. ▶

NEW FOREST WATER PARK

NEW FOREST CYCLING TOURS

NEW FOREST ACTIVITIES

BURLEY VILLA SCHOOL OF RIDING

420 ⊘ morebus.co.uk) operates buses X1 and X2 from Lymington to Bournemouth via New Milton and Christchurch.

Rural routes cover Lymington, Boldre, Beaulieu, Hythe, Burley and Ringwood. **Salisbury Reds** (✆ 01202 338420 ⊘ salisburyreds.co.uk) runs the X3, which goes between Salisbury and Bournemouth, passing through Downton, Breamore, Fordingbridge and Ringwood. Salisbury Reds also operates the X7 from Salisbury through the northern Commons area and into Southampton, plus rural route 44, which passes through Downton and Woodfalls.

Note that bus routes can change from one day to the next, so it's wise to check the websites before setting out. Within the Forest, the open-topped hop-on, hop-off **New Forest Tour** bus (⊘ morebus.co.uk) is worth considering if you want to travel by bus and bicycle. The bus has three routes that you can switch between: the red route travels around the north and west; the green route covers the south and east areas; and the blue route is coastal areas. The tour bus runs from the end of June until mid-September with regular stopping points, including connections to public bus routes. Bus travel from Southampton, Bournemouth and Salisbury is free if you buy your New Forest Tour ticket on local buses run by Bluestar, More or Salisbury Reds. You can also purchase tickets online or from the driver. Multi-day tickets are available. A ticket also includes discounts to some attractions around the national park. Up to four bikes can be carried on the bus; you could take the train to Brockenhurst or Ashurst and ride the bus to a cycle-hire shop and explore without ever needing a car.

CYCLING

The New Forest has 100 miles of marked trails so in theory you can cover a lot of ground on a bike. Unfortunately, not all the trails are linked so to get from one area to another often involves riding on roads. It's frustrating but it has improved and continues to do so with new trail markings and maps. A cycle map (available at some bike rental shops and tourist information centres or downloadable from ⊘ newforestnpa.gov.uk) shows cycle routes as well as smaller roads. The greatest concentration of designated trails is in the central Forest around Brockenhurst, Burley and Lyndhurst. You can also cycle on bridleways and Forestry England tracks that are dedicated cycle routes, but not on footpaths. Do not even think about cycling on the Open Forest. Cycling off marked routes can damage the Forest and possibly disrupt wildlife so it carries a maximum fine of £500.

Off-road cycling is a contentious issue in the Forest, mostly concerning organised events involving large groups because these often interfere with commoning work (page 15). There is sometimes conflict between off-road cyclists and horseriders and walkers but that's usually when cyclists ride aggressively through trails shared by various users. Hard-core off-road cycling in the traditional sense is frowned upon in the Forest; cyclists are expected to be gentle and respectful of the landscape.

If you're intimidated by cycling on your own, consider joining a guided tour. Various companies offer **organised excursions**. **New Forest Cycling Tours** (℘ 07976 688437 ℰ newforestcyclingtours.com) offers guided tours in the Forest ranging from two hours to full days; **Likie Bikie** (℘ 07894 987292 ℰ likiebikie.co.uk) specialises in electric bike excursions in and around the north Forest on various terrains; and **New Forest Mountain Biking** (ℰ newforestmountainbiking. co.uk) categorises its guided mountain bike tours by ability level. **Pedall** (ℰ pedall.org.uk) is an inclusive cycling charity dedicated to making cycling accessible to all. It offers guided rides for those who need support, whether that is emotional support and confidence building or mobility issues.

Note that electric bikes must be EAPC compliant.

CYCLE HIRE

The following are rental options at key points in the Forest. Staff are often knowledgeable about suitable routes for your group; definitely ask for guidance.

Cyclexperience Railway Station Car Park, Brockenhurst SO42 7TW ℘ 01590 624808 ℰ cyclex.co.uk. One of the oldest and most reliable cycle hire companies in the New Forest, this is also the most convenient cycle hire if you're arriving by train and want to travel without a car. If you have a car, parking is free for 45 minutes in the Brockenhurst Railway Station car park. Book ahead online to avoid disappointment.

Forest Leisure Cycling The Cross, Burley BH24 4AB ℘ 01425 403584 ℰ forestleisurecycling.co.uk. Bike shop that prides itself on offering free parking – which is actually incredibly helpful – and has quick access to the Forest. There is a huge assortment of bikes, including electric, and delivery is available with 48-hours' notice. Great option for families due to the huge stock. Book ahead via the website to guarantee your order.

Jaunt-Ebikes Keyhaven Rd, Keyhaven SO41 0TH ✆ 0707846 395684 ⌂ jaunt-ebikes.co.uk. Variety of electric bikes for rental. The shop also offers activity experiences that include a picnic. Free on-site parking.

New Forest Activities Hazel Copse Farm, Beaulieu SO42 7WA ✆ 01590 613377 ⌂ newforestactivities.co.uk. Bikes are bookable online for collection. No childrens' bikes or trailers due to location on busy road; all riders must be over 12 and able to fit on a full-size bike.

New Forest Bikes Quay St, Lymington SO41 3AS ✆ 01590 679793 ⌂ newforestbikes. co.uk. Located just five minutes from Lymington train station (on the branch line from Brockenhurst), making it possible to travel without a car. Delivery available with 24-hours' notice. In summer, there is a two-hour twilight rental option between 18.00 and 20.00.

The Woods Cyclery 56 High St, Lyndhurst SO43 7BG ✆ 023 80282028 ⌂ thewoodscyclery. co.uk. One of the biggest and most versatile cycle-hire companies, with a large fleet that includes e-bikes. Free delivery for four or more bikes within a five-mile radius.

WALKING

There is plenty of scope for walking in the Forest, across incredibly varied terrain of open heath, woodland and seaside. There are loads of designated footpaths, bridleways and cycle trails throughout the entire Forest; although there is no law against walking away from designated paths, doing so can seriously harm wildlife. From February to August, some areas are restricted in order to protect ground-nesting birds (page 34). If you are unsure where to go, there are suggested routes from the National Park Authority (⌂ newforestnpa.org). You might also want to consider a guided walk to enhance your appreciation of the area. In addition, I feature in full detail some of my personal favourite routes in this book. A word of caution: at certain times of year the gorse can be high and very prickly throughout the Forest. You might not want to wear shorts, and proper walking shoes are essential. Just about anywhere you walk in the Forest can be muddy and/or waterlogged after heavy rainfall.

"There is plenty of scope for walking in the Forest, across incredibly varied terrain of open heath, woodland and seaside."

Stories abound about people and animals getting stuck in bogs. Although infrequent, it does happen, albeit more often to ponies than humans. When an animal wanders in, it can sink up to its neck – the Lyndhurst Fire Department even has a special crane to pull unfortunate animals out from sticky situations. Although it's unlikely that you will get stuck, this is one of the many reasons the National Park Authority urges people to remain on marked trails.

The cream of the crop of walking tours are run by **Wild New Forest** (⌀ wildnewforest.co.uk), the wildlife consultancy. Dedicated researchers and Forest enthusiasts, Professor Russell Wynn and Marcus Ward, lead a variety of walks in the Forest that complement their ongoing research work. They know just about everything about every inch of wildlife. Both men have extensive experience leading conservation projects and wildlife surveys and numerous credentials. They offer a number of regularly scheduled 90-minute introductory 'Welcome to the Forest' tours and also longer, more specialised walks at various points in the Forest. They also run hugely popular Beaulieu River boat trips with specialised commentary. One of their greatest initiatives is a series of wildlife adventures aimed at young people aged eight to 16, which take place on the third Saturday of every month. Bespoke private walks and cycle rides can be arranged, too.

The National Park Authority (⌀ newforestnpa.gov.uk/things-to-do) has an app of walking routes for self-guiding.

Some notable **long-distance paths** run near or through the New Forest. Much of the **Avon Valley Path** (⌀ hants.gov.uk/thingstodo/countryside/walking/avonvalley), a 34-mile walking route that runs from Salisbury to Christchurch following the course of the River Avon, is within the west and north New Forest. The path is divided into five sections that make ideal day trips but it can be waterlogged or flooded from December to May. The sections through water meadows have an open, pastoral quality quite different from the New Forest itself and a walk from the Forest into the Avon Valley can be rewarded by some striking scenic contrasts. Further east, the **Solent Way** (⌀ solentway.co.uk), a 60-mile footpath linking Milford with Emsworth Harbour, near Portsmouth, passes along the eastern edge of the Forest. Breaking it into day-trip segments is a good way to visit many coastal highlights, including Hurst Castle, Buckler's Hard, Beaulieu and the village of Hythe.

HORSERIDING

Horseback is an appropriately Slow way of seeing the Forest. Stables throughout the Forest are adept at guiding first-time riders as well as the more experienced, and you'll soon find yourself in remote reaches of the Forest. Below is a sampling of stables that cater to all abilities. It is essential to book ahead, particularly during summer and school holidays.

STABLES

Arniss Equestrian Godshill SP6 2JX ℰ 01425 654114 ⬧ arnissequestrian.co.uk. Located in one of the most beautiful parts of the Forest, about two miles east of Fordingbridge. Riding lessons, hacks into the Forest and training days for all abilities from the age of four. British Horse Association approved.

Bagnum Equestrian Centre Bagnum Ln, Ringwood BH24 3BZ ℰ 01425 476263 ⬧ bagnumequestrian.co.uk. Located about four miles south of Ringwood. Popular stables that offer a variety of lessons and ride-outs for all abilities and ages from four.

Brockenhurst Riding Stables Warren Farm, Balmer Lawn Rd, Brockenhurst SO42 7TT ℰ 01590 624747 ⬧ brockenhurstridingstables.co.uk ⊙ Easter–mid-Oct. Situated off the A337, just north of Brockenhurst. Friendly, flexible stables that accommodate all abilities.

Burley Villa School of Riding Bashley Common Rd, New Milton BH25 5SH ℰ 01425 610278 ⬧ burleyvilla.co.uk. Located roughly equidistant between Burley and Lymington. The only stable in the Forest to offer Western riding for anyone over 12: this is riding in a wide saddle, which is easy to balance in and is ideal way to ride if you've never been on a horse before. Kids' lessons offered in the arena. No direct access to Forest.

Coombe Stables Coombe Ln, SO41 6BP ℰ 07989 971865 ⬧ coombeequestrian.com. This riding school in Sway offers one-hour rides into the Forest for more experienced riders. Booking ahead required.

FEEDBACK REQUEST

At Bradt Guides we're aware that guidebooks start to go out of date on the day they're published — and that you, our readers, are out there in the field doing research of your own. You'll find out before us when a fine new family-run hotel opens or a favourite restaurant changes hands and goes downhill. So why not tell us about your experiences? Contact us on ℰ 01753 893444 or ✉ info@bradtguides.com. We will forward emails to the author who may post updates on the Bradt website at ⬧ bradtguides.com/updates. Alternatively, you can add a review of the book to Amazon, or share your adventures with us on social:

🄵 BradtGuides   🄸 BradtGuides & emilylaurencebaker1
🄣 BradtGuides

JOIN

THE TRAVEL CLUB

THE MEMBERSHIP CLUB FOR SERIOUS TRAVELLERS
FROM BRADT GUIDES

Be inspired
Free books and exclusive
insider travel tips
and inspiration

Save money
Special offers and
discounts from our
favourite travel brands

**Plan the trip
of a lifetime**
Access our exclusive concierge
service and have a bespoke
itinerary created for you
by a Bradt author

Join here:
bradtguides.com/travelclub

Membership levels to suit all budgets

Bradt GUIDES

TRAVEL TAKEN SERIOUSLY

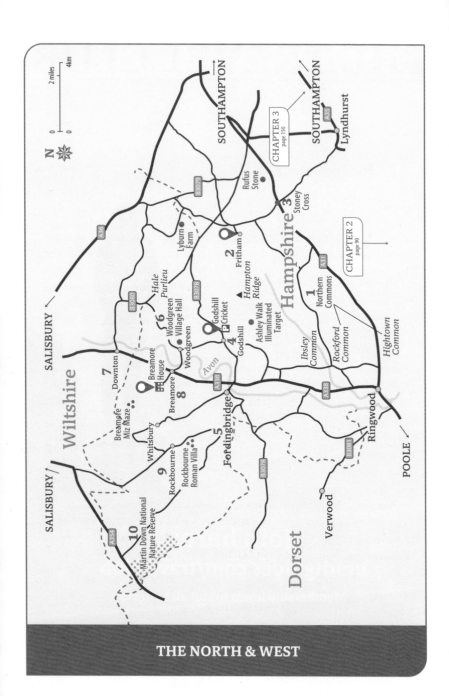

THE NORTH & WEST

1
THE NORTH & WEST

Residents of the north Forest are protective of their quiet corner and rightly so. Fewer tourists come here than other parts of the Forest (with the exception of Fritham), largely because there are not as many attractions and you need to work a bit harder to get a feel for the landscape. Outdoor types are happy here – those who want to ride, cycle, fish and, most of all, walk. In short, this part of the Forest translates to a truly Slow experience, especially as you move north towards the Wiltshire border. During an all-day trek you will be rewarded with varied terrain of rolling hills, chalky and boggy ground, dark conifer woodland and the more dappled ancient and ornamental woodlands. There are also distant views of Wiltshire and Dorset farmland, quite a different backdrop from what you encounter in the central and southern Forest.

Cycling is particularly pleasant in the north Forest as roads tend to be quieter than in the south. **Hampton Ridge**, which cuts east–west through the Forest between Fritham and Frogham, is an ideal cycling path with views towards Dorset and Wiltshire. The area west of the A338 is not part of the national park but the quiet, hedged lanes around **Breamore** are peaceful and rewarding cycling territory. From here, it's not too far to **Martin Down National Nature Reserve** and **Cranborne Chase** where there are plenty of quiet roads through the Area of Outstanding Natural Beauty (AONB).

North Foresters are proud of their hilly topography; I've heard more than one speak disdainfully of the flatter landscape of Brockenhurst and the coastal areas. It's certainly true that some of the choicest views in the entire Forest are here: **Piper's Wait**, at 422ft, is the highest point in the Forest; **Stagbury Hill**, which has seven barrows and overlooks the northeast Forest; and **Bramshaw Telegraph** – such a good vantage point that it was the site of an optical shutter station that formed part of a signalling chain between Plymouth and London during the Napoleonic wars (1803–1815).

NORTH FOREST: THE NORTHERN COMMONS, FRITHAM & FORDINGBRIDGE

The north Forest is the easiest place to gain a sense of how the Forest might have been before it became such a popular tourist destination. With no direct trains from London, it's that little bit quieter than the south and you are more likely to find yourself alone with just birdsong as a backdrop, rather than human sounds. It's also easier to get away from traffic noise, as there are fewer large roads. Geologically speaking, the land slopes gently down from north to south, where it flattens out

A YOUNG COMMONER'S PERSPECTIVE

'Keeping cattle has become quite challenging,' said Tom Hordle, as we climbed one of the hills that characterise Rockford Common in the west Forest. 'I have to file papers every time I move a cow, even if it's just a mile down the road. I need to keep medical records, have tuberculosis checks and maintain buildings.' But he insists that it's worth it because keeping cattle on the Forest is critical to its survival as we know it.

As a full-scale commoner (page 15), Tom maintains the farming tradition that has underwritten the Forest since Anglo-Saxon times. Fewer commoners now graze cattle on the open Forest but Tom is chipping away at those statistics by turning out a herd of cows that has been steadily increasing during the past ten years.

'Ponies and cattle graze differently and this ultimately will affect the composition of the landscape. Ponies nibble but cows graze deeper and eat rough plants like heather and tough grasses. If we lose too many cows, the large expanses of green lawns in the Forest could become overgrown,' Tom explained to me.

Tom supplies local restaurants with beef from cows that he has personally bred. 'Supplying beef off the Forest is challenging because I have to keep cows for twice as long as a traditional farmer because it's hard to fatten them up. But on the other hand, grazing cattle on the open forest means I'm able to keep more than I'd be able to elsewhere because they have so much grazing space.'

At 32, Tom is considered a 'young commoner'. 'If you are under 40, you're still classed as young because so many commoners tend to be older,' said Tom, into the Solent Coast. The hillier terrain of the north naturally translates to views and from a high point like Hampton Ridge or Telegraph Hill, you get a real appreciation for how truly precious this largely untouched landscape is in one of the most developed regions of England.

While researching this book, I became enamoured with the watercolours of **Heywood Sumner** (page 58), an artist active in the Arts and Crafts movement, who painted scenes conveying the stillness and beauty of the Forest that still prevails. As I delved deeper into the history of the north Forest, I learned that Sumner is best known for his archaeological contributions which, although not completely accurate regarding Bronze and Iron Age settlements, shed much light on Roman influence in the Forest. Now it seems impossible to me that someone could come to this part of the Forest and not appreciate the varied works of Sumner. His writings and illustrations on his home in Gorley were republished in 1987; page 14.

chuckling. He explained that at the moment, there are few commoners in the 40 to 60 age group. This might be because a generation of commoners discouraged their offspring from pursuing full-time commoning as it is so hard to earn a living, something mirrored with Tom's own family.

But Tom pointed out that there has been keen interest from younger people in recent years, possibly thanks to government grants that have benefitted the commoning community. Whether those will continue is unclear but, unlike many people, Tom is optimistic about the future of commoning.

He does, however, point out that the dynamics have changed. 'Years ago, all commoners would have worked full-time in the Forest. But today's younger commoners all have full-time jobs that sustain them so they practise commoning in evenings and on weekends – just when recreational users want to be in the Forest.' This means commoners (and everyone involved with Forest management) have to manage their animals amid dog walkers and recreational horseriders.

There are so many obstacles to the commoning life that one might question, why do it? But to Tom and other commoners, this is a way of life, one that is as integral to the Forest as the land itself. And if commoning disappears, so does the New Forest as we know it.

Tom's pride was palpable as we stood atop the hill, from where we could see towards Fordingbridge and beyond. 'They say that commoning is in your blood and I think that's true. Even though it skipped two generations, this is what I've always wanted to do. I love it and I can't imagine doing anything else.'

I leave it to this expressive artist and writer, who so deeply loved it here, to describe the riches of this region.

> Here, on the Northern side… we have long rolling hills, capped with plateau gravel and clothed with heather, fern, and furze, worn into five parallel ridges and furrows by streams that trickle in dry, and rush in wet weather, down gravelly courses to the broad valley of the Avon. Here and there the hills are covered with thickets of holly, thorn, yew and crab-apple; with old woods of oak, beech, yew, holly, thorn and whitebeam and with enclosures of Scots pine, larch, oak, and sweet chestnut. But the main features of our side of the New Forest are heather uplands, winding moorland streams, and scattered woods. The open country is never far distant.
>
> Heywood Sumner *Cuckoo Hill: The Book of Gorley*

1 NORTHERN COMMONS

⌂ The Bell Inn (page 222)

The National Trust, the second largest landowner in the Forest, owns 3,300 acres of mostly 'adjacent commons', traditionally privately owned lands that bordered the Forest but were not subject to its rules, which were brought into Forest borders as recently as 1964. As these lands were originally privately owned, the commoners here were granted rights from the lords of the manors and were known as manorial commoners. Today, these manorial commoners are not governed by the Verderers, as commoners on Crown lands are. That's why this is the only place in the Forest where you will see pigs all year round, as the commoners here possess that unusual right, and it is also one of the only places you will see sheep grazing. Although the National Trust owns most of the Northern Commons, some remains privately owned.

The former adjacent commons are collectively called the Northern Commons but this term can be confusing because the areas are relatively widely dispersed, ranging from Hightown, Ibsley and Rockford in the far west by Ringwood, to Hale Purlieu north of Fordingbridge, and then Bramshaw further east. Taken as a whole, the Northern Commons present diverse landscapes. 'Ibsley and Hale Purlieu are pristine heathland sites while Hale boasts a rich mosaic of habitats including dry and wet heath, mires and woodland, all of which are grazed by commoners' animals,' said Dylan Everett, Countryside

---

1 Heather on Rockford Common, part of the Northern Commons. 2 Highland Cow. ▶

HELEN HOTSON/S

DEREK TIPPETTS

Operations Manager of the National Trust. 'Hightown, the smallest of our holdings, serves as an excellent gateway to the Forest because it's close to Ringwood. Bramshaw Commons traditionally is a stronghold of livestock commoning, which you don't see to the same extent in all parts of the Forest.' Certainly, if you walk through Bramshaw Commons, you are very likely to encounter cows munching their way across the acid grasslands that characterise this area.

You are also likely to catch some great views at **Stagbury Hill**, the New Forest's second highest point at 200ft (park at Half Moon Common car park). Climbing to the top grants a rare opportunity to see the Forest from above and to appreciate how expansive this untouched land is in an otherwise very developed region of England. It also provides a wonderful contrast to the more enclosed areas that tend to make up much of the New Forest. You'll also get spectacular views from the hills at Rockford and Ibsley. The National Trust details several moderate, level walks, including one at **Hale Purlieu** that showcases vistas across the mires and valleys of the Northern Commons. Butterfly lovers also head to Hale to observe protected silver-studded blue butterflies, which feed within the heather in summer. Another highlighted walk is from Ibsley and incorporates wartime history with a look at the Huff Duff, a World War II directional station.

"Butterfly lovers also head to Hale, to observe protected silver-studded blue butterflies."

The New Forest National Park Authority (newforestnpa.gov.uk/things-to-do) outlines two downloadable walks in **Rockford Common**, one of which is accessible to all on surfaced tracks. The longer route points out landscape features that illustrate the history of the area, including a disused sand quarry, ancient trackways, a Bronze Age barrow and a World War II gun site. There is parking at Half Moon, Bramshaw, Rockford, Hale Purlieu and Hightown commons. Note that there are no toilet facilities at any sites.

The National Trust also owns **Foxbury Plantation**, a former conifer plantation, about ten miles northwest of Southampton. The Trust has been working to restore this 350-acre site to the open heathland and broad-leafed woodland that would have been here in the 19th century. The work here is reflective of a trend throughout the Forest, to reinstate lands as they originally were and allow native species to thrive. Foxbury is also able to help reduce impact on heavily used areas of the New

Forest, both by humans and animals. The now thriving wetlands have enabled stock from the over-worked land at Bramshaw to graze here, allowing Bramshaw to recover.

The use of Foxbury could point towards the direction of land usage in the wider Forest in the future. Although Foxbury is not open to the public at present, the National Trust hosts large groups for activity days and events that significantly reduce recreational impact in other parts of the Forest. The basecamp cabins here regularly host school and other youth groups for educational activities and the team hopes to host activity days and guided walks for the public in the future.

¶¶ FOOD & DRINK

Le Frog at Les Mirabelles Nomansland SP5 2BN ⌀ 01794 390205 ⌀ lesmirabelles.co.uk. An incongruous setting for a quietly sophisticated French restaurant but a welcome treat in Nomansland, a tiny village in Wiltshire, about 10 miles southeast of Salisbury but within the boundaries of the national park. The owner is French and the authentic food has been delighting Salisbury and Forest residents for 18 years. Booking essential at weekends, as it's very popular.

Rockingham Arms Canada Rd, West Wellow SO51 6DE ⌀ 01794 324798 ⌀ redcatpubcompany.com ⌀ 11.00–22.00 Mon–Sat, noon–19.00 Sun. Delightful and friendly pub located amid the Northern Commons, about 15 minutes north of Cadnam. The pub has direct access to Canada Commons so you can walk off your lunch. There is lovely outdoor seating in summer (get there early) and a few drinking spots by the car park. The interior is welcoming and cosy in winter. There is a wide selection of above-average pub food, including a gluten-free menu. Real ales from Ringwood Brewery and various guest breweries. Dog friendly but not in restaurant.

2 FRITHAM

🏠 **New Forest Shepherd's Huts** (page 222)

Walkers flock to Fritham, partly for refreshment at the **Royal Oak** (page 57), one of the Forest's best-loved pubs, and partly because within a small area you can see a variety of Forest landscapes. Although the village seems quiet today, in the late 19th century, it was headquarters for the **Schultze Gunpowder Factory**, which manufactured smokeless gunpowder popular with the hunters of the day. The factory was probably established here because of the remoteness of the site and also because black powder had been manufactured here in the 1860s from the abundant charcoal in the Forest.

DEREK TIPPETTS

JOANA KRUSE/A

The business began in three huts with transport conducted by just one man and a wheelbarrow but grew to ultimately include 70 buildings and employ about 100 workers. The transport system evolved from a wheelbarrow, to horse and carriage, to cars. Wages were considerably higher than for agricultural work, prompting some workers to walk many miles daily for factory jobs. Water from Eyeworth Pond, today a tranquil spot with water lilies and waterfowl, was used to power factory machinery.

The factory boom was relatively short-lived and by the early 20th century manufacture had ceased in this area. You can still see evidence of the gunpowder heyday in addition to Eyeworth Pond: a blackened letterbox at the edge of the car park; Powder Mill Road (now a cycle trail that leads from Eyeworth Pond to the B3078), originally designed so that dangerous substances wouldn't have to be ferried through the village; and Eyeworth Lodge, initially a hunting lodge and later the research lab where Schultze's head chemist worked (now a private home).

You can walk directly out onto open Forest from the car parks located just up the road from the Royal Oak, and there are plenty of opportunities for gentle strolls or more ambitious hikes. Many people don't venture much further than Fritham Plain, located just beyond the car park and often picturesquely arrayed with grazing ponies. Carry on, however, and you will be rewarded with the opportunity to walk within ancient woodlands and several different inclosures (page 23), where you are very likely to find yourself alone amid a chorus of birdsong. You can even walk all the way to Frogham (where the Foresters Arms pub awaits) by climbing up to **Hampton Ridge**, a combination walking and cycling trail that lies west of Fritham (see step 12 of the Heywood Sumner walk; you would turn left here instead of right; page 63.) The five-mile trail (from its start at Abbots Wells) has some of the best views in the entire Forest.

¶¶ FOOD & DRINK

Royal Oak Fritham SO43 7HJ ✐ 02380 812606 ⟁ royaloakfritham.co.uk ⏱ 11.00–21.00 Wed–Sat, noon–21.00 Sun. 'Meet me at the Royal Oak,' is a phrase used among Forest residents regularly and has been for hundreds of years. Only simple Forest food is served here, and then only at lunch (noon–15.00) – ploughmans, pork pies, a very popular smoked

◀ **1** The famous Royal Oak at Fritham. **2** Sloden Inclosure.

IN THE FOOTSTEPS OF HEYWOOD SUMNER

The west and north New Forest strongly influenced the works of Heywood Sumner (1853–1940), whose writings and drawings vividly depict all aspects of Forest life. Sumner was good at so many things and slots into no single category: he was a pioneer archaeologist whose recordings of excavations at New Forest Roman potteries paved the way for scholars behind him; a naturalist who painstakingly noted observations of wildlife and vegetation as they changed seasonally; and an artist whose drawings and watercolours still evoke the serenity to be found during a walk deep in the woods. The combination of those attributes continues to provide unparalleled insight to the Forest.

A leading light in the Arts and Crafts movement, Sumner worked as an artist in London designing tapestries, wallpapers and furniture, as well as illustrating books and crafting sgraffito murals and church stained-glass windows. He then moved to Bournemouth, allegedly because of his wife's ill health, although the overriding factor might have been that he had tired of the London scene and sought a more tranquil existence. In any case, Bournemouth soon proved to be too suburban for his liking and he set his sights on a home in the Forest.

Sumner built a house at Cuckoo Hill in Gorley and it was from here that he began to make a name for himself as an archaeologist at sites in Cranborne Chase and the New Forest. The first archaeologist to scientifically investigate and record the New Forest potteries, he also discovered and excavated the first intact pottery kiln at Ashley Rails. Many artefacts he unearthed are kept at the Salisbury Museum. What distinguished Sumner was his detailed analysis in which he identified which areas of the Forest pottery came from. Meticulously, Sumner recorded his findings of storage pots, platters and bowls, along with educated conjecture about kilns and how the pottery was made.

duck pâté and, in winter, homemade soup – making use of ingredients from the family farm or within 40 miles. In summer, visiting vans serve up fish and chips (Sat) and pizza (Tue & Fri) in the evenings. To experience the true Forest flavour of the pub, go in winter when the small network of rooms is filled with locals and dog walkers. Muddy boots and canines are the norm and convivial laughter fills the rooms heated by log fires. Beer connoisseurs go out of their way to visit the Royal Oak for the outstanding selection of cask ales – up to eight at any time. Special events such as musical evenings are held throughout the year. Accommodation is also on offer (page 222).

3 STONEY CROSS & AROUND

When you stand out on Stoney Cross today, the 1882 writing of John Wise, arguably the best chronicler of New Forest life, still makes sense:

His archaeological notes were spiced with observations of Forest life and drawings that only someone who loved every aspect of the Forest could provide.

I was lucky to retrace his routes around Fritham and through Sloden and Pitts Wood Inclosures with local historian Henry Cole; part of the walk is detailed on page 60. Not surprisingly, Henry believes that Sumner would be disappointed in some elements of the Forest today. 'He would have been horrified at the number of people who visit the Forest and the number of cars. But he also would have been pleased that so many people want to look after the Forest and that there are so many restoration projects underway.' Henry also thinks that Sumner would have been thrilled by modern technologies like the use of ground-penetrating radar and Lidar (page 24) for archaeological discoveries.

The artist went everywhere on his bike, possibly travelling as many as 60 miles a day, explained Henry. 'I can't help but think how exhausted he would have been to cycle on rough trails from Ibsley and then conduct excavation work when he got here.'

One of Sumner's greatest gifts to us was encouragement to leave the beaten track and explore out-of-the-way pockets of the Forest. 'Many of the views Heywood Sumner painted are similar today, although he did take liberties with moving things around to suit his ideal view,' said Henry, who has made countless excursions to the Forest to identify views that Sumner painted.

Heywood Sumner's original books are now out of print, but there are modern reprints still available. *Cuckoo Hill: The Book of Gorley*, a 1987 facsimile adaptation of Sumner's original three volumes, is highly readable and features beautiful watercolours of the north Forest. New Forest libraries have copies of many of his books in Local Studies reference sections, as does the Christopher Tower Reference Library in the New Forest Centre (page 157).

> If any one wishes to know the beauty of the Forest in autumn, let him see the view from the high ridge at Stoney-Cross. Here the air blows off the Wiltshire Downs finer and keener than anywhere else. Here, on all sides, stretch woods and moors. Here, in the latter end of August, the three heathers, one after another, cover every plain and holt with their crimson glory, mixed with the flashes of the dwarf furze.
>
> John R Wise, *The New Forest: Its History and its Scenery*

Located just over two miles south of Fritham, Stoney Cross feels much the same today; the windswept expanses of heathland and the long (often empty) roads can feel otherworldly. If you visit at dusk, you might be treated to herds of deer munching their way across the heath and, as darkness falls and traffic subsides, you can feel the sense of remoteness that Wise undoubtedly experienced regularly. This is

A walk from Fritham through Sloden Inclosure
By Henry Cole, Forestry Commission volunteer ranger and local historian

❋ OS Explorer map OL22; start: Forestry Commission car park, Fritham ♀ SU231141;
5 miles; moderate.

Our journey follows a gravel forest road into the depths of Old Sloden wood, a route taken many times by Heywood Sumner (page 58) in the period just before and after World War I. The route is uneven underfoot and there's one fairly steep descent; it can be muddy and probably isn't suitable for very young children. The archaeological features cited in this walk can be difficult for the amateur to see but, even if you can't make out the ancient ditches and banks, just knowing all that has gone on here before you should be reward enough. This is one of the most remote places in the entire Forest; I think it's safe to say that your only encounter will be with a surprised deer.

1 At the far end of the main car park, take the gravel track heading out across open heathland (to the left of the 'Additional Car Park' sign).

2 Continue straight on the track for about one mile and just before you enter Old Sloden Wood, by an intersecting track on the right, you can detour into the trees on your left. Here you will find the remains of a World War II sawmill. All that is left are the loading ramps and some lumps of concrete. This is one of several long-forgotten sawmills located around the New Forest that played their part in the war effort. Back on the track and venturing on a little further you will see to your right the fence, banks and ditches of Sloden Inclosure, but more about that later.

3 Continue on the main track – as soon as you enter the woods, you will see a less clear path veering off to the right. Follow this trail directly into woods; after a short while it becomes wide and grassy. The inclosure fence will be on your right – your distance from it will vary but keep the fence on your right all the way until you emerge from the woods at the clearing a bit further ahead. You are walking in Old Sloden, which Sumner described as 'the most beautiful wooded hillside… nowhere in the Forest do yews and whitebeams grow in such profusion'. Standing in the tranquillity of this setting, it is not impossible to imagine an elderly bearded gentleman dressed in tweeds cycling towards you, ready for a day's archaeological investigation. Thankfully little has changed since Heywood Sumner's day.

4 It's very difficult to see but if you look carefully you will find banks delineating the eastern edge of the medieval coppice, after about 220yds from where you first entered the woods. The practice of enclosing areas of woodland and renting them out by the Crown for coppicing goes back to medieval times, when it was a very important source of revenue during the

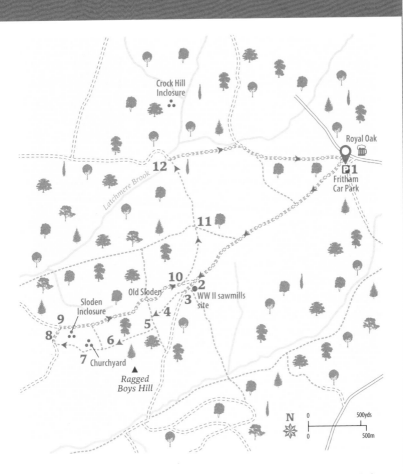

Crock Hill
Inclosure

Royal Oak

P1
Fritham
Car Park

12

Latchmere Brook

11

10

Old Sloden

2

3 WW II sawmills
site

Sloden
Inclosure

4

9

5

8

6

7 Churchyard

Ragged
Boys Hill

N

0   500yds

0   500m

reigns of Henry VIII and Elizabeth I. Continue forward, keeping your eye to the left, and after about 160yds you will come across a large clearing to your left. Make your way towards it, and then walk along the right edge of the clearing, continuing in the same direction you've been walking. This is the site of one of the Roman potteries that Sumner excavated and recorded. The New Forest produced huge amounts of pottery between the late 3rd and late 4th centuries. The landscape must have looked very different from today with the area being covered with potters huts and kilns and small market gardens. Sumner ▶

A walk from Fritham through Sloden Inclosure (continued)

◀ investigated 17 kiln sites and plotted many more spoil heaps; additional sites have been found in recent years.

5 Exit the clearing straight ahead, on to the wide grassy track. You are now walking within an ancient and ornamental woodland (normally just referred to as A&O woodland). There is no precise definition of A&O woodland but it normally refers to unenclosed woods going back to the 18th century or earlier – the term was first used in the New Forest Act of 1877.

Notice that many of the yews for which Sloden was famous are in poor condition; the cause of deterioration is unknown.

6 Continue heading west atop a ridge, with the fence on your right now below you. After about 500yds from the clearing, you will cross the first side of small rectangular earthwork known as the Churchyard. Each side is about 47yds long. Sumner surveyed it in 1915 after sketching it in 1913; he thought it was an animal enclosure but it is now believed to be one of at least six medieval hunting lodges built in the Forest. A short distance on, the woods become less dense and you will see where the land slopes down on the left. Ahead of you on the left is one of the most enormous oak trees in the Forest. It has been pollarded (page 112) so long ago that the branches are almost as thick as the trunk. There is another one on the other side of the track, on the right. We don't know how old these trees are but we can be certain that these two oaks were fairly mature in 1698, as that was the year when pollarding was made illegal by William III because the government required tall straight timber from maiden (unpollarded) trees for the Royal Navy.

7 Follow the path between the two oaks for 110yds. The path narrows and then you will emerge from the wood to enjoy a glorious view. Looking ahead you can see right across to Ogdens and Abbotswell, with the inclosure in the middle ground and slightly to the left is Hasley. On the far side of Hasley are the humps and bumps of quarrying work carried out by the Roman-era potters – they needed lots of heath stone to make their kilns. On the nearer side is a track composed of red sand due to its high iron content. The 'red sands' are a favourite gallop for local horseriders as it is fairly soft if you fall off. The hill where you are standing is known as Ragged Boys. Sumner investigated local place names and believed that 'boys' was a corruption of the French 'bois' meaning wood – so a literal translation would be Ragged Wood. Descend the hill towards the gravel track. There is no defined path and you may have to pick your way among undergrowth, depending on the season, but it is an easy descent with plenty of clear spaces, especially as you move to the right. On reaching the main track, turn right and head towards the inclosure.

8 After about a couple of minutes, enter the inclosure through a gate and keep going straight on until you reach a T-junction, in about 250ft. Sumner described Sloden Inclosure as

having been planted in 1864 with oak, ash and Scots pine with a few well-grown Douglas and Silver firs. The taller Douglas firs are probably the ones Sumner mentioned and are likely to be some of the first introduced to England, by David Douglas in the first part of the 19th century.

9 Turn right at the T-junction and follow the wide, clear track until you reach the vehicle access gate to Sloden Inclosure, after about three quarters of a mile; exit here. (Note that from here you can opt instead to follow a track uphill on the right to rejoin the original track you had walked out on from the car park. A sharp left at the top of the hill will lead you back to the car park.)

10 Just outside the vehicle gate from where you exited Sloden Inclosure, you will see a well-worn track that bears left away from the gravel track you are on. Follow this straight ahead. After passing through a mix of heather and gorse, the track goes through a large group of very old hollies, known locally as a 'holm', in about 550yds.

11 At this point, on your left, you will see an impressive bank and ditch, which is visible for two miles. Sumner believed that it was a demarcation boundary defining the pottery areas. It is worth exploring here for a little while and marvelling how these banks have survived for some 1,600 years. Continue along the path, which is a bit rutted in places but takes you through a lovely varied part of the Forest. After 400yds, you will enter Crock Hill, part of Island Thorns Inclosure. Sumner suspected the name derived from the large amount of very fine Roman pottery shards found in the area. You can still find bits of pottery here that workers discarded. After 220yds, you will meet the main track and cycle route that runs from Fritham to Frogham.

12 Turn right on to the gravel track (away from the bridge) and follow it uphill back towards Fritham. After about 750yds, you will see paddocks to your left. On the far side of the field is a grassed-over mound that is the last surviving blast-proof storage building from the gunpowder factory at Eyeworth. Follow the track back to the car park, roughly half a mile away. Just past the vehicle barrier at the entrance to the car park, look out for a small black postbox on your left. The Powder Mill Post was installed by the Schulze gunpowder factory (page 55) so that the postman did not need to enter the works. This was probably not just for the benefit of the postman but more likely for the safety of the workers in case the postman was a smoker.

Henry Cole (✆ 07748 026230 ✉ henrycole@sky.com), a volunteer ranger with Forestry England, lectures on Heywood Sumner and New Forest Airfields to interested societies.

also a great location for stargazing; the levels of light pollution here are relatively low and there is plenty of space to spread out a blanket. The only downside is the presence of the A31; come prepared to block out the noise of the relentless traffic.

But it's not all about the wide-open prospects. One of the joys of walking near here is the diversity of landscape, easily seen in a six-mile circular route from Stoney Cross. If you head west past the Ocknell Campsite and through Ocknell Inclosure (away from the A31), you can explore numerous inclosures, including South and North Bentley, King's Garn Gutter and Long Beech, as well as the ancient, unenclosed woodlands. You'll be serenaded by diverse birdsong among the trees and spot plenty of butterflies and dragonflies in the undergrowth.

Perhaps most significantly, you'll be walking in history. During World War II, this area was buzzing with activity, as Stoney Cross played a major role in air-force preparations to support the D-day invasion of

FROM MILK TO CHEESE: CHANGING WITH THE TIMES

Lyburn Farm Lyburn Rd, Landford SP5 2DN 🕽 01794 399982 👌 lyburnfarm.co.uk

Mike and Judy Smales have been farming at the northern tip of the New Forest since 1970. Their farm now encompasses an impressive 500 acres. They decided to start making cheese when the price of milk sunk so low that they were losing money on their dairy herd. The family still produce milk because, as Mike told me, 'we have the infrastructure so it would be foolish not to continue'. But the cheese is the main focus here, with 50% of their annual 1.4 million litres of milk turned into cheese – 80 tonnes of it, to be precise.

All of Lyburn's cheese – which is predominantly Old Winchester, Stoney Cross and Lyburn Gold – has won national and international awards. 'We knew when we started that we couldn't compete with the cheddar market so we decided to make

gouda-style cheeses. Our niche is Old Winchester, a hard, crumbly vegetarian cheese that can be used for grating, as a substitute for pecorino or parmesan, both of which use an animal rennet,' Mike told me.

The farm is now run by Mike's and Judy's oldest son, Jono, who oversees the daily management of 170 cows and fields of organic vegetables, which include runner beans, courgette, sweetcorn and pumpkin. These are all delivered to Riverford and Able and Cole who use them in their box deliveries.

The Smales are proud of their eco-friendly initiatives. Because the milk is used for cheese-making straight after milking, there is no refrigeration energy drain, and since everything is done on-site, there is no transport of milk either. Most impressively,

Europe in 1944. Stoney Cross was one of three major airfields to be built in the New Forest (the others were at Beaulieu Heath and Holmsley South). The most visible wartime remnant here is the road to Linwood, part of which served as a 2,000yd runway. When you stand out in the open land today, it's easy to imagine the drone of airplanes and feelings of tense anticipation among the pilots and ground crew who were based here. Today, however, you're most likely to hear trickling streams, snorting ponies and the gleeful whoops of children delighting in this open ground.

The airfield here was one of the largest in the New Forest and was used by both the Royal Air Force and the US Army Air Force. Former US president Barack Obama's maternal grandfather arrived at Stoney Cross in 1944 and served here for a brief time until D-day.

Other remainders are less obvious, such as the former service roads that have been incorporated into Ocknell and Longbeech campsites.

most of the electricity used in cheese-making is generated by solar power.

A good time to visit Lyburn is during the annual **Hampshire Food Festival** (⊘ hampshirefare.co.uk/news-events). For a few evenings in July, Mike and his family take visitors on a tour of the 450-acre farm in trailers attached to huge tractors. Seated on hay bales, you bounce along over the fields and learn about the challenges involved with growing organic vegetables. You'll get a close-up view of grazing cows and experience the flavour of a truly family-run operation. You're also likely to hear Mike talk about the doom that supermarkets, 'purveyors of mediocrity', bring to dairy farmers. 'When supermarkets reduce milk prices to such a large degree, producers can only operate at a loss,' Mike explained to our group, although this has changed recently due to milk shortages. 'There needs to be more equal distribution among producers, processors and sellers.'

After the tractor ride, guests are treated to a cheese supper laid out on picnic tables. All food is truly local: bread from a nearby bakery, lettuce from the Hayward farm 'down the road', Hill Farm apple juice, wines from Setley Ridge (page 119) and other vineyards, and courgette chutney made by Judy. It feels just like a family supper on the farm.

Mike has chosen to bypass supermarkets by appealing to a 'small but discerning percentage of the market'. You can purchase Lyburn cheese at farm shops throughout the New Forest or at the small shop on the farm, which is usually open weekdays from 8.00 until 16.30 but it's advisable to call to be sure.

The National Park Authority's New Forest Knowledge website (page 12) has further information, including personal memories.

Rufus Stone

All is not what it seems at the Rufus Stone, just over a mile northeast of Stoney Cross and one of the most visited sites in the Forest. Even the original stone, 'having been much mutilated', was replaced by this three-sided memorial in 1841. The present-day cast-iron pillar, with inscriptions that tell the legend, encases the original stone. The accompanying history and geography might be on dodgy ground as well. The story that is regularly repeated and that prompted the erection of the original stone in 1745 is that during a hunting expedition in 1100, William II, known as William Rufus, was enjoying his hunting ground when his finest archer, Sir Walter Tyrell, aimed at a stag but the arrow ricocheted off an oak tree, striking the king in the chest and killing him immediately. The question of whether the incident was an accident or a deliberate plot to remove the unpopular monarch has long surrounded the tale.

In more recent years, debate has concerned the location of the event. Historians now believe that the memorial is on the wrong side of the Forest. New Forest historian Richard Reeves thinks that the death took place at Truham, now known as Througham, on the Beaulieu Estate. So how did the monument end up near Fritham? 'It's possible that Truham was misidentified as Fritham,' Richard told me.

So go along and visit this memorial but do so to stir your interest in history, not necessarily because you are standing where it really happened. Fortunately, it's lovely to walk among the many oak trees here, possibly relatives of the long-gone oak that might have caused Rufus's demise. The stone is located close to the car park and there are clear walking trails through the woods. One caveat is that you do hear the hum of cars from the A31 from here.

The easiest way to reach the Rufus Stone is from the eastbound carriageway of the A31, about 1.3 miles east of Stoney Cross. It is also accessible from the hamlet of Brook by taking the road opposite the Bell Inn. The stone is on the right, about a mile after the Sir Walter Tyrell pub.

---

1 New Forest pony at sunset, Stoney Cross. 2 Ponies being rounded up on a drift.
3 Running at Hampton Ridge. 4 The Rufus Stone. ▶

IANREDDING/S

DEREK TIPPETTS

NEW FOREST NATIONAL PARK AUTHORITY

DEREK TIPPETTS

A walk through Ditchend Bottom & Pitts Wood Inclosure

❄ OS Explorer map OL22; start: Godshill Cricket car park ♀ SU181150; 5 miles; moderate.

This is an ideal route for history buffs and view lovers alike. It takes in a sampling of the valleys, conifer woodlands and wide vistas that characterise this area, as well as some exciting evidence of World War II bomb testing. The route is particularly lovely in autumn when copper-hued ferns shimmer on the hillsides. Look out for pillars that are remnants of when the woods were originally enclosed in 1775. The route involves a few hills, including two steep ones at the end, and can be wet depending on rainfall – there are a few stream crossings along the way. For excellent perspective on the wartime activities that took place here, see the drone tour or bomb testing sites on the National Park Authority's youtube channel (📺 NewForestNPA).

1 Begin at Godshill Cricket car park. With the car park behind you, keep to the right of the cricket ground, walking straight from the cricket hut to the edge of the trail. Bear right as you come down the hill, following the wide, deeply grooved track to Ditchend Bottom. Cross two streams (depth varies according to how rainy it has been but you can usually hop across) and head towards the woods.

2 Make a sharp left to follow the track straight into the woods. Follow the track uphill, bearing right, to where it widens. Continue straight up the hill, past another two junctions of tracks.

3 About 600yds from where you first entered woods, take a sharp right turn at three pillars, leaving the woods on a narrow, rough path. When you reach the top of the hill, remain on the same trail as it curves around to the left and emerges on to open land. The track joins another that goes left in a Y shape; this can be hard to see as it is grassy underfoot but it will become clear as you begin to approach the wide Hampton Ridge cycle trail. Bear right and continue as the trail joins first one dirt track, and then another. This second is the Hampton Ridge cycle trail (about 500yds after leaving the woods).

4 Turn right on to the cycle trail; you'll see a post marked 7 on the right. Walk for about half a mile until you see a well-defined clearing on the left. If you look carefully, you will see rectangular blocks in the grass, about 25 steps away from the edge of the trail. Walk to them and just beyond you will see the rectangular cement blocks that form the shaft of an arrow pointing over the edge of the ridge to where an illuminated target lay in the valley during World War II. Both the directional arrow and the target could be lit by a diesel generator to direct bomber pilots during night Air Force practise sessions.

5 At the tip of the arrow, turn left on to the narrow white gravel path that arcs around to the left and rejoins the cycle trail. Cross the cycle trail and join the wide grassy path on the other side. Follow this until it joins a horse trail a short distance on. Turn right on to the horse path. This runs parallel to the cycle trail but provides a stunning view of the inclosure and landscape beyond. After about 250yds, you will begin to see the cycle trail on your right. Continue on until the track joins with the

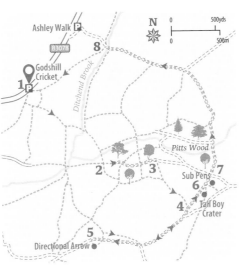

cycle trail at a four-way junction. Turn left on to Hampton Ridge Cycle Trail and return to the post marked 7. Just beyond this post, turn left off the cycle trail to follow a smaller dirt path marked at the beginning with a no cycling symbol. This path can be waterlogged after heavy rains but you should be able to detour around the puddles.

6 After about 300yds, you will come to a large, grassy mound ahead to the right of the track. Just in front of it is a pond that varies in size according to rainfall but is a well-frequented drinking spot for animals. Known as the Tallboy Crater, this is one of the most visible remains of the bomb-testing sites in this area. The mound is known as the Sub Pens, a World War II bomb-testing structure. Feel free to leave the track and climb one of the paths up it. In 1945, this was the target for the Grand Slam, the largest bomb ever dropped by British forces. The huge concrete structure was covered over with earth in 1946. When you have finished, climb down on the side you came up, and turn right back on to the trail. Walk downhill to a T-junction. Cross the intersecting path and pass between two wooden posts marking the entrance to Pitts Wood Inclosure. Just past them on the right is a small stone marker dedicated to Gerald Lascelles, a much-lauded deputy surveyor of the Forest from 1880 to 1914.

7 Follow the track down until you reach a stream. Cross – there is a bridge but it can be wet – and continue up the hill on the other side. As you climb the hill, notice bricks in the path, which are ▶

A walk through Ditchend Bottom & Pitts Wood Inclosure (continued)

◀ leftover reinforcements from World War II. At the top of the hill, where you emerge into the open air, follow the track straight on. Another track joins from the right; continue straight as the track passes through a small cluster of trees and downhill towards Ditchend Brook. As you walk downhill, you will see large concrete slabs underfoot. Again, these are reinforcements left from World War II.

8 Cross the bridge and immediately turn sharp left (the main track continues uphill towards Ashley Walk car park), on to a rough path that alternates between grass, sand and gravel. Rise to the opposite side of the cricket ground where you started.

---

4 GODSHILL & AROUND

🏠 **Sandy Balls** (page 222) ▲ **Harry's Field** (page 223)

The Godshill area is a good base for exploring the north Forest. The village itself is split by the B3078 (Roger Penny Way) and consists of a pub, village hall and a cricket club, from where the walk detailed on page 68 begins. The difference in landscape between the flat, boggy heathland in the south Forest and the wide vistas visible from the ridges and hilltops of the north Forest is readily apparent in the many walking trails carved out here. The stretch of the B3078 from Bramshaw Telegraph along Deadman Hill and on to Godshill is an exceptionally pretty drive, although notorious for a high number of road accidents involving ponies.

World War II history abounds here. Inert bombs were tested throughout the **Ashley Walk** area and some traces can be seen, although much has disappeared. In 1940, animals were removed from a 5,000-acre tract of land, which was fenced off and turned into a bombing range. You can still see concrete directional signals near Deadman's Hill on the Godshill to Cadnam road and concrete light boxes at various points near Hampton Ridge. Near Hampton Ridge, outside Pitts Wood, is also where you can see what are known as the **Sub Pens** (or Submarine Pens), and other wartime scars. These are highlighted in the walk on page 69.

¶¶ FOOD & DRINK

Foresters Arms Frogham SP6 2JA ✆ 01425 652294 ⌁ the.littlepubgroup.co.uk/the-foresters-arms. There's lots to look at in this good old-fashioned, red-walled pub with no music, just friendly conversation. It has a relatively small bar area but boasts a good local selection of real ales. Lots of dogs at lunchtime in the large garden. Popular with authentic Forest folk.

Hockey's Farmyard Café South Gorley SP6 2PW ✆ 01425 652 542 ⟡ hockeys-farm. co.uk ☉ seasonal; check online. Delightfully local, licensed café on a farm. Especially good for breakfast but also serves cooked lunch, including home-made soups, sandwiches and yummy cakes. Friendly staff and an overall pleasant ambience. Situated next to an award-winning, family-owned farm shop that supports local farmers and producers. A personal favourite.

The Potting Shed Fordingbridge SP6 2QB ✆ 01425 655392 ⟡ pottingshedhyde. co.uk ☉ 09.00−16.00 Tue−Sun; kitchen closes at 14.45. Quirky café with tables set up in greenhouses and the main building. Dedicated to homegrown and local produce; you are surrounded by the vegetables you eat. Also has a fully licensed bar. Occasional evening events, including themed dinners and live musicians. Dogs are properly feted.

5 FORDINGBRIDGE

⌂ **The Three Lions** (page 222)

Named after the medieval bridge with seven arches that majestically crosses the Avon, Fordingbridge is officially a New Forest town but has a slightly different feel because of the more open landscapes that surround it compared with towns in the south. The quiet high street reflects tough economic times but the town's setting by the River Avon redeems the neglected ambience and after a riverside walk among the willows – and perhaps a run-around in the children's play area – you begin to appreciate this former market town.

It's well worth visiting the **Fordingbridge Museum** (King's Yd, SP6 1AB ✆ 01425 655222 ⟡ fordingbridgemuseum.co.uk ☉ Easter–Oct), especially for the small collection of paintings and sketches by Augustus John of his children. At one time considered Britain's leading portrait painter, John lived at Freyerns Court in Burgate, near Fordingbridge, for the last 31 years of his life until his death in 1961.

A timeline at the front of the museum explains Fordingbridge's historical context and other items show how life has changed for town residents. The well-presented displays grew from the private collection of former town residents John Shering and his brother Richard, who amassed some 9,000 artefacts from house clearances and shop closings. A large Victorian doll's house donated by a local is meticulously furnished. A visitor information centre is adjacent to the museum.

¶¶ FOOD & DRINK

Bridges 26 High St, SP6 1AX T ✆ 01425 654149 ⌂ bridgescoffeeanddining.com ⊙ 09.00–16.00 Mon–Sat, 09.00–15.00 Sun. This small tea room at the centre of the high street is a pleasant spot for breakfast and lunch or a slice of cake in the afternoon.

The George 14 Bridge St, SP6 1AH ✆ 01425 652040 ⌂ georgeatfordingbridge.co.uk ⊙ Wed–Sun. This has the prime location for viewing the Avon and its resident swans that swim right past your table. In summer, the few tables on the outdoor terrace are in high demand but you still get a good view from the conservatory or the large back room with a fireplace. The interior is cosy and welcoming although service can be slow during busy times. The best pub food in town.

La Lambretta 1 Shaftesbury St, SP6 1JF ✆ 01425 656192 ⌂ lambrettafordingbridge.com ⊙ 17.30–21.00 Mon–Sat. Cosy Italian serving comforting and reliable pizzas and pastas.

6 WOODGREEN VILLAGE HALL

🏠 **Undercastle Cottage** (page 223)

Woodgreen, near Fordingbridge SP6 2AQ ✆ 01725 513828 ⌂ woodgreenvillagehall.uk

The sleepy ambience of **Woodgreen**, a village four miles north of Fordingbridge, belies the community spirit beneath. Not only did

WOODGREEN COMMUNITY SHOP

Hale Rd, SP6 2AJ ✆ 01725 512467 ⌂ woodgreenshop.org ⊙ 08.00–18.00 Mon–Fri, 08.00–17.00 Sat, 08.00–11.00 Sun

'This is the pride of our village,' said Andrea Finn, Woodgreen resident, gesturing to the shelves neatly stocked with jams, herbs, chutneys and sauces, all made and grown by residents of Woodgreen and other nearby villages. Further back, fridges containing local meats and cheeses and shelves with wines and household goods awaited the day's customers. We sat at a table by the large window that overlooks the lane and fields beyond. The post office window was open and a new day began at the Woodgreen Community Shop.

As people came in and waved to Andrea, it was hard to believe that this shop, like so many others nationwide, was threatened with closure in 2006. 'When the couple who ran the previous shop and post office had to give it up, a group of us placed a notice in the parish newsletter urging people to get involved and try to save it,' Andrea told me. Responses were enthusiastic and in just six weeks concerned citizens from Woodgreen and the nearby villages of Breamore, Godshill and Hale, all of which had lost their shops, raised over £16,000 in shares and donations. In January 2007 the Woodgreen Community Shop Association took over the running of the village shop and post office.

villagers unite to save their community shop, but they are fiercely proud of their village hall where life in the 1930s is depicted in a series of Grade-II-listed **wall murals.** For a period of 18 months from 1932–33, two Royal College of Art students were paid £100 to live in the village and paint local scenes. Displaying their mutual passion for early Italian frescoes, each artist painted one side and one end wall. One of them, Robert Baker, who went on to become an Oxford professor, loved Woodgreen so much that he retired here; he is buried in the village cemetery.

Every inch of wall is painted with scenes of village life, including a flower show, cider pressing, a Sunday school gathering and a dance contest. It is touching to realise that many of these events still take place. You can also see black cherry trees, known locally as Merry Trees because villagers used to concoct a drink from the cherries that made them merry. Residents of the village were models for the paintings. Only one person appears twice. The local poacher, who is shown with his gun in a scene illustrating the River Avon from Castle Hill, returns to the village on the opposite wall as a respectable citizen playing his

Supporting the local community was central to the association's goals from the outset. The shop stocks goods sourced as locally as possible, including New Forest Marque items (page 30).

'That ongoing support to local businesses is one of the cornerstones of the shop's ethos,' said David Mussell, vice chairman of the association and one of the people involved with carrying the shop forward from the planning stages to day-to-day operations. 'Enabling local businesses to thrive can only be good for the New Forest and surrounding areas.'

The shop also boosts the social fabric of Woodgreen and surrounding hamlets. Young students often have their first work experience here and they are an important source of paid help in after-school hours. The shop is maintained by a group of paid staffers, and all the rest of the work, including carrying and unloading boxes, stocking shelves and clearing rubbish, is done by volunteers.

There is also the overseeing committee of eight, all of whom bring diverse skills and backgrounds from current or previous professions. Many of this group volunteer some 30-40 hours per week to keep the shop afloat. 'So much goes on behind the scenes that customers don't see,' explained David. 'All of us are using lifelong experience to operate a major commercial venture. It's far more complicated than one might think.'

JANE RIX/S

ADRIAN BAKER/S

FORDINGBRIDGE MUSEUM

NEW FOREST DESTINATION PARTNERSHIP

accordion. Flanking the stage are representations of the morning cock crowing and an owl hailing darkness.

Perhaps the most wonderful aspect of the murals is that they are not tucked away for safekeeping. The village hall is still a central point in village life and hosts regular meetings, displays and community events.

If you want to see this representation of bucolic village life, you can attend the public afternoon tea usually held on the second Wednesday of every month. Bring a book or jigsaw puzzle because the locals will be keen on exchanging. Check the booking calendar on the website to be sure.

¶¶ FOOD & DRINK

The Horse & Groom High St, SP6 2AS ⌀ horseandgroom-woodgreen.com. It's no surprise that the car park at the Horse & Groom is regularly full; this is the stand-out pub in the area. Situated in the centre of tiny Woodgreen, the pub is a focal point for residents and walkers. It serves standard pub fare but a cut above its rivals. The large garden is popular in summer; come early if you want to snag a table in the evening. On cold days, the wood-burner by the entrance provides a warm welcome, as do the staff. There is a good selection of local ales.

Woodgreen Community Shop Hale Rd, SP6 2AJ ⌀ 01725 512467 ⌀ woodgreencommunityshop.org; page 72. An excellent resource for people self-catering in the area. Also a good place to stop for coffee and a snack; there are outdoor tables and a few inside by the window.

NORTH & WEST BORDERS: WEAVING IN & OUT OF THE NEW FOREST

It's fun to criss-cross in and out of Hampshire, Dorset, Wiltshire and back again as you venture into the areas bordering the New Forest. You can feel the presence of Wiltshire as you head to the **northern reaches** of the Forest, possibly because the views of patchwork fields are such a marked contrast to the woodland and heaths traditionally associated with it. The relative quiet and absence of tourist attractions is a striking change from the busy southern region.

◀ **1** Cranborne Chase. **2** Blacksmithing display, Fordingbridge Museum. **3** Folk band at Downton Cuckoo Fair. **4** New Forest Marque local produce is promoted by outlets such as Woodgreen Community Shop.

You are constantly reminded of archaeology when visiting the northern and western regions of the New Forest and its surrounds, especially further west towards **Martin Down** and **Cranborne Chase**. The chalk plateau that runs through Dorset, Hampshire and Wiltshire is where Augustus Pitt Rivers, considered to be a founding father of British archaeology, excavated ancient ruins on his private estate. Here I include a small corner of the Cranborne Chase and West Wiltshire Downs AONB at **Martin Down**; for more on the area, see the Bradt guide, *Slow Travel Dorset*. Although not part of the New Forest National Park, these wonderfully unspoilt landscapes are certainly worth further exploration for the abundant wildlife and gentle slopes of grass.

7 DOWNTON

🏠 **Newton Farmhouse** (page 222)

Downton, originally within the borders of William the Conqueror's New Forest, but today just to the north of the Forest boundary in Wiltshire, has been populated for over 7,000 years, making it one of the oldest settlements in the area. It still qualifies as the quintessential English village with its thatched cottages, cosy pubs and the River Avon flowing through. Amenities are minimal, which makes it an especially charming town to wander around; this is not somewhere that attracts the souvenir-hunting crowd. Situated just six miles south of Salisbury, Downton is worth visiting to explore the Norman castle ruins at the Moot (see below). The **Downton Heritage Trail** (⊘ downtonvillage.co.uk), which is available online or as a leaflet at the library on Church Leat, just off High Street, is an absorbing delve into the best of the area outlining some of its varied history. The trail begins at the 13th-century **cross** at the heart of The Borough, the most eye-catching part of town with its long, narrow green lined with thatched houses. From there, the route continues out to the **water meadows** where you still can still see the old sluice gates that were controlled by 'drowners' to flood the meadows and encourage early grazing. A visit to the **old mills and tannery** site is a reminder of the importance of the River Avon in this village's industrial history. Tanneries, where animal hides are prepared for production of leather goods, were recorded here as early as 1215. The last one closed in 1998.

The Heritage Trail passes **The Moot** (⊘ downtonmoot.co.uk) an 18th-century garden created from the site of a Norman castle built by the bishop of Winchester. These peaceful and unusual eight acres abut

WELCOMING SPRING WITH THE CUCKOO FAIR

cuckoofair.co.uk

Historians believe that Downton hosted market fairs from 1249 but the first proper cuckoo fair was probably held in 1530. Cuckoo fairs evolved to celebrate the arrival of warm weather, so named because the cuckoo is a migratory bird that returns in spring.

World War I brought an end to most village fairs and Downton was no exception. But in 1980, Steve Addison, a newcomer to the area, led a group of volunteers in re-establishing the fair. It's been running ever since, as an annual, non-profit event held on the Saturday of the first May bank holiday weekend. Its growth to the huge occasion that it is today, with some 20,000 people attending, is testimony to what volunteers can achieve.

Stalls line the green strip of The Borough, one of Downton's most attractive streets with its profuse showing of thatched roofs.

Crafts, jewellery, woodcarvings, paintings and lots of home-baked goods are on offer. A car park is turned over to food producers, which include local butchers, jam- and honey-makers, bakers and wineries. Some of the exhibitors display the New Forest Marque (page 30).

There is, of course, a maypole that local children dance around throughout the day. If you arrive at the start, you can witness the crowning of the princess and the procession from the Bull Hotel to the maypole that officially opens the event.

In keeping with the ancient tradition of minstrels and performers who would come to the village during the fair, there are lots of local bands and entertainers as well as a field with fairground rides and games. It's a great, old-fashioned day out and well worth a special trip.

the banks of the River Avon. The Moot is just a short distance from the library (where you might be able to find a leaflet to help guide you, though there are brief descriptions in the gardens) and centre of town; go up High Street and then turn right into Moot Lane – the entrance is on the right, opposite **Moot House**. There is a car park just beyond.

The original earth structure here was built by the Bishop of Winchester, brother of King Stephen, to control the crossing of the River Avon and was destroyed after the bishop's death in 1154. In 1700, when Moot House was built, the earthworks were landscaped as a garden. The gardens were separated from Moot House in 1972, at which time they became overgrown; local residents formed a charitable trust in 1988 to restore them to the way they were in 1909.

You have to use a lot of imagination to figure out what might have been here in the 12th century, but the gardens are delightful to walk through.

The best surviving feature of this time is the **amphitheatre**, made up of six tiers of grass that overlook a small pond. You can still very clearly see the inner and outer ditches – the area between the two was used for livestock and people lived here when an invasion was feared. The two mounds in the centre are the remains of the castle keep. Climb up **Bevis Mount** (it's steep and not suitable for everyone) for a far-reaching view of Wiltshire hillsides toward Cranborne Chase and Clearbury Rings, an Iron Age hillfort.

¶¶ FOOD & DRINK

The Goat 62 The Borough ✆ 01725 535353 ⌂ thegoatatdownton.co.uk ⊙ noon–23.00 Mon–Sat, noon–20.00 Sun. Residents of both the northern New Forest and Salisbury frequent the Goat for its charming atmosphere and good (although sometimes inconsistent) British classics. The garden is a lovely place to be on a summer day. And you can bring the dog.

8 BREAMORE

Life in this bucolic spot seems to be continuing on seamlessly from the 16th century, when the original Breamore House was built. The village's history stretches back to Saxon times, when the church of St Mary was founded, and beyond. In the Roman period, the land most likely was part of the estate at the Roman Villa at Rockbourne. Today, Breamore is still a charming village but unfortunately bisected by the A338, the main route between the New Forest and Salisbury. On the west side, you'll find peaceful country lanes, enviable residences and the centrepiece of this area, the Breamore Estate.

St Mary's Church, at the base of the drive leading to Breamore House, was built roughly around AD1000 and is one of the finest surviving Saxon buildings in southern England. It has an unusually long nave and the walls are made of whole flints with large quoins of irregular long and short work (a characteristic feature of Saxon church building) and pilaster strips of green sandstone and ironstone. The original stones on the northeast quoin of the chancel are still visible. Another remarkably well-preserved feature is the strikingly clear Anglo-Saxon inscription above the door from the tower through to the south porticus, believed to mean 'Here is

"It's easy to imagine children racing up and down the staircase or elegant ladies taking tea in the drawing room."

manifested the word to thee'. Seven of the original Saxon windows also remain: two can be seen high in the wall on the north side of the nave and another in the south transept. Others have been altered.

Although it is not technically a cruciform church, St Mary's represents an evolutionary step in the cruciform plan due to its integration of tower and transepts of the same width, all connected as one structure. Before the 12th century, the church was a minster, serving the needs of surrounding communities. The original church was larger and is thought to have been part of a royal estate, but in the 15th century parts of the building that had fallen into disrepair were destroyed. By then the community did not need such a large church because the population had declined due to the Black Death, and there was insufficient money for repairs.

Breamore Estate
⁂ 01725 512858 ⁂ breamorehouse.com. ⊙ Apr–Oct: house selected afternoons (check website); museum 10.00–16.00 Tue–Sun Apr–Oct. Café: Tue-Sun 10.00-15.00

This is a great chance to visit an Elizabethan manor house that's been in the same family since 1748. The current owner of **Breamore House**, Sir Michael Westrow Hulse, is the 11th baronet. But the history of the house and its land goes back to AD508 when a battle on the outskirts of Breamore village may have determined the boundaries of the New Forest. Today, the exterior of the house looks much as it did in 1583, when it was built by William Dodington. His family still holds a claim in a portrait of his widow that hangs in the Great Hall. According to the current owners, a condition of sale in 1748, when the Hulse family purchased the house from the Dodingtons, was that the portrait would never be moved. The Great Hall has a more recent claim to fame: during the planning of the D-day invasions, General George Patton headquartered here for a short time while allied troops waited and camped in the nearby Forest.

Visits to the house are by guided tour only, but there are lots of quirky tales like this that you will hear from your guide as part of it. Despite the rigidity of having a guided tour, Breamore is charming and it's easy to imagine children racing up and down the staircase or elegant ladies taking tea in the drawing room. The art collection is notable: I spotted a Rembrandt, four Van Dycks and a large rural scene by David Tenniers that hangs in the Great Hall. The two 17th-century

Brussels tapestries here are in excellent condition and help soften the otherwise rather long room.

The most important art is in an alcove above the main staircase where the earliest known set of ethnological paintings hangs. The

A walk of farmland & ancient sites around Whitsbury

✱ OS Explorer Map OL22; start: car park by Breamore House tea rooms (The Pantry Barn)
♀ SU151187; 5 miles; moderate.

- -

This route incorporates the Breamore Estate (including the mizmaze), the site of ancient Whitsbury Castle, Whitsbury Stud Farm and St Leonard's Church, as well as fabulous, expansive views, farmland and woods. It obviously combines well with a visit to the house but you can do it even when the house is closed by parking in the museum car park (⊙ 09.00–18.00 daily) and walking on the public footpath past the house and into Breamore Woods.

1 Follow the directions to the Breamore Mizmaze on page 82.
2 After viewing the mizmaze, retrace your steps out to the white sign and bear left down the hill to rejoin the bridleway, keeping the large hedge on your right and fields on the left.
3 At the first metal kissing gate, take sharp left at footpath signposted to Whitsbury. Follow the footpath downhill, along the edge of the field. After about 300yds, enter a wooded path (there is small yellow arrow on the post on the left marking the footpath). Keep straight ahead on this track, past a large barn and ultimately between two tall hedges, then head downhill to a wooden stile.
4 Turn right on to a larger path after passing over the stile, then immediately turn left to follow the path up a steep hill. (A blue arrow on the right marks the bridlepath that you are on.) Climb the hill, with tall trees on your left and a fenced field on your right. At the top of the hill, you will see a large farm below you, to the right.

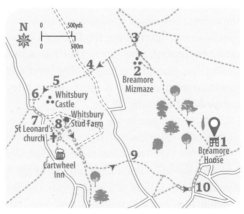

5 Follow the track, with the woods on your left. If you look

14 paintings by an illegitimate son of the Spanish painter, Murillo, show the intermarriages of Spanish, African and indigenous Mexican populations in colonial Mexico. The kitchen is warm and inviting and has an abundance of copper pans and kettles arrayed on shelves. 'The

carefully into the woods on the other side of the fence, you can see the ramparts and ditches of Whitsbury Castle, the 16-acre site of an Iron Age hillfort. You will be walking here shortly. Continue on the path uphill, towards a barn.

6 At the top of a small hill – the path becomes paved – go through the opening between fences and turn right on to a farm track, walking alongside the barn of Whitsbury Stud Farm on your left. As you pass the barn, curve around to the left and head out towards the main farm entrance.

7 Exit on to the main road, then make a sharp left towards a metal gate signposted 'St Leonard's Church and Stud Office'. Pass through a pedestrian gate (note that it is locked between 20.00 and 07.00) to reach the site of Whitsbury Castle ruins. Now you can clearly see more ramparts on your left. Follow the paved farm road straight ahead to where it becomes a dirt track and you'll see a sign for St Leonard's Church. To visit the church, follow the track as it curves right and leads to the churchyard. After visiting the church, retrace your steps, turning left outside the gate and take the first right that leads in between paddocks, signposted 'Footpath'.

8 Follow the path between paddocks and turn right just before a red-brick house. Follow this paved road downhill; it becomes a dirt track and then narrows to a walking trail through woods. At a four-way junction of bridlepaths, keep straight, following the middle path downhill with a fence on your right. At the next junction, continue straight on and walk downhill on a grassy track between wire fences (which may be hidden in summer by vegetation). At the bottom of the hill, go through the gate and turn right on to a dirt track. Walk a short distance and then take the first left (slightly backwards), passing through the gap to the right of the fence, signposted 'Footpath'.

9 Follow the trail along the right edge of the field, keeping a tall hedge on your right. At the top of the hill, go through the metal kissing gate marked with a yellow footpath arrow. Follow this wooded trail up and down hills, past a gate where the footpath merges with a bridleway and out to a paved road (Rookery Lane).

10 Follow Rookery Lane out to the main road and then turn left, passing houses on the left; the museum car park will be on your left in about 700yds.

Hulse family had only sons,' explained our guide, 'so the copper stayed here with the girls.'

Just inside the gates of the estate is the **Countryside Museum**, where you can get a genuine feel for local 19th-century village life. (The café is also here; see opposite.) The life-size shops and farmworker's cottage illustrate how villages were once self-sufficient. Each person in the community was dependent on the others and in this way the village survived daily life. An impressive collection of horse-drawn and steam-operated farming equipment fills the barns. Although these are interesting enough in themselves, they impressively come to life during the museum's **working weekends** in the spring and autumn. You might get to see the grinding mill churning away or the Dreadnought, a 1926 haulage tractor that takes two-and-a-half hours just to get started. It certainly gives you the impression that some people back then worked hard; just a quick glance at the village laundry is enough to convince you that today's domestic chores aren't really so bad.

"Just a quick glance at the village laundry is enough to convince you that today's domestic chores aren't really so bad."

Less than a mile from the rear of the house is **Breamore Mizmaze**. To get there, follow the trail that leads from Breamore House's drive, with the octagonal bell tower on your right. Follow the wooded bridleway uphill through Breamore Woods. Within these woods and throughout its various terrains, the Breamore Estate nurtures environments for endangered species by planting winter food sources and preserving corridors of habitats that span neighbouring land. These environmental initiatives are co-ordinated with nearby farms as part of the Allenford Farmer Cluster. Just before the woods end in a clearing (do head out to look at the view of Downton and Salisbury on your right), follow the bridleway around to the left. You will emerge at the base of a hill; ahead of you, at the top of the hill, you will see a large white sign that indicates the entrance to the mizmaze.

The mizmaze, technically a labyrinth because it has no junctions or crossings, is fenced for protection but you still experience a mystical sensation with the encircling yew trees and atmosphere of secrecy. It is one of only eight surviving turf labyrinths in England. In the nearby woods you can see temporary shelters built from logs and ground cover – a sure sign that this site is still used for sacred pilgrimages. It is thought that in its early days, the mizmaze was used by monks from Breamore Priory who absolved their sins by crossing the turf on their knees, saying prayers at specific points. Whether or not their sins were forgiven, this would have kept the chalky paths visible. Now, there are tales of modern-day fertility ceremonies and spooky encounters with apparitions, but I've been there several times on my own and have only encountered peace and quiet.

FOOD & DRINK

The Cartwheel Inn Whitsbury SP6 3PZ ✆ 01725 518362 ⌂ cartwheelinnwhitsbury.com ⊙ 11.00–15.00 & 17.00–22.00 Wed–Fri, 11.00–22.00 Sat, 11.00–19.00 Sun. A popular local pub with friendly staff, three miles northwest of Breamore. The 18th-century building was once farm cottages and a bakery; you can still see the original oven next to the bar.

The Pantry Barn Breamore SP6 2DB ✆ 01725 511955 ⌂ thenewforestpantry.com ⊙ Apr–Oct 10.00–16.30 Tue–Sun, Nov–Mar 10.00–15.00 Tue–Sun. Although situated in the courtyard of the Countryside Museum, this independent café can be visited separately from it and the house. This cosy, dog-friendly place serves light lunches and cream teas with home-baked sweets. The outdoor courtyard is especially pleasant.

9 ROCKBOURNE

One of the most photogenic villages in Hampshire, Rockbourne is laid out in a linear pattern typical of the area. Thatched houses line the meandering main street with patchwork fields beyond. It makes a pleasant amble, combined with lunch at the Rose & Thistle, the centrepiece of the village.

Rockbourne Roman Villa

Rockbourne SP6 3PG ✆ 01725 518541 ⌂ hampshireculture.org.uk/rockbourne-roman-villa ⊙ Apr–Sep

Who would believe that a ferret could uncover Roman ruins? But that's what happened in 1942. A farmer who was digging out a ferret from a rabbit warren found an oyster shell and tile. Morley Hewitt, a local estate agent and antiquarian recognised the potential significance of these items and dug a trial hole that immediately uncovered a mosaic floor. He subsequently bought the land but, because it was wartime, excavations didn't begin until 1956. Digging continued annually in the summer months but unfortunately early excavators discarded some useful finds like animal bones and pottery shards. They also failed to

ANDREW HARKER/S

GRAHAM MCANDREW/S

JIM CHAMPION CC-BY-SA

HAMPSHIRE CULTURAL TRUST

SANDRA STANDBRIDGE/S

SUSAZOOM/S

record the exact archaeological contexts that might have shed light on how the Roman villa had been laid out.

Even so, experts have worked out how buildings might have been arranged and the villa, which would have contained about 40 rooms together with farm buildings at its peak in the 4th century, is now marked out in the field, less than one mile from Rockbourne village centre. There are explanatory plaques explaining the different areas and how the inhabitants might have lived when the villa was in use.

"By the 5th century, the villa was abandoned and walls were demolished and quarried for stone."

One highlight is the **hypocaust**, the foundation of the underfloor heating system, which heated the bathhouse. It is unusual here in comprising curved roof tiles cemented together to form the supporting *pilae* rather than a stack of flat bricks. You can also see portions of mosaic floors that have been restored and relaid. Archaeologists have determined that the first phase of building featured one simple rectangular house over the remains of an Iron Age timber roundhouse.

It's best to start inside the **museum**, which explains how the remains were discovered and excavated. Display cases contain artefacts including coins, jewellery, hairpins, basic tools and a roof tile of Purbeck stone. In 1967, an undoubtedly delighted summer volunteer discovered a pottery jar filled with 7,717 bronze coins. There are many unanswered questions about Rockbourne but one particularly tantalising one is about what the occupants were anticipating when they buried their coins. Perhaps they were frightened or maybe they buried their hoard as an offering to the gods. By examining these coins, experts were able to determine that the site was occupied for about 350 years. By the 5th century, the villa was abandoned and walls were demolished and quarried for stone.

Nature notes displayed alongside archaeological information add another dimension to the site. There is also a family-friendly trail around the site. During school holidays, special activities are conducted for children designed to inspire them to see the ruins as more than a big

◄ **1** Breamore House & Countryside Museum. **2** St Mary's Saxon church. **3** Breamore Mizmaze. **4** Rockbourne Roman Villa. **5** & **6** Martin Down Nature Reserve is home to rarities such as the grey partridge and bee orchid.

field with a few stones laid out. You can even picnic in the grounds with your dog.

From the ruins you can see the somewhat incongruous tower of the **Eyre Coote Monument**, which stands in the grounds of West Park. Its aesthetics are questionable but the 100ft column is a great way to orient yourself when walking in the fields surrounding Rockbourne.

¶¶ FOOD & DRINK

Rose & Thistle Rockbourne Rd, P6 3NL ✆ 01725 518236 ⌂ roseandthistle.co.uk ⊙ Tue, Wed & Fri–Sun. A 16th-century pub that has gone gastro without losing its charm. The low ceilings and huge fireplace make this a cosy place for lunch or dinner and the food, more restaurant than pub fare, is an added bonus. Book ahead as there are few tables. In summer the small front garden is a prime lunch or post-walk drinking spot.

10 MARTIN DOWN NATIONAL NATURE RESERVE

SP5 5RQ

This 860-acre stretch of chalk downland is prized as one of the best places in the country to observe a large variety of **butterfly** species. The southern section of the reserve is located near **Martin**, the most westerly settlement in Hampshire and a top contender for quintessential chocolate-box village.

Martin Down has two car parks: one signposted off the A354, the road that runs between Salisbury and Blandford Forum, which serves the northern part of the reserve; and the other at the eastern edge of the reserve at Sillens Lane, just under a mile from the village of Martin.

The northern part of the reserve contains some 45 acres of scrubland and woodland that is carefully trimmed to provide optimum habitats for birds, butterflies, snakes and other woodland wildlife. In the area called **Kitt's Grave** (directly across the busy A354, north of the reserve's car park), woodland butterflies flourish: on a summer morning I counted ten different types, including white admiral, silver-washed fritillary, marble white and dark green fritillary. Between April and September, a weekly census is taken to monitor butterfly populations. This land is not grazed and cutting is done on rotation during the winter so as not to disturb any nesting wildlife. 'This is where the staff work because the work on

"This land is not grazed and cutting is done on rotation during the winter so as not to disturb any nesting wildlife."

the Downs is all done by sheep,' a staffer joked, referring to the grazed downs on the other side of the A354. A bit of folklore surrounds the legend of the grim name for this area but the most frequently heard story is that a gypsy called Kitt died on the boundary between two parishes, neither of which would pay for her burial. So she was buried where she was found and the copse was named after her.

Throughout this woodland are numerous reminders of the past. Near the main road, the remains of a Roman road are visible just inside the entrance gate. After passing around the cattle grid, go through the first gate on the right into **Vernditch Chase**. Archaeologists believe that the mound on the left with the ditch running alongside it is a vestige of the Roman road. In spring and early summer you have a chance of seeing several species of rare orchid here, including bee and butterfly orchids, but you need to look closely, as they grow very near to the ground. There are at least eight species of orchids at Martin Down.

This is also a **Neolithic long barrow** in the woodlands. To get there, at the entrance to Kitt's Grave, go straight on to the main trail. If you follow this around in a 'U' shape, the barrow, excavated in the late 19th century by Augustus Pitt Rivers, is on the left. Many of the recovered materials are in the Pitt Rivers Museum in Oxford.

"In spring and early summer you have a chance of seeing several species of rare orchid here, including bee and butterfly orchids."

On the other side of the A354, straight behind the car park, is a linear prehistoric earthwork, **Bokerley Dyke**, which runs near the former World War II firing range. Butterflies thrive in the sheltered environment. The downland here has been unploughed for centuries since the first farmers cleared the woodland in Neolithic times. The open spaces were grazed by animals and today Natural England keeps about 120 sheep here in summer and close to 800 in winter, supplied by local graziers, to keep the scrub at bay. The unploughed land allows many wildflowers to flourish in the ancient chalky soils where grasses cannot compete. In the middle of summer, the reserve is carpeted in purple scabious and knapweed.

If you park at **Sillens Lane** on the eastern side of the reserve, you can walk up the hill to the ridge for a view of the New Forest on one side and Hampshire and Wiltshire farms on the other. The gorse and tree growth at the top does not permit an unimpeded view but it's worth the climb. There are well-cleared tracks on the hillside but part of the pleasure here is that you can wander wherever you please and find yourself completely alone. If you are looking for butterflies, walk west from the car park keeping the hedgerow on your right and the field (flower-filled in spring and summer) on your left.

FOOD & DRINK

The Compasses Inn East End, Damerham SP6 3HQ ⚲ 01725 518 231
⚲ compassesinndamerham.co.uk. Dog biscuits at the bar are the first indication of the relaxed atmosphere at the Compasses. Staff are friendly and it has a quiet, peaceful atmosphere. The very spacious and well-landscaped garden makes a delightful lunch spot and the main dining room and bar are cosy places to eat in the evening. There is a good selection of real and craft ales. The inn is located just six miles from the A354 car park at Martin Down.

The award-winning Slow Travel series from Bradt Guides

Over 20 regional guides across Britain.
See the full list at bradtguides.com/slowtravel.

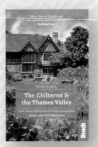

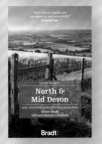

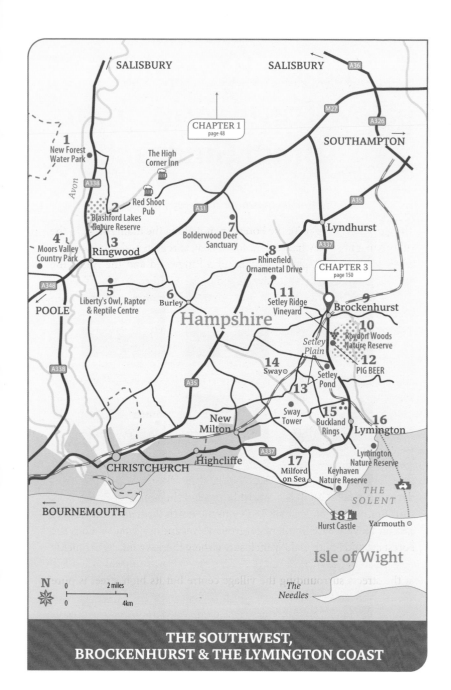

SALISBURY

SALISBURY

A36

M27

A326

CHAPTER 1
page 48

SOUTHAMPTON

1
New Forest
Water Park

The High
Corner Inn

Avon

A338

2 Red Shoot
Pub

A31

Blashford Lakes
Nature Reserve

A35

7
Bolderwood Deer
Sanctuary

Lyndhurst

4
Moors Valley
Country Park

3
Ringwood

A337

8
Rhinefield
Ornamental Drive

CHAPTER 3
page 150

A348

5
Liberty's Owl, Raptor
& Reptile Centre

6
Burley

11
Setley Ridge
Vineyard

9

POOLE

Hampshire

Brockenhurst

10
Roydon Woods
Nature Reserve

A338

*Setley
Plain*

12
PIG BEER

14
Sway

Setley
Pond

A35

13

16
Lymington

New
Milton

Sway
Tower

15
Buckland
Rings

Lymington
Nature Reserve

CHRISTCHURCH

Highcliffe

A337

17
Milford
on Sea

Keyhaven
Nature Reserve

*THE
SOLENT*

BOURNEMOUTH

18
Hurst Castle

Yarmouth

Isle of Wight

N

0   2 miles

0   4km

*The
Needles*

THE SOUTHWEST,
BROCKENHURST & THE LYMINGTON COAST

2

THE SOUTHWEST, BROCKENHURST & THE LYMINGTON COAST

The glories of this part of the Forest are not along the main roads. In the suburban and somewhat rushed south central region and southwestern edges of the Forest, particularly around Ringwood and the A338, the area loses some of its distinctive qualities. But within seconds of leaving major roads, you can be on a quiet country lane or even deep within Forest woodland.

Ringwood is a busy market town, made all the more so because of its proximity to the A31 and its natural affiliation with points further west. For shopping, Ringwood and coastal Lymington are the most useful of all the villages and towns in and around the New Forest. If you need something, you are likely to find it here.

By contrast, **Burley** and **Brockenhurst** very much belong to the New Forest. Animals roam freely throughout the streets, almost as if the towns are afterthoughts and the Forest has surrendered a bit of land to accommodate human residents' needs. The boundaries of both flow seamlessly into the Forest, especially in Burley where the main shopping area is tiny. It is a tourist haven, but the beauty of Burley is its surrounding Forest. Leaving Burley to the north through Burley Street and on to Vereley Hill offers gorgeous views and walking, as does the Forest around South Oakley Inclosure (where there is a bike trail quickly reached from the village centre). Brockenhurst has a more suburban feel in the streets surrounding the village centre but its high street is pure village. It is my favourite of all Forest enclaves, a lovely place to potter around and have a coffee, often in the company of the ponies and cows that regularly wander around.

If you're looking for a glimpse of really small-town life, a weekend at the tiny hamlet of **Sway** will provide it. Surprisingly, this wee village has a mainline train station, a charming hotel, restaurant, pub, deli, art gallery and a first-class butcher. It also has good access to the Forest so if you don't want to travel far afield, you can easily stay here without a car.

Easy **cycling** is especially rewarding around the south and south central Forest (south of Lyndhurst). The Forest network of cycle paths is centred around the southern village of Brockenhurst, including a disused

FOREST BATHING

I was in a patch of woodland I'd been in many times on my daily walk, where I'm usually thinking about the work I need to do when I get home, what mischief the now-disappeared dog is in, and even, shamefully, glancing at my fitness monitor to see how many steps I've taken. But this day was different. I was, for once, not marching. I was walking, ambling, loitering even. Standing still! And it was bliss.

I joined Brockenhurst environmental therapist and forest-bathing practitioner Sam Lewis (arttherapyhampshire.co.uk) for a leisurely stroll that encouraged me to see the Forest in a completely new way. 'We are going to slow our pace and breathing way down in order to focus on engaging all our senses,' she explained at the start of the walk. I might not have chosen the optimum day, as temperatures had plunged and the leaves beneath our feet were iced with traces of white, lacy frost.

As we set out, we paused beneath an impossibly tall canopy of conifers where Sam asked me to stand motionless and completely engage with the space around me. 'Take in a deep breath of air and then let it go,' she said, almost whispering. 'Push your feet into the forest floor so that you almost merge with the landscape.'

I closed my eyes and the bird sounds got louder; I could distinguish several different calls. I was dismayed to hear traffic sounds in the distance, but the longer we stood there, the more I was able to block them out. I just stood. And it felt great. 'Look,' Sam whispered. Ahead of us, camouflaged in the brown tree trunks and ferns, stood a lone deer, staring at us intently. 'We become part of their world,' Sam whispered. 'We exist in their time frame.'

One of the reasons Sam wants people to move slowly through the Forest is so that they can understand their impact on the natural world. 'We change the dynamic of the Forest as we move through it,' she said. 'By slowing down and being more mindful, we can think carefully about the impact we leave.'

As we neared the end point, I was relaxed and yet at the same time, invigoratingly refreshed. Sam motioned to a huge fallen tree bathed in sun, with an invitingly flat edge. We sat comfortably and she produced a warm flask of pine tea made from pine needles and heather. We sipped companionably, noting colour changes in the ferns as the sun's rays shone through the trees. I was, in that moment, anyway, at one with the Forest.

railway line that provides a wide, flat route. You have to cycle on minor roads for a short time to access this from Brockenhurst village but not for very far (it's also easy accessible from Sway). The other problem, as with many New Forest cycle tracks, is that it doesn't go in a continuous loop and you need to double back. But this works well if you've rented cycles in Brockenhurst. There are also several cycle trails in the woods around the Rhinefield Ornamental Drive; the area around Ober Water and Puttles Bridge just as you enter the Forest at Rhinefield Road (before the Ornamental Drive) is especially gratifying. The New Forest National Park Authority (⊘ newforestnpa.gov.uk) outlines a gentle ten-mile circular, mostly off-road route. Cycling within the Forest is relaxed and family-orientated; adventure-seeking mountain bikers will be happiest at Moor Valley Country Park, which has purpose-built circuits.

From the very Forest flavour of Brockenhurst, it's a short distance to the coastal atmosphere of **Lymington** where it's all about boats and the Solent. The town overflows with visitors in summer because there is so much to do, from crabbing by the quay, swimming in the saltwater pool, walking along the marshes at Keyhaven or taking a ferry to the Isle of Wight. The main roads through here are not that appealing; stick to the coast and especially **Keyhaven**. The **Solent Way** passes right through Lymington, so it's possible to walk about ten miles east or west towards Beaulieu or Milford on Sea respectively. The Forest is not far – **Beaulieu Heath** is an easy cycle ride away and **Setley Plain** is a good place to walk to for its expansive views and concentration of prehistoric barrows. In summer, my family is frequently found among the strawberry vines of **Goodall's Pick Your Own**, conveniently situated across from the ferry port.

RINGWOOD & BURLEY

The Ringwood area is about so much more than just the New Forest, as the landscape here is defined by the River Avon and its water meadows. The southern stretch of the Avon Valley Path runs from Fordingbridge in the north, through Ringwood and on to Christchurch on the western fringes of the Forest. There are wonderful contrasts here, from open stretches of water meadows to the sunlight-dappled trails through the ancient woods around Burley where the trees have been commanding the landscape for centuries.

Busy **Ringwood** ranks as one of the most useful of all the villages and towns in and around the New Forest for shopping and town amenities, and offers easy access to the heart of the Forest and the beaches around nearby Christchurch, to the south. The **River Avon** and its water meadows add a different dimension to this part of the Forest, with fishing and abundant aquatic wildlife-viewing. Many sites cater to families. At **Blashford Lakes** there are excellent nature programmes for children, including pond dipping and mini-beast tracking; the bird hides give opportunities for observing a host of duck species. Further north on the A338, the focus is more on play at **New Forest Water Park**, which offers waterskiing, wakeboarding, kayaking and paddleboarding with tuition for all ages. **Burley** offers carriage rides and deer safaris, while the holiday-camp atmosphere of **Moors Valley Country Park** is a contrast to the New Forest, with structured activities and instruction that can be a lot of fun for families.

1 NEW FOREST WATER PARK

Ringwood Rd, near Ringwood SP6 2EY ✆ 01425 656868 ⬦ newforestwaterpark.co.uk
☺ Easter–Oct

You can hear the squeals of exhilarated children as you drive on the long, winding approach to the clubhouse that overlooks the two small lakes between Ringwood and Fordingbridge. Watersports include kayaking, cable-powered wakeboarding and waterskiing, paddleboarding, open-water swimming and two aqua parks with inflatable obstacle courses. The cable system, which is modelled on a ski lift, is an environmentally friendly alternative to traditional power boats. Beach towels are flung across railings, balls whiz through the air while children await their turn boating and there is a true summer camp atmosphere.

2 BLASHFORD LAKES NATURE RESERVE

Ellingham Drove BH24 3PJ ✆ 01425 472760 ⬦ hiwwt.org.uk ☺ 09.00–16.30 daily

The nature reserve at Blashford Lakes, just outside Ringwood, shows what use can be made of abandoned gravel pits. Administered by the Hampshire & Isle of Wight Wildlife Trust (HIWWT), these flooded gravel pits host thousands of birds and this 370-acre site (both

1 Canada geese at Blashford Lakes Nature Reserve. 2 Kingfisher. 3 Bird hide. 4 Great crested grebe. 5 Peregrine falcon. ▶

DEREK TIPPETTS

STEFAN-KADAR/S

STEFAN-KADAR/S

MARK CHRISTOPHER COOPER/S

wheelchair and pushchair friendly) is now a popular birdwatching site and education centre.

This means human noise can be quieter here than in other parts of the Forest making it a splendid place for a peaceful walk with birdsong as a backdrop. It's particularly lovely in the autumn when trees are in colour and reflected in the lakes. Birds here year-round include kingfishers, lapwings and oystercatcher. In the winter, you are treated to great viewing of the hundreds of birds that return here each year, including great bittern, bearded tit and great egret. Because the River Avon is a north–south migration route, unexpected species can just drop in, especially to the area around Ibsley Water, one of Hampshire's largest bodies of freshwater.

Unfortunately, the west side of the reserve is bordered by the A338 and you can hear it much of the time. But, in an odd way, this actually can enhance your appreciation of this precious, protected spot. The hum of the A-road is a poignant reminder of an issue that faces the entire New Forest: how urban development on the fringes of the Forest is encroaching.

Wildlife Watch Group sessions, which aim to raise children's awareness of the wildlife that surrounds them, are offered throughout the year. I attended an evening event here in which children gathered to observe wildlife. The Education Officer showed us a variety of animal skulls, deer antlers and plaster impressions of animal footprints. When she presented her samples of poo and explained to children how to examine it for clues to animals' lifestyles, there were no cries of 'Eeew, gross,' but instead rapt concentration. The group leader then helped the children each make a humane trap, which they later hid in the undergrowth in hopes of catching a mouse for observation. The children returned the next morning to find their traps and release the mice that had spent a cosy night in the box with food and hay.

"The children were thrilled to spot rabbits, a pheasant strutting its bright red colours and lots of small woodland birds."

At dusk, we walked out to one of the bird hides in the woods to observe wildlife. The children were thrilled to spot rabbits, a pheasant strutting its bright red colours and lots of small woodland birds. The pièce de résistance though were the bat monitors, small handheld devices that bleep when bats are nearby. The success of spotting them seemed incidental to the excitement of working the monitor and being in the woods at nightfall.

3 RINGWOOD

⌂ **Upper Kingston Farm Cottages** (page 223) ▲ **Fernwood Glamping** (page 223), **Red Shoot Camping Park** (page 223)

Traditionally known as the western gateway to the Forest, the ancient town of Ringwood is positioned at what was historically a key crossing of the River Avon. Nowadays, residents often choose to live here because of the town's proximity to both Dorset beaches (to the south) and the Forest (to the east). History abounds here: Henry III granted a market charter in 1226 and every Wednesday the Market Place at the western end of town still bustles (☉ 08.00–15.30 Wed). You won't find the live animals of days past but you can still have fun perusing stalls that stock clothing, games, household items and, of course, fresh produce, baked goods and preserved foods.

"Nowadays, residents often choose to live here because of the town's proximity to both Dorset beaches and the Forest."

Also on Market Place, the Church of St Peter and St Paul is a 19th-century construction but there has been a church on this site since the 11th century. As suggested by the tower, which is visible from quite a distance, the interior is huge and worth a visit. The stained-glass windows are particularly lovely.

From here, the High Street meanders east and retains an old-world character. Shops are mostly independent, with a sprinkling of cafés among them. The eastern end of town is dominated by the Furlong, a shopping centre created from the town's cattle market, which closed in 1989. Here you'll find many recognizable UK high street shops. On the last Saturday of every month, there is also a farmers' market by the Furlong Car Park (⌖ hampshirefarmersmarkets.co.uk ☉ 10.00–14.00 Sat).

Just south of the shopping centre, **Ringwood Meeting House** (22 Meeting House Ln, BN24 1EY ☏ 01425 480656 ⌖ ringwoodmeetinghouse.org ☉ 10.00–noon Fri–Tue, 10.00–14.30 Wed) is an extremely fine example of an early 18th-century Presbyterian meeting house, and one of only two original meeting houses existing in the UK. The building, which no longer serves a religious function but is clearly well cared for by the charity that looks after it, is Grade II listed because of its original box pews and balcony. The nominal admission charge includes a cup of tea or coffee at a table in the box pews, so you can easily imagine what it might have been like

RINGWOOD'S CARNIVAL

Residents put a lot of effort into the annual carnival, held in September (⊘ ringwoodcarnival.org). The all-day event features local marching bands, entertainers, a lengthy afternoon procession and a smattering of famous heavy horses. It's good old-fashioned, small-town fun.

as a non-conformist worshipper in the 1700s, and a visit to the history exhibits that line the walls and balcony. The replica organ is used for recitals and there are other regular shows and events hosted here; the building has exceptional acoustics, making this a wonderful venue for choral groups.

The western end of town, near the River Avon, is the most pleasant, although you do hear the relentless traffic of the A31. Still, there are a few walks along the river from here, most notably the **Avon Valley Path**. One of the prettiest sections heads north for seven miles to Fordingbridge, passing through Blashford Lakes where you will undoubtedly see and hear many waterbirds, into woodlands near Ibsley and on to the water meadows outside Fordingbridge. You can also walk south to Sopley (about 6½ miles) and even on to Christchurch (a further 3½ miles) but the scenery is not as pleasant. Please note that the Avon Valley Path is at its best in summer, and can be waterlogged from December through May.

Ringwood Brewery

Christchurch Rd, BH24 3AP ✏ 01425 470303 ⊘ ringwoodbrewery.co.uk.

Beer has been an integral part of Ringwood's development since medieval man mixed River Avon waters with the malted barley of Hampshire. As a prominent market town, Ringwood required plenty of hostelries and pubs to refresh early salesmen who travelled here with their goods. There were as many as four breweries in Ringwood at one time but all had closed by 1925.

When CAMRA (the Campaign for Real Ale) was formed in the 1970s to encourage development of good quality cask ales, Ringwood local Peter Austin founded the brewery in a former bakery in an old Ringwood railway yard. He began brewing Best Bitter, still Ringwood's best seller. By the mid-1980s he was producing more varieties, had acquired a partner and had moved into larger premises that – fittingly –

had once been a brewery. Peter Austin became a leader in Britain's craft brewery market. Ringwood and surrounding towns are proud of their local brew, even though it is now owned by Carlsberg Marston's Brewing Company. Brewery officials insist it is still run like a family business.

It certainly feels that way when you step into the small shop and tap room. It's a friendly atmosphere and people come from all over the world to sample the local offerings. Old Thumper, the flagship beer that won a CAMRA award in 1988, ultimately fostered the company's success. It has a complex peppery, spicy flavour that is deliciously distinct. The newest offering, Circadian, is termed an 'everyday IPA'. It has citrus and pine-like aromas.

The shop stocks t-shirts, bottled beers and souvenirs. The marketing emblem of the Hampshire Hog was chosen because the hop flower isn't definitive enough, and indeed the friendly-looking statue in the car park seems an apt welcome to the brewery that is fondly known as 'the Winding Downs'.

¶¶ FOOD & DRINK

BakeHouse 24 8–12 Lynes Ln, Ringwood BH24 1BT ✐ 01425 485170 ⬦ bakehouse24. com. Comforting coffee stop where you can watch (and smell) the speciality sourdough breads and sweet treats as they emerge from the oven. It doesn't get fresher than this.
Frampton's High St, BH24 1BQ ✐ 01425 473114 ⬦ framptonsbar.co.uk. This eclectic café starts the day as a coffee shop serving pastries and cakes and transitions to light lunches and then a wine bar in the evening. Located in the building that once belonged to Frampton and Sons, a pet supply and garden shop that had been here for 175 years, the café has retained some original features, including shelving, floors and panelled walls. At the back is a sofa and some relaxing seating, while the front has communal tables. It all translates to a welcoming atmosphere.

THE CASTLEMAN TRAILWAY

From Ringwood you can cycle over 16 miles of old railway trackbed, formerly the Southampton to Dorchester line, by taking the Castleman Trailway into Dorset (⬦ dorsetcouncil.gov.uk), through West Moors, Ferndown Forest and with a final section along the River Stour before ending in Poole. It's a fairly flat, mostly off-road route and a great place to cycle with children because you don't have to worry about cars or big hills. Note though that the rough, gravel track is best suited to off-road bikes with thicker tyres.

4 MOORS VALLEY COUNTRY PARK

Horton Rd, Ashley Heath BH24 2ET ✆ 01425 470721 ⬧ moors-valley.co.uk ⊙ from 08.00 daily; check website for closing times

Deciduous woodland, coniferous forest, lakes, ponds and rivers make up the 250 acres of this country park. Activity trails for all ages are set up throughout the woods: there is one each for exercise buffs, cyclists and walkers, and for those who want just to play, and nearly all are push- and wheelchair friendly. The adventure play area for older children is particularly good, with a zip slide and lots of climbing challenges. It's possible to hire cycles, join a Go Ape programme for both juniors and adults (book ahead online), golf, fish and use the permanent orienteering course that caters to all ages and abilities. Children also love the steam train (it's kid-sized), which takes 20 minutes to run the mile-long track. If that doesn't keep you busy enough, you can explore the forest on a hired Segway through Go Ape.

Despite its activity park atmosphere, Moors Valley earns a place in a Slow itinerary because of its excellent programmes that foster family togetherness while simultaneously teaching about the countryside. The structured activities – which might include a torchlight safari, nature walks and holiday treasure hunts – provide a good contrast to the wild setting of the New Forest and might give confidence to those who find the open Forest intimidating. The park gets very busy when school is not in session but even on crowded days you can find a corner for yourself. Technically, you could stay all day for just the price of parking but it's worth spending extra for some of the guided activities inside the park.

"The adventure play area for older children is particularly good, with a zip slide and lots of climbing challenges."

For me, the most eye-opening feature at Moors Valley is the **orienteering**. The permanent course was mapped out by Wimborne Orienteering Club and you can challenge yourself with maps from the visitor centre, which offers courses for different levels. There is even a challenge to run among the points and beat the speed record. This can be a great introduction to walking in the New Forest where basic map-reading and navigation skills are hugely helpful.

Fishing is permitted on Moors Lake during fishing season (⊙ June–mid-Mar). The artificial lake stocks roach, tench and perch, among others. In summer, rangers hold fishing tuition for children. Equipment is provided for those taking courses only. You don't have to take a course to fish but securing a swim (the specific places where you fish from; at Moors Valley they are mostly small gravel inlets) can be competitive, so come early. All fishers must have a rod licence from the Environment Agency.

There is loads of space in the park for picnics; note though that there are no rubbish bins so you take your refuse home with you.

5 LIBERTY'S OWL, RAPTOR & REPTILE CENTRE
Crow Ln, Ringwood BH24 3EA ✆ 01425 476487 🖉 libertysfalconry.co.uk ⏱ Mar–Oct daily, Nov–Feb Sat, Sun & half terms

'Reptiles do not make good pets,' said Lynda Bridges firmly as she gazed at the enormous boa constrictor that she originally took in as an underfed, abused snake. 'People buy them as pets and then realise reptiles basically only eat and sleep so they neglect or abandon them.' Most of the reptiles at Liberty's are rescued, like the now healthy and seemingly happy constrictor.

'Perhaps it's because I have a farming background, I don't know, but I like animals and want to see them properly cared for,' Lynda explained in a tour around the small reptile house. A common green iguana that Lynda adopted when the owner was surprised how large it had grown, gazed out at us from behind its glass shield and seemed to smile. 'There are now more reptiles than dogs in captivity,' Lynda lamented.

Because this is a relatively small wildlife centre, with birds in large cages lining a walkway and reptiles tucked away in their own house, you'll get more out of your visit if you come for the daily flying displays of birds of prey. Here you can see these magnificent creatures spread their wings, even if it is in a contained setting, with informative commentary and a chance to ask questions. Demonstrations usually take place in the middle of the day but Lynda recommends phoning ahead to be sure.

Lynda opened her menagerie, which she named after her prize Alaskan bald eagle, Liberty, in 2005 and then revamped the rundown buildings that were part of the owl sanctuary that had previously been here – she took over the site in 2003 when she heard that the entire facility was going to be razed and the animals put down. Her mission is an expensive and daunting one but the rescued owls don't seem to mind that some of the housing here is a bit tired and that renovations take

A LITTLE PARCEL FROM THE NEW FOREST

newforestshortbread.co.uk

Many marketers of baked goods use the expression 'baked with love'. Tracy Thew doesn't but, having visited her kitchen, I can assure you that New Forest Shortbread is baked with love. Tracy lives about as deep into the Forest as one can live and she produces her shortbread, which holds a Great Taste award from the New Forest Marque, from her Forest idyll outside of Burley.

'That's my secret machine,' Tracy told me proudly as we inspected the contents of the kitchen where her shortbread is baked. Needless to say, I am not at liberty to describe her machine but her home-made contraption enables her to circumvent the drawbacks of a commercial machine. 'Commercial machines require oil and that changes the flavour and texture,' Tracy explained earnestly. 'Oil makes the shortbread denser and you lose the flakiness that shortbread should have.' And, of course, that oil also dilutes the fabulous melt-in-your-mouth butter flavour that makes shortbread, well, shortbread.

Tracy had been making her biscuits for friends and family for 50 years when she realised she could have a business supplying local outlets. Her kitchen above her husband's workshop is small but efficient. Tracy and her sole assistant make as many as 5,000 pieces a day, including special flavours, during peak periods when Tracy travels around to local food fairs and outdoor markets to sell her biscuits. She also supplies a range of local hotels and holiday cottages, where these parcels of sweetness are often left on tea trays in bedrooms.

Tracy's packaging is as sumptuous as the shortbread itself. The tops of each box fold out into cards that can be cut and saved as mementos. The paper souvenirs highlight a small fact about the New Forest and are illustrated by a local artist. 'They are stories that you would only learn if you talked to a local,' explained Tracy. 'So visitors take away a little piece of the Forest. Maybe later on, they will be somewhere else and pull one of those cards from their pocket and remember the wonderful time they spent in the Forest.' Tracy got the packaging idea when she was running a B&B in Brockenhurst and she noticed her guests couldn't always remember even recent trips to other parts of the country. 'They were vague about the details,' she explained, 'so I thought it would be good to give them a keepsake with something specific to remember about the Forest.'

New Forest Shortbread is available from many retail outlets throughout the Forest, as well as online.

time. 'I hope that when people come here they leave not only having learned about the animals that are here but about the importance of global conservation,' said Lynda. 'We need to make sure that children understand the need to care for animals so that their future is safe.'

Lynda has expanded her mission to include breeding programmes that support some of the most endangered species on the planet. Her favourites are the vultures, which she feels are often misunderstood. 'Vultures aren't what we consider traditionally beautiful but they are so useful to humans by keeping diseases at bay. People leave here with a better understanding that we are surrounded by birds of prey in this part of the world and how important they are to our survival.'

¶| FOOD & DRINK

Crow Farm Shop 169 Crow Ln, Ringwood BH24 3EA ✐ 01425 473290 ☺ 09.00−16:30 Mon−Sat. Family-run farm shop that serves award-winning pork pies and sausages. Full selection of local meats, artisan bread supplied by BakeHouse 24 in Ringwood, and a wider selection of vegetables than is often available at other local shops. Outdoor tables for coffee and a snack.

6 BURLEY

🏠 **Wilf's Cabin** (page 223)

Burley's claim to fame, which it's not shy about heralding, is its connection to **witchcraft**. Much of the hype centres on a white witch, Sybil Leek, who lived here in the 1950s and wrote several books on astrology and the occult. She founded **A Coven of Witches**, a shop selling broomsticks and spells for modern witches. Some people say that white witches still live in the Forest but none parade around with a jackdaw on their shoulder as did Sybil. If you do have inclinations towards the supernatural, head here in the summer when the New Forest Fairy Festival (⌂ newforestfairyfestival.com) takes place.

Many local historians feel the witchcraft connection is no more than a clever marketing campaign and that the village's true history is centred around **smuggling**. Having landed on the Solent coast, probably near Lymington and Beaulieu, smugglers escaped into the Forest and apparently used the **Queen's Head** pub here as a stopping point. During renovations, workers found old coins, bottles and pistols, hidden beneath floorboards.

The village itself is spread out; the main shopping area, with quaint, thatched cottages, lies at the bottom of a steep hill. The ponies and cattle that share the pavements with people almost require you to be Slow here: all you need to do is potter. Wander in and out of shops, have a cup of tea and some ice cream in one of the tea rooms and imagine what it was like when this settlement consisted of '14 villagers and six smallholders with seven ploughs', as recorded in the Domesday Book of 1086.

The true prize of Burley is its surrounding environment. The Forest is easily accessible from the centre of town, either by walking or driving. To the north lies acres of pristine, peaceful woodland: Woods Corner Car Park is only a mile out of town and a bit further on is Oakley Car Park, both of which are well situated for walks. To the east of the village, Burley Cricket Car Park makes a good starting point for a circular walk that heads south to Holmsley Ridge with its good views. This is also near the White Buck Inn, a great lunch stop (page 105).

Burley Wagon Rides

BH24 4DJ ✆ 07958 231336 or 01425 672910 ⌖ nandjheavyhorses.co.uk ⊙ Feb half term & Easter–Oct half term

It would be easy to dismiss Burley Wagon Rides as a tourist gimmick but there is an honourable tradition behind them. The wagon rides have been running from the car park behind the Queen's Head for more

---

NEW FOREST DEER SAFARI

Safaris leave from the farm shop behind the Queen's Head Pub near Burley public car park ⌖ newforestsafari.co.uk ⊙ summer noon–17.00 daily

To a Forest resident, paying to ride out and view deer might be a laughable proposition. But that's what I found myself doing, all in the name of book research of course, with New Forest Deer Safari. Much to my surprise, it was enormous fun. I piled into a wagon with what seemed like an overwhelming number of young children and bounced along behind a tractor a couple of hundred yards or so over to Burley Park where a herd of red deer were obligingly waiting, knowing that the wagon contained goodies for them. As we jolted across the field, I could just make out very still antlers poking out from the long grass. Then gradually I could see more young red deer emerging from the woods as the tractor approached. When they realised we did indeed have food, they trotted towards the bucket and gave us a perfect view as they devoured the meal. The biggest treat was seeing an enormous stag with antlers so large that it seemed as if he would keel over. He viewed the proceedings with interest but clearly it was beneath him to indulge in such easy pickings. As I watched two young males butt each other and grapple for food, I realised that the best views I normally have of deer in the Forest (aside from those who feast in my flower garden) are usually of their tail ends scampering away.

than 40 years, making this splendid pastime one of the oldest tourist institutions in the New Forest. The proprietors, Neil and Julia Kitchen, take guests out for either a 20-minute or 30-minute trip on country lanes around Burley and in the Forest.

This is a great opportunity to get a close-up view of heavy horses at work. They are trained to work as a team by just one person standing behind them operating the reins. Then gradually, sound and weight are introduced so that horses learn to cope with any situation. That can include animals in the Forest, loud noises in the street or even the sound of a band at a special event. The horses have a busy diary; they are hired for ploughing, heavy horse musical shows, weddings, and films.

If you want to guarantee your ride it's best to book online, but you can also just turn up on the day and wait for the horses to be ready.

♚ FOOD & DRINK

The Cider Pantry Pound Ln, BH24 4ED ✎ 01425 402193 ○ 08.00—noon daily. Located in front of New Forest Cider, a breakfast here is a pleasant way to start the day, especially in summer when the garden is open.

New Forest Cider Pound Ln, BH24 4ED ✎ 01425 403589 ♂ newforestcider.co.uk. Dry, medium and sweet cider from local apples. Unless you are a cider fanatic, it's probably not worth a special trip but the small shop is interesting to peruse if you're in Burley. Every autumn, this family-run business hosts an open weekend featuring traditional craft demonstrations and wagon rides from the village.

The Old Farmhouse Restaurant and Tea Rooms Ringwood Rd, BH24 4AB ✎ 01425 402218 ○ 09.00—16.00 daily. Decent food, known for its big portions at breakfast. Service can be slow at busy times but it is a good alternative to the larger pubs in the area. It's especially fun to sit inside this thatched cottage, knowing that meals have been served here continuously for 100 years.

Three Tuns Ringwood Rd, Bransgore BH23 8JH ✎ 01425 672232 ♂ threetunsinn.com. The car park is always full at the Three Tuns, located three miles southwest of Burley and just outside the national park. Copious hanging flower baskets make this extremely popular thatched inn look quite a picture in summer. Inside, the low-ceilinged main bar is laden with old-fashioned character. The kitchen serves modern takes on pub classics; seasonal menus mean interesting regular changes. The atmosphere is lively and fun and staff are friendly.

White Buck Inn Bisterne Cl, BH24 4AZ ✎ 01425402264 ♂ whitebuckburley.co.uk ○ food noon—15.00 & 17.00—21.00 Mon—Sat, noon—16.00 & 17.30—20.00 Sun. Located just one mile east of Burley and worth the effort. This former country house became a hotel in the

1960s – when Gerry and the Pacemakers played here – and has now had an ambitious refurbishment by Fullers. There is a wide-ranging menu with burgers, fish, pies, pasta and Sunday roasts, but the stand-out is the outdoor terrace. Booking essential; terrace not guaranteed.

BROCKENHURST & AROUND

🏠 **Cottage Lodge** (page 223), **The Pig** (page 223) ⚑ **Aldridge Hill Campsite** (page 223), **Long Meadow Campsite** (page 223), **Roundhill Caravan & Camping Site** (page 224)

Brockenhurst is an ideal spot to base yourself in if you are travelling without a car. The Forest's main railway station and a bike rental shop (page 43) are here, along with many restaurants, cycle trails and places to stay that are within walking distance of the station. The village's population swells by thousands in the warmer months due to large campsites nearby and the annual **New Forest Show** (page 114), held here at the end of July. Some 95,000 people attend, so for three days the stretch of the A337, the Lyndhurst Road, between Lyndhurst and Brockenhurst is virtually impassable. It's best to avoid this area at opening and closing times, or go around via the A35.

Near the southern border of the New Forest and about 1¼ miles from Brockenhurst, **Setley Plain** is a large stretch of heathland with views of Three Beech Bottom towards Sway and, on clear days, the rounded humps of the Isle of Wight in the opposite direction. It is a historic and varied landscape with a mix of ancient barrows, mires and great expanses of heath that bloom cheerful yellow in summer and soothing purple in autumn. As brilliant as the colours are in sunshine, the brooding skies of cloudy days suit this landscape best, making it easy to imagine previous generations of horseriders galloping away to distant parts of the Forest.

7 BOLDERWOOD DEER SANCTUARY

Bolderwood Arboretum Ornamental Dr, SO43 7GQ ⌀ forestryengland.uk/bolderwood

Bolderwood, a recreational area, is something of a Forest hot spot with its large car park, picnic area, deer sanctuary and flat green spaces at the edge of the woodland. In the Information Unit by the car park,

---

1 Moors Valley Steam Railway. **2** Moors Valley Country Park. **3** Pigs rooting for acorns at Burley. **4** Bolderwood Deer Sanctuary. **5** Ringwood Brewery. **6** A Coven of Witches, Burley. ▶

LOIS GOBE/S

DAAN KLOEG/S

STEFAN-KADAR/S

DAVE HEAD/S

LOIS GOBE/S

DEREK TIPPETTS

at weekends from Easter until September and daily during summer afternoons, you can speak to a volunteer ranger about deer, the royal hunting lodges that used to be on this land and ask general questions about the New Forest. The rangers also have an excellent collection of antlers which you can touch. You'll have a good chance of seeing deer at the **observation platform** across the road from the car park. Although they have plenty to eat in the Forest, the keeper for this area sometimes feeds them in the meadow during the summer so that people have the opportunity to view and photograph them.

This area is truly the land of the kings as this is where medieval rulers built hunting lodges. The first record of a hunting lodge here is from 1325 but in 1358, when Edward III took over the Forest, he built four hunting lodges. The largest of these was at Bolderwood, then known as Hatheburgh, and was situated where the picnic area is now. A series of lodges followed, the grandest of which was for the 1st Earl de la Warr, the Master Keeper in the early 18th century. Master Keepers viewed their role as a mark of distinction but the Under Keepers were the ones who

THE WORK OF A FOREST KEEPER

Andy Shore looked up with a sheepish grin as he sprinkled feed on the ground by the observation platform at Bolderwood Deer Sanctuary. 'They don't need to be fed,' he explained, 'this is just to help visitors see them. Otherwise they prefer to hide in the Forest.' He called softly; the animals know and trust him and, sooner or later, they will appear here. He pointed to a distant hill: 'There's one old woman up there, trying to decide whether to come down to the meadow.'

I wouldn't even have noticed the lone female but to Andy, one of Forestry England's most experienced keepers, she's like family. He knows many of the deer in his 'patch', as he calls it, around the Bolderwood area. It's also his job to cull them when their numbers

get too high, but he doesn't feel sentimental about it; he views culling as essential to Forest maintenance and ultimately, preservation of the species themselves (page 35).

As a Forest keeper, a job that has been in existence since the 16th century, Andy is exercising ancient protection of 'vert and venison,' 'vert' being defined under the Forest law instituted by William the Conqueror, as 'everything that grows and bears a green leaf that may cover or hide a deer.' 'My job has changed little since those early days, except for maybe policing visitors.' Each of the Forest's ten keepers is responsible for a specific area, or beat. In addition to controlling the deer population, they are responsible for squirrels, hares and rabbits. They also liaise with the patrolled the Forest looking for poachers and wood thieves, and were the predecessors of today's Forest keepers.

The fate of deer changed considerably as rulers came and went. The Normans took hunting so seriously that William I instilled Forest Law to protect the animals at the expense of Forest residents. Punishments were serious for those who interfered with the king's hunting ground. By the time of the Tudors, the Forest was viewed as a source of timber, so deer were perceived as pests that ruined trees, leading to widespread culling in the 17th century. James II, who ruled from 1685 to 1688, was the last monarch to hunt here. After that, timber interests really took over. By 1851, sentiments had come full circle and the Deer Removal Act authorised complete removal as they were a threat to the timber plantations and interfered with commoners' interests. A few fallow deer escaped the hunters and were able to bolster the numbers when demand for timber once again died down. Today, the population is carefully controlled by culling or else deer would destroy the Forest (page 35).

public and have the power to deal with civil offences, usually involving people camping in a non-official site, parking in forbidden areas, or lighting a campfire.

Andy has been looking after the Bolderwood area for 35 years. Part of his job involves late night phone calls to attend to road accidents in which deer have been hit by a car or sometimes breaking up a late night party in the woods. More often than you think, Andy is summoned to pull a tourist from a bog deep in the Forest.

He describes his work with people with humour and perhaps a slight tinge of incredulity. 'People are only animals but highly predictable. I can tell who's going to be in the woods late at night just by the way their car is parked in the afternoon.'

As someone who has lived in the Forest his entire life and respects the ancient traditions, Andy is passionate about the Forest and his job. 'People forget that when it was established hundreds of years ago, the New Forest was given massive protection, even from the government. That protection is why we still have what we have today.' He laments the loss of oral traditions that cease to be passed on as Forest life becomes diluted by outside forces. 'Not too long ago, 80% of the people living in the Forest also worked here. All that's changed as more people come from other areas and the Forest has become accessible to so many people. Society's detachment from nature means a loss of understanding for how the Forest works.'

You don't have to venture far from the car park to see traces of these elusive animals, though have to know what to look for. When deer rub their antlers on trees, they leave gashes and eventually cause the tree to die. You can also tell when they've been in the area by observing the graze line on trees – the line of greenery that is eaten below head level of a deer.

8 RHINEFIELD ORNAMENTAL DRIVE

This famous stretch of road is a bit less ornamental since the scourge of Sudden Oak Death, a disease that infects and kills oaks as well as numerous other New Forest species, including ash, beech, larch and conifers. Rhododendrons, which are not native to this area, can harbour spores of the fungus that can be transmitted to other species in rainwater. In the early 2000s, spores were found in rhododendrons on the ornamental drive so the Forestry Commission removed them in the hopes of preserving the ancient Forest. Formerly you could drive along here and experience thrilling bouts of colour but now the ornamental drive is more about the grace and majesty of the tall conifers that were planted in the mid 19th century when it was fashionable to experiment with exotic trees. The road was originally the drive leading to **Rhinefield House**, a private home until the 1950s and now a hotel.

After Rhinefield House, the forest becomes thick with conifers. You can happily get lost amid towering trees that cast dark shadows or cool yourself down in the shade on a hot summer day. Midway along the drive is **Blackwater** car park. Of the many trails through the woods, a good one to do with children is the **Tall Trees Walk**, a mile-long circular route between Blackwater and **Brock Hill** car parks. Plaques along the trail highlight information about trees you see on the trail, including some of the oldest Douglas fir trees in Britain and a giant sequoia, a type of redwood native to America. You'll also pass an inclosure bank and ditch that dates from 1848 and illustrates how foresters used to exclude animals from young trees without fencing. Benches throughout invite you to slow down and contemplate the magnificent heights that surround.

Also across from the Blackwater car park is **Blackwater Arboretum**, a small area displaying trees from around the world. The wheelchair-

Autumn colours at Blackwater Arboretum on Rhinefield Ornamental Drive. ▶

BRITPIX/A

accessible sensory trail encourages people to experience trees in an almost spiritual way, by suggesting how calming they can be, as well as just pretty to look at. On the other side of the very busy A35, Rhinefield Ornamental Drive becomes **Bolderwood Ornamental Drive** where, just off the north side of the A35, you can see the famous **Knightwood Oak**, one of the oldest and most majestic trees in the Forest. The famous tree is on the opposite side of the road from its eponymous car park and well signposted. There are prettier trees in the Forest but the Knightwood is a fantastic example of an ancient pollarded tree (page 112).

9 BROCKENHURST

Brockenhurst is the largest village by population (about 3,500 residents) within the New Forest but it doesn't feel that way when you're pottering about here. There is no surrender to modern chain stores, just an old-fashioned high street, Brookley Road, with an independent hardware shop, art gallery, butcher and cafés. It's not uncommon to see cows meandering through the centre of the village. Glance out of a shop window and you might see a pony's or donkey's face pressed against the glass, peering in.

The North and South Weirs converge right in the centre of town, often to the inconvenience of motorists unable to cross the **Water Splash**, the ford at the base of the Brookley Road; it's easily bypassed by using The

POLLARDING IN THE FOREST

Like coppicing, pollarding is a long-established pruning system of forcing a tree to continually produce new growth. In pollarding, cuts are made above the browse line, meaning above where animals can reach, so it was useful in woodlands where animals grazed freely. In ancient times, the new wood would have been used for hedges, fences, houses, firewood and sometimes for animal feed. Branches would be left on the ground for commoners' animals to feed on.

From 1583, attempts were made to stop pollarding as it ruined trees for timber harvesting. The 1698 Inclosure Act prohibited pollarding in oak and beech trees in order to produce tall, straight trees for shipbuilding. That means that most pollarded trees, certainly the large pollarded oaks, that you see today in the Forest are more than 300 years old. But, of course there are exceptions. Pollarding has resumed in recent years to a limited extent, mostly on holly trees to produce feed for ponies and also to allow light to reach the forest floor, thereby increasing woodland diversity.

Rise, the parallel street. Open forest lies just beyond the high street at **Beachern Wood**, off Rhinefield Road.

Easily accessible from here is one of my favourite **cycle rides** in the Forest: following **Rhinefield Ornamental Drive** all the way through until it becomes Bolderwood Drive on the other side of the A35 (four miles) and then on to the road's end near **Rockford Common**, a total distance of 13 miles. The short distance boasts almost every terrain the Forest has to offer, from pasture to the dark woods of the ornamental drives with their summertime shocks of magenta foxglove, through to the undulating heaths of the west Forest.

To do this route yourself, leave Brockenhurst via Brookley Road, then go right on to Burley Road for a short distance until it becomes Rhinefield Road and leads on to the Ornamental Drive. After this you simply keep to the same road. You'll need to dismount and cross the busy A35 to continue on to **Bolderwood Ornamental Drive** where you cycle through some of the tallest trees anywhere in the Forest. Past Bolderwood, there is a long cruise downhill to the underpass of the busy A31, then it's

"Glance out of a shop window and you might see a pony's or donkey's face pressed against the glass, peering in."

back up the other side to emerge into open heathland. At the top, by **Holly Hatch**, you can see across Fordingbridge all the way to Wiltshire and the hills of Salisbury. If you're feeling peckish, you can cut right across the rough dirt track that leads to the signposted **High Corner Inn** (Linwood BH24 3QY ⊘ butcombe.com), where you can enjoy a drink or basic pub food in the huge garden. The main road then passes through woodland again before emerging into the open, where the **Red Shoot Pub** (Toms Ln, Linwood BH24 3QT ⊘ redshoot.co.uk) offers another welcome respite to refresh yourself before retracing your way back to Brockenhurst.

Church of St Nicholas

Church Ln (away from the main part of the village, on the east side of the A337), SO42 7UB
⊘ 01590 624584 ⊘ brockenhurstchurch.com

As the oldest church in the New Forest – Brockenhurst is the only New Forest village for which a church is mentioned in the Domesday Book – St Nicholas's Church and its setting boasts a lot of history. Historians believe that the hill on which it stands is partly artificial, suggesting that a pagan temple or Romano–British church once stood here. If you approach the church on foot (it's a short walk from the station) it's easy to imagine how this church might have appeared to its parishioners hundreds of years ago. Indeed, the words of John Wise, writing in 1862, are apt today:

> For a quiet piece of quiet English scenery nothing can exceed this. A deep lane, its banks a garden of ferns, its hedge malted with honeysuckle and woven together with byrony, runs, winding along a side space of green, to the latch gate.

He would be dismayed to hear the distant road noise today but, if you can block that out, the lane feels as tranquil as it might have been so many years ago. Wise was less complimentary about the 'wretched brick tower… patched on at the west end' – to the modern eye, though, it seems fitting. Inside are eight bells.

St Nicholas's has an odd shape for a modern congregation; the north aisle, from where it can be difficult to see proceedings, was built in 1832 to provide seating for the expanding population. The compact building

THE NEW FOREST SHOW

New Park, SO42 7QH ✆ 01590 622400 ⏶ newforestshow.co.uk ☉ late July

For three days in late July every year, the fields behind New Park Manor near Brockenhurst become a mini village that takes several weeks to set up and a full year to plan. I've been to the New Forest Show many times and have yet to leave feeling that I've seen everything. Programmes vary from year to year but the overall flavour is the same – everyone is here to slow down, have fun and celebrate this region's agriculture and rural pursuits.

Continuously running since 1921, the show officially incorporates all of Hampshire County but there is a New Forest emphasis, especially if you find your way to the back, where there is a special area dedicated to New Forest displays. The focus, of course, is the agricultural events, which include judging of sheep, horses and cows in show rings. The animals are housed in huge tents so you can wander in and say hello when they are not showing off in the ring. Farmers are happy to chat, especially at the end of the day when things slow down.

One attendee who shows off his cattle every year, explained that exhibiting in the ring can be trying. 'You're out there trying to make everything look perfect and of course hoping the judge doesn't look around at that one moment your cow does the wrong thing. You just don't know how she might react when the judge fondles her udder.' I'm guessing his sense of humour reduces the stress.

reveals many remnants from its long history. Roman masonry is built into the south porch, and just inside the doorway, to the left as you face the door, you can see Saxon herringbone masonry. A 12th-century font stands in the west end corner of the nave, and nearby behind a curtain a Tudor arch spans the entrance to the ground floor of the tower.

The churchyard, which cascades down the hill to the west of the church, is just as atmospheric. The enormous yew tree by the porch, which has a girth of 20ft, was carbon dated in the mid-1980s and found to be more than 1,000 years old. The churchyard contains 106 graves from World War II, 93 of which are New Zealanders who served beside British troops and were brought to the No. 1 New Zealand General Hospital established nearby at Balmer Lawn. Brockenhurst was chosen in 1915 to become a centre for several field hospitals because it was close to the port of Southampton and had good railway connections, as well as many large homes and available land. Soldiers were transported here from the Western Front for treatment and rehabilitation. Information boards at the base of the hill describe Brockenhurst's role in the war,

One of the best aspects of the show is that it's not assumed that visitors understand everything. Ring events feature running commentary that bridges the gap between ordinary citizens and rural workers. During the very popular 'One Man and his Dog' (or often *her* dog, I've noticed) demonstration, the audience learns traditional sheep dog commands and sees the level of patience required to train a dog to herd sheep. Dairy farmers give milking demonstrations so that visiting children can understand that the milk they drink doesn't originate in bottles. Equestrian events take place nearly all day.

An undercurrent of humour runs through the show and the best is found in the Countryside Area where dogs perform impressive and sometimes just funny feats. A real crowd pleaser is the terrier race when show attendees are invited to enter their dogs in a race to catch a 'ferret' (all humanely artificial). Getting the dogs to line up is a show in itself.

Even if you are not interested in agriculture, there is something for you here. The shopping is as good as any urban mall with jewellery, handbags, shoes and toys – and, of course, an abundance of farm gear. You'll be convinced you need a handsomely carved walking stick or fur-lined wellies, or perhaps a lawn mower.

A few visitor tips: it can be hot or rainy and either way there are few places to hide. Don't wear open-toed shoes because either the dry dust or the mud will get all over your feet. There is a picnic area if you don't want to be captive to the food stalls.

where some 24,000 wounded troops were admitted to hospital. You can imagine the impact on the 2,000 Brockenhurst residents, many of whom volunteered in the hospitals.

Brusher Mills, known locally for his snake-catching abilities, also has his final resting place here. Legend says that Mills lived in a hut in the woods and caught some 30,000 snakes in his lifetime. He was a popular Victorian figure and people came from all around to watch him at work.

FOOD & DRINK

Commoners 66–68 Brookley Rd, SO42 7RA ✆ 01590 718155 ⏣ commonerswinebar.com ⊙ 11.00–23.30 daily; food until 21.00. Smack in the centre of Brockenhurst's high street, this large, airy space is more than a wine bar because it is open all day. There are cosy sofas in the windows and bar tables for food and drink, plus a large outdoor terrace. Food is standard pub fare in a restaurant setting. On weekends there is sometimes live music and a large screen is used for major sporting events. A convivial feel, but best when it's busy.

The Pig Beaulieu Rd, SO42 7QL ✆ 01590 622354 ⏣ thepighotel.com. There is relaxed sophistication here that's hard to find in the Forest, as well as really good food prepared from ingredients that mostly come from the grounds. It's not cheap but good value for the quality and ambience. In summer and into autumn, The Pig hosts 'Smoked & Uncut' ('uncut' referring to a live performance), Sunday evening sessions with small bands that play on the lawn while chefs manning the Mediterranean oven turn out flat-bread pocket sandwiches.

Rosie Lea Bakery 76 Brookley Rd, SO42 7RA ✆ 01590 622797 ⏣ rosielea.co.uk ⊙ 09.00–16.30 Mon–Fri, 09.00–17.00 Sat & Sun. Definitely the place to come for home-baked cakes and other baked goods in Brockenhurst village. There are a few tables but be prepared to take your treats away.

Rosie Lea House Southampton Rd, SO41 8PT ✆ 01590 622908 ⏣ rosielea.co.uk ⊙ breakfast, lunch & afternoon tea daily, & seasonal dinner hours; check website in advance. This large café, operated by the same owners as the Brockenhurst bakery, is ideally situated if you've been walking in Roydon Woods. The expansive garden is a lovely setting for cocktails made from local spirits, as well as locally produced craft ales and cider. Just off the main restaurant is a very pleasant roofed terrace. Parents of young children love it here because there is space for little ones to run around.

The Thatched Cottage Hotel Tea Room and Gin Bar 16 Brookley Rd, SO42 7RR ✆ 01590 622005 ⏣ thatchedcottage.co.uk ⊙ from noon daily. How often do you have coffee in a 400-year-old thatched cottage? This cosy interior is a comforting atmosphere for tea and cake after long Forest walks and a great alternative to some of the busier nearby cafés. In summer, the gin bar moves to the outdoor terrace, which is a pleasant spot to sample a gin-tasting flight from some of the 300 available tipples.

DE-STRESS WITH A DONKEY

Brockenhurst Donkey Walks, South Weirs, SO42 7UQ ✆ 07721 068579
⏚ brockenhurstdonkeywalks.com

'Donkeys love people and people love donkeys,' said Jean Smith, proprietor of Brockenhurst Donkey Walks, as I began to brush Mr Macgregor, one of Jean's prized donkeys. I had signed up for a short walk into the forest with a donkey but first I had the opportunity to spend some time with him and beautify him for our outing. As I ran the brush along his back, it seemed as though he was smiling. We were going to get along fine. I found myself saying ridiculous things to Mr Macgregor but, as I cooed at him, I could feel myself relaxing and feeling the way I did as a child when time seemed to be only for things like this.

When Jean deemed him tidy and ready to go, I led 'my' donkey out towards the trail into the Forest and Jean walked alongside. As we walked, she told me donkey tales but Mr Macgregor remained silent, preferring to just plod along companionably at a delightfully slow pace. I regretted that I hadn't met Jean when my children were young because this is an experience made for youngsters. But Jean told me that actually some of the people who love it most are the elderly. When we returned to the yard, I gave the donkey who had stolen my heart a little treat and reluctantly turned away. I missed him already.

White Tails Restaurant Cottage Lodge Hotel, Sway Rd SO42 7SH ✆ 07503 120474
⏚ whitetails.co.uk ⏲ 18.00–22.00 Tue–Sat. This feels a bit like an exceptionally good dinner party. The small dining room adjacent to Cottage Lodge Hotel is cosy and intimate, with food carefully prepared and presented by chef Ramsey Hammad. Service is attentive and personal. Vegetarian options available; no children under ten and booking essential.

10 ROYDON WOODS NATURE RESERVE

Main entrance at Setley ⚲ SU315009 ⏚ hiwwt.org.uk; no on-site parking.

Against the many woodlands of the New Forest, Roydon stands out for the surprisingly diverse landscape of ancient woodland, conifers and streams within its 950 acres. Not too many people come here, even though the woods are only a mile southeast of Brockenhurst village. I've wandered through countless times and seldom seen another person. You can download self-guided walks from the website, and I've also featured the woods in the walk on page 124.

The land, owned and managed by the Hampshire & Isle of Wight Wildlife Trust, has protected status as a Site of Specific Scientific Interest (SSSI). Timber felled during woodland management is used to make fencing, gates and bridges for use in Roydon Woods and other trust

MICK HARPER/S

NICRAM SABOD/S

GORAN_SAFAREK/S

ONDREJ PROSICKY/S

WIRESTOCK CREATORS/S

reserves. Oak and softwood products are also sold to the public, as well as venison from deer that are culled. In spring, the dense woods at Roydon burst into colour with some of the best bluebell displays in the area, along with a profusion of other wildflowers and plentiful butterflies. But for me the delight of Roydon is its tranquillity. I live in the heart of the Forest but frequently choose to come here because I always have the sense I am a guest of the deer that remain hidden but watching.

The annual and increasingly popular **Woodfair**, when local woodsmen demonstrate traditional crafts like making besom brooms and walking sticks, is usually held in late spring; details are posted in advance on the website. New Forest Marque members (page 30) attend and sell their products.

11 SETLEY RIDGE VINEYARD

Lymington Rd (A337), SO42 7UF ℘ 01590 622246 ⌂ setleyridge.co.uk.

When Paul Girling purchased Setley Ridge Vineyard in 1999, it was in need of tender loving care. After he was laid off from his job as a surveyor in a big London firm, he decided he wanted to return to the area where he'd grown up and make a complete life change. 'Even though I didn't set out to buy a vineyard, I wanted a challenge and I thought the neglected site with its many outbuildings and the beautiful setting presented a lot of opportunities.' Setley Ridge is now a respected and well-known vineyard.

Producing wine in the non-agricultural New Forest is not easy but in the early days, Paul took courses and got help from other English wine producers. Setley Ridge now produces reds, whites, rosé and sometimes sparkling wines, depending on the conditions, and wines are bottled on-site. The vines are mostly German in origin and therefore suit the cooler climate of the Forest. Typical British weather could be one of Paul's greatest challenges but the recent hotter summers work to his favour. 'Every season is different and you never know what nature is going to throw at you, so we are always learning and are getting better at managing the vineyard,' Paul told me when I visited his bucolic setting.

◀ **1** Elizabethan Tudor architecture by the River Beaulieu. **2**, **3**, **4** & **5** Residents of Royston Woods Nature Reserve include insectivorous sundews, six-spot burnets, badgers & fly agarics.

Although Setley wines are not officially organic, Paul does not use pesticides and any (albeit rare) spraying is with Soil Association-approved materials. He prefers to work with nature by planting hybrids that are more resistant and maintaining the balance of beneficial predatory insects with those that are harmful to his crop. 'I don't see myself as unusually environmentally friendly,' he told me as we strolled amongst the tidy rows of early summer grapes. 'It's just common sense. If we destroy our environment, we won't have anything left. Because we are part of the national park, it's great to be able to produce a crop that is not having any impact on our sensitive environment.'

Paul's love and respect for the Forest are obvious. 'You can see our environment is healthy because of the varied wildlife we have living here. I regularly see birds of prey, toads, adders, butterflies and a variety of other birds. If we were seriously commercial, we wouldn't have hedgerows but I like them because they attract wildlife and look nice.'

As a member of the New Forest Marque scheme (page 30) Paul is dedicated to the concept of supporting local businesses and reducing food miles. 'When people traditionally went on holiday to Europe, they enjoyed seeking out local foods and wines,' he said. 'Now it's the same thing in the UK. The country has better palates and when people travel domestically, they want traceable food with a story from local producers.'

You can visit the vineyard on a guided tour, which includes tastings, bookable through the farm shop (page 122).

¶¶ FOOD & DRINK

Daisy Tea Garden Lymington Rd, SO42 7UF ✆ 01590 622912 ⌗ daisyteagarden.co.uk ⊙ 09.00—17.00 daily. A charming café that's part of the Setley Ridge family. In summer, there are outdoor tables with plenty of shade overlooking the garden centre, while in winter the former greenhouse is a cosy setting for breakfast, light lunch, and afternoon tea. Afterwards, you can browse the garden shop and farm shop. Not surprisingly, it's well-loved by locals.

Filly Inn Lymington Rd, SO42 7UF ✆ 01590 700270 ⌗ fillyinn.com. This beautifully restored 16th-century inn has a wonderfully cosy bar area in winter and a large garden with outdoor dining in summer. The menu is standard pub fare, not innovative but on par with many pubs in the area.

---

1 Fresh produce from a local hotel's kitchen garden. 2 Vegetables with the New Forest Marque. 3 Locally produced cheese. 4 New Forest rosé wine. ▶

THE MONTAGU ARMS HOTEL

NEW FOREST DESTINATION PARTNERSHIP

NEW FOREST DESTINATION PARTNERSHIP

NEW FOREST DESTINATION PARTNERSHIP

Setley Ridge Farm Shop Lymington Rd, SO42 7UF ⊙ 09.00–17.00 Mon–Sat, 10.00–16.00 Sun. Setley Ridge wines are sold in their shop, which is located in front of the vineyard, on the A337. Run by Paul and his wife Hayley, they stock numerous foods from the Forest, many of which hold the New Forest Marque. In addition to meats and dairy products, there are homemade cakes, jams, chutneys, marinades and other sauces. There are also pies and pasties and many groceries. Non-Forest stock is still reasonably local, coming from the Isle of Wight, Hampshire and Dorset.

12 PIG BEER

Baynhams Brewery, Lymington Rd, SO42 7UF ⊘ baynhamsbrewery.com

There is a bit of a craft beer frenzy in the New Forest, particularly in the Brockenhurst/Lymington region where there are three small breweries. But Baynhams Brewery, makers of PIG BEER, stands out for its staunch commitment to conservation.

'We like to challenge the way things are done,' said Tom Baynham, co-founder of Baynhams with his brother, Lawrence, and cousin, Harry.

"On summer weekends, the Baynhams fire up a woodburning oven for pizza and people gather at outdoor tables."

The trio is clearly not afraid of challenges. In 2017, while all of them were working in other careers, they purchased a former pig farm on the A337, planted a field with hops behind the original farmhouse and converted the former pigs' barn into a brewery. All three knew little about beer other than that they liked to drink it but they added to their learning curve by brewing beer – traditionally not an environmentally friendly process – with innovative, eco-conscious techniques.

'Growing hops is a water-intensive process and beer production generates a lot of wastewater,' explained Tom. 'About four pints of water are wasted for every pint you drink.' In response, they installed 20,000-litre tank (now beneath the car park) where rinse water from the brewing process is collected. This is then filtered to a drip irrigation system for the field.

But using grey waste is not even their most impressive environmental initiative. Making beer naturally generates what is called 'spent grain', the by-product of soaked and cooked grain. Although brewers traditionally pass spent grain on to farmers who use it as animal feed, it needs to be done almost immediately because spent grain is very wet and goes off in about 24 hours.

'The quick turnaround involved with using spent grain is extremely difficult to implement,' explained Tom. 'But we've developed a process in which our spent grain is ensiled, eliminating the time pressure of when a farmer needs to claim it. Now farmers pay us for our ensiled spent grain and we dramatically reduce waste.'

At the moment, there are seven beers in the range, including STORM, a popular IPA, BLAK, a milk stout, and SESSION, a light, citrus-led ale.

On summer weekends, the Baynhams fire up a woodburning oven for pizza and people gather at outdoor tables and in the tent outside the shop, which for the moment, serves as the brewery's taproom. They've also purchased a mobile bar to enable them to serve fresh brew at food fairs and festivals. And another barn is being converted to a more permanent taproom.

PIG BEER is available in local farm shops, online or from the brewery shop. The shop is usually open weekdays and weekends, but check the website to be sure.

13 SETLEY POND & SETLEY PLAIN

The very natural-looking **Setley Pond**, just over two miles south of Brockenhurst, originated during World War II when gravel was extracted for construction of runways at Stoney Cross, further north near Fritham. I've seen children swimming here, and of course dogs (though I don't recommend it for either) but mostly this is the local drinking spot for ponies and cows, who often come from quite a distance, nearly always in groups. There is something so fundamentally comforting about seeing the animals plodding with purpose across the heath, or along a wooded gravel track, almost as if they are gathering for a pre-arranged social hour at the watering hole.

Setley Pond is also known for the model boats that ply this suitably-sized body of water. The **Solent Radio Controlled Model Boat Club** (srcmbc.org.uk) has been operating here since 1978 when club members cleared the bottom of the pond to form an island and created a launching area. Sunday mornings, people (usually men of a certain age) gather to cruise their craft. It's all very sociable – many bring fold-up chairs and set up camp for the day. Because the club pays a fee to Forestry England to use the pond for sailing boats and because their boats are very expensive, members can seem a bit protective of their turf. But it's fun to watch, especially on a busy day when sailboats vie

A walk around Brockenhurst, Roydon Woods & Setley Plain

✳ OS Explorer map OL22; start: Brockenhurst Station ♀ SU301022; 6½-miles; moderate.

This walk is a splendid mix of deep woods, historic heathland and a New Forest village. If you do it on a Sunday, you might see model sailboats at Setley Pond (page 123). You're also likely to encounter deer in Roydon Woods, ponies at Setley Pond and, in summer, cows on the heathland surrounding Brockenhurst. Halfway around, Rosie Lea House, a former pub reincarnated as a tea shop, has a pleasant garden, and makes a good stopping point for sustenance to continue the journey. At the start and finish of the walk, Brockenhurst village has a number of tea shops and pubs. This walk also can be muddy and very wet in places. You can shorten the walk by taking the bus back to Brockenhurst halfway round (see point 6).

1 From Brockenhurst station, turn right on to the A337. Cross the railway and after 30yds, cross the main road and then turn left on to a lane signposted 'St Nicholas Parish Church'. Walk up past the church and after it, continue on the road as it curves around to the right.

2 After 200yds, turn left at the top of the hill, across from Birch Tree Cottage, and go through the narrow opening between gates. Walk between fences through Brockenhurst Park until the gate marking the entrance to Roydon Woods Nature Reserve. Once inside the reserve, the path goes up and down hills, and curves around but is easy to follow.

3 About one mile after the gate, the path intersects a main track. Go left down the hill and pass a red-brick cottage. Continue all the way to the bottom of the slope and then back up another slope for about 200yds.

4 At a little clearing on the left, there is a small path opposite, to the right of the main track, signposted 'Bridleway'. Follow this over a small stream and uphill through woods until the ground levels out. Pass through a gate and carry on straight across the turf, with a fence on your left, heading for houses and the road. Pass through a kissing gate just before the road, then cross the road and go through a second kissing gate marked 'Hampshire County Council'. Follow the path between hedges until you reach a gate and then follow the path downhill through a wooded area until you reach another gate, just before a small road.

5 Directly across the road, enter the woods by a footpath signpost. Follow the path a short distance downhill to a footbridge and stile. The ground is nearly always wet here; you can usually cut to the left to stay dry. Continue uphill after the stile on a wooded path to another stile. Cross the stile and walk uphill on the left edge of a field to a further stile. Cross it and then follow the narrow path along the left edge of the woods (you will begin to hear the noisy A337) until it emerges on to the right edge of a field.

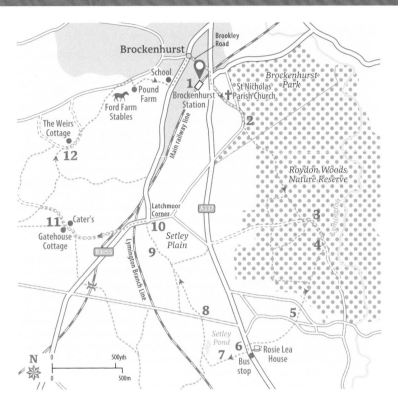

6 After about 130yds, pass through the metal kissing gate on to the verge of the A337. Take care here; cars go fast and it's a narrow verge. Turn left and stay close to the building on the left, which is the Rosie Lea House, a good place to pause for refreshments (page 116). There is a bus stop here if you want to go back to Brockenhurst or reconnect with the green route New Forest Tour bus. Otherwise, cross the A337 at the large Rosie Lea sign; directly opposite, to the right of the house, is a narrow entrance with a stile to a public footpath. Climb over the stile and walk on the narrow path that runs beside the property. At the end of the narrow path, climb another stile to emerge in open heathland.

7 With open forest on your right, head straight on towards a red-brick house. Just before the house, follow the track around to the right. After 30yds, cross an intersecting gravel track and ▶

A walk around Brockenhurst, Roydon Woods & Setley Plain (continued)

◄ follow a wide, open grassy path that gradually narrows and runs to the left of Setley Pond. At the end of the pond, continue on the same track until you come to a 'Horseriders' sign on the right, with an arrow pointing away from you. (It might be slightly obscured by gorse.) Follow this, with the car track on your right, out to the main road.

8 Cross the road, where you will see a wooden post to the left of a wide track. You will also see a slightly less distinct track on the left, which veers off from the wood post in a 'V' shape from the wide track. Take this left-hand track. You will be crossing the heathland of Setley Plain for about three-quarters of a mile; there are gorse clumps on your left but a clear view of the wide expanses towards the north. Soon you will see the bright green cladding of the railway bridge in the distance. The track gradually becomes more defined gravel; after heavy rain, you may have to dodge pools of water. Stay on the main track and ignore all intersecting paths. The path goes slightly uphill and narrows, then curves to the left and then to the right.

9 After about half a mile, you will come to a V junction; take the left-hand path. Follow the stony path as it winds downhill between gorse bushes. The path curves left then right, and then becomes slightly less distinct. Bear to the right, keeping the green railway bridge on your left and slightly behind you as you continue making your way towards the main road.

10 The path passes to right of a house (Latchmoor Corner) and comes out on a main road. Cross the road and turn left towards the railway bridge. Take care here – it is a minor road but a busy one. Walk along the road verge for about 350yds, passing under the railway bridge. Just after passing beneath the bridge, turn right on to the cycle track that passes under a second railway bridge (this is the main line leading to Dorset). Follow this for about 750yds until you reach two houses.

11 Walk straight on between Gatehouse Cottage on the left and Cater's on the right, ignoring a cycle trail that joins from the left. Pass through a barrier on to a track that heads into a

for space with miniature ferries and noisy power boats. Non-members can sail during Scale Section days on Thursday and Sundays from 10.00 but visitors must consult with club members in order to avoid a clash of radio frequencies. There is also the matter of a small insurance fee to pay, as stipulated by Forestry England. The Setley Cup, held annually on Boxing Day, is a junior model yacht race that is a 'must' on the local calendar.

Setley Plain, to the north of Setley Pond, across the road from the car park by the A337, has three extremely rare Bronze Age **disc barrows** on wooded area. After about a quarter of a mile, just before a clump of trees on your left, turn sharp right on to a wide track. This becomes indistinct at times but keep the power lines on your right and after a further quarter of a mile the path bends sharply left, at which point you will see a bridge (it can be muddy here). Cross the bridge and carry on along the main track as it continues to bend left away from the power lines and into a thicket of trees. After 250yds, cross another stream by a plank bridge. Continue straight, up a slight hill.

12 At the junction with a dirt track, turn right and walk towards houses. At the barrier, continue on to a gravel track by The Weirs Cottage, on your left. Follow this for 300yds until the main track curves left. Take the smaller track straight ahead and at the end, by a house, go through the kissing gate into a field that sometimes has sheep and other times alpaca, to a kissing gate at other end. (You will now begin to see yellow arrows marking the footpath.) Go through a gate to cut across the corner of a farm field and then over a stile into a field with a stream on your right. Walk on a narrow path with a fence on your left and a stream on your right until you emerge on to track at Ford Farm Stables. Turn left to reach the main road and then turn right along it, passing a dirt track on the right (after about 150yds) and continuing on to the next track where you turn right on the driveway to Pound Farm. Cross a bridge at the entrance to the drive and, just before the farmhouse, turn left past the hurdle (there is no defined path) and walk along a grassy clearing with a stream on your left. (Note: if this area is waterlogged, go back to Pound Farm driveway and walk along the main road until taking the first right, opposite Armstrong Lane.)

13 After 200yds, with another footbridge on your left, turn half right on a path that leads toward red-brick buildings and ends at a school. Turn left when you reach the main road and walk past the school until the junction with Brookley Road. Turn right to return to the station; alternatively, a left turn will take you to the village centre.

the northwest side. They are the only ones of this type in the New Forest. Mostly found in Wessex, disc barrows are distinguished by being round platforms within a circular ditch and bank; those at Setley Plain include the only pair of overlapping disc barrows in England. They are marked on Ordnance Survey maps as tumuli. The barrows can be hard for the untrained eye to see amid the vegetation, but there is a more visible circular one just beyond the Setley Pond car park, before reaching the main road as you exit. You pass all of these in the walk detailed on page 124.

14 SWAY

🏠 **The Manor at Sway** (page 223), **The Old Mill** (page 223)

The community flavour of Sway is palpable from the moment you step off the train, making this tiny village a delightful place to visit and perfect for a Slow weekend. For such a small, seemingly sleepy place, there is a lot going on. Sway is best known for its folly tower (see below) and locally for its early summer carnival (usually July). In the run-up to celebrations, residents decorate their houses and streets with scarecrows in a fierce competition. Lots of Hampshire towns hold scarecrow festivals but Sway approaches theirs with special zeal. It's not unusual to see entire streets decorated, with each house hosting a home-made scarecrow.

Sway's other claim to fame is that Captain Marryat, the 19th- century author of *Children of the New Forest*, lived here. The children of the story learn to live off the Forest land surrounding Sway while hiding from their Roundhead oppressors during the English Civil War. Literary fans journey here to walk in the story's landscape.

There is not a huge amount going on in Sway – which is precisely the joy of visiting. That said, it's a small place that punches well above its weight, with a hotel, pub, deli, butcher and several restaurants. There is

SWAY TOWER

From most every angle in the flat heaths surrounding Sway, you can glimpse the 218ft-tall Sway Tower, also known as Peterson's Folly, a 19th-century structure built by a wealthy judge who had worked in India, retired to the New Forest and fancied a monument to himself using Portland cement. A more altruistic take on the tale is that he wanted to prove that concrete was a viable building material and also provide work for local men. In any case, Peterson, a spiritualist, had apparently been communicating with the by-then long-deceased architect, Sir Christopher Wren, who allegedly urged him to build it. At the time of its construction, the tower was a record-breaker and it is believed (by locals anyway) to be the tallest non-reinforced concrete structure in the world.

It is, however, no longer a folly. In the 1970s, the tower was converted to a private home, an act that could only be described as a labour of love. It supposedly contained some 18 tons of pigeon droppings before the owners made it a stunning four-bedroom home with an indoor swimming pool and spread over 14 floors. But selling wasn't so easy. In 2019, the desperate owners auctioned off the structure after it had been on the market for three years. It was last listed for sale in 2021 for £2.75 million.

even an inspiring art gallery called Spudworks (Station Rd, SO41 6BA ✎ 01590 682260 ⌖ spud.org.uk), which hosts changing exhibitions, sometimes focused on the Forest. The goal of this national arts and education charity is to foster community spirit and personal wellbeing. For the visitor, this translates to thought-provoking installations that engender an understanding of this area. Exhibitions often highlight voices

"Lots of Hampshire towns hold scarecrow festivals but Sway approaches theirs with special zeal."

traditionally not heard in the Forest. Shows have included a Queer Almanac about what it means to be queer in the Forest and interactive events exploring equal access to nature.

Sway is on the South West Main Line from Weymouth and Bournemouth to Southampton and London Waterloo, so it's an easy and worthwhile place to stay without a car. There is good access to the Forest, which is just a half-mile walk away from the village centre, at Adlam's Lane, from where you can explore the heath and woodland of Wilverley, Longslade and Wooton Bridge. Bike trails are accessible from the village from small, rural roads. Particularly good for cycling families is the bike trail along the former railway line 'Castleman Corkscrew', which originally ran from Southampton to Dorset. The trail begins in Brockenhurst and a flat section passes through the Setthorn Campsite near Sway; you can do a ten mile loop around Setthorns and Sway that is suitable for younger children. The National Park Authority website has details.

¶¶ FOOD & DRINK

In addition to the places listed below, **Sway Deli & Coffee Shop** (3 Middle Rd, SO41 6BB ✎ 01590 683393) is good for coffee and snacks.

Hare & Hounds Durnstown SO41 6AL ✎ 01590 682404. About ½ mile to the northeast of Sway village, and a pleasant walk away, is this family-orientated pub with decent food and an even better drinking atmosphere. Good selection of ales, including Ringwood and Itchen Valley. Well situated for walks around Sway, Brockenhurst and Setley.

The Old Mill Silver St, Hordle SO41 6DJ ✎ 01590 682219 ⌖ theoldmillnewforest.co.uk. This 18th-century water mill makes a stunning setting for a restaurant and hotel, and it's only two miles from Sway. The riverside terrace dining is splendid on a sunny day and there is also a garden out the back that has a separate menu featuring lighter fare. In winter, the restaurant is cosy by the fire but you can also sit in the conservatory overlooking the water. Food quality is better than most nearby pubs.

The Silver Hind Station Rd SO41 6BA ✆ 01590 683900 ◌ silverhind.co.uk ◷ 12.00-15.00 and 17.00-20.30 Mon-Thu; 12.00-20.30 Fri-Sat; 12.00-17.00 Sun. A pleasant restaurant that serves pub classics but is yearning to be a bistro. Really friendly service and decent food, especially the pies. The building itself is important to locals; developers have been staved off several times and the village is lucky to have this restaurant.

LYMINGTON & ITS COAST

As you move towards the Solent, the atmosphere changes distinctly from other parts of the Forest. The major town of this area, **Lymington**, is not part of the New Forest geographically or spiritually, although it is included within the national park. Yacht enthusiasts come from all over the world to experience Solent sailing, to which the huge number of moored craft, two sailing clubs (three if you count the one run by and for children) and two large marinas attest. You only need to spend an afternoon wandering around the quay or watching seabirds at **Keyhaven** to appreciate the very different essence that ocean air brings. To visit Lymington and say you've been to the New Forest would be inaccurate but to come to the New Forest and not explore the coastal areas around Lymington, especially Keyhaven, would be to miss a key element.

15 BUCKLAND RINGS

122 Southampton Rd, Lymington SO41 8NA ✆ 01590 674656 ◌ hants.gov.uk

Traffic whizzes by this ancient site and it's only when you look closely that you notice the gate leading into what is one of the best-preserved Iron Age hillforts in this part of Hampshire. Buckland Rings was occupied sometime around 600–100BC, before it was abandoned. The ramparts on the eastern side were flattened sometime in the 18th century but on the southern and especially the northern side you can clearly see the ditches and banks that once surrounded the six-acre settlement.

There are two marked trails around the rings. The yellow trail follows the wide, open meadows (which you might share with grazing animals) and gives perspective on how high this settlement was. The red trail takes you into the woods to see the defensive structures that now are covered with thick woodland. Oddly, although trees would not have been here back when the fort was first built, the essence of the site is most apparent when you walk through the woods and appreciate the scale of the ditches.

Although the fort undoubtedly had some military purpose, historians believe that Buckland was an Iron Age community living in roundhouses and using small square buildings elevated on posts to store crops in winter and keep them safe from pests. Locally produced salt also would have been used for food preservation. What's not immediately clear is that the site is very close to the Lymington River, providing its occupants access to the coast. You can no longer see the river because of the trees planted here during the 18th century when nearby Buckland Manor was landscaped.

Be sure to explore the whole thing; it is not very big and both trails (of about 460yds) are rewarding. It's particularly lovely in autumn when you walk on a carpet of colour on the red trail. And don't miss the *Hilltop Benches* sculpture on top of the hill overlooking the fort.

The site is best accessed from the main gate off the busy A337, about 150yds past the Ampress Park Roundabout heading south on the A337, or 100ft from Marsh Lane when heading north. There is no designated parking but you can usually find a spot in one of the residential roads off nearby Marsh Lane.

 ## FOOD & DRINK

Mabel's Café Shallowmead Nurseries, Boldre Ln, SO41 8PA ✆ 01590 672550
⌘ shallowmead.co.uk ◷ 09.00–16.00 daily. Set within a garden centre, Mabel's is one of the best places for breakfast (until 11.30) in the area. Light meals are served all day in a bright setting that overlooks a landscaped garden. In summer, the outdoor seating is lovely.
Monkey Brewhouse 167 Southampton Rd, SO41 9HA ✆ 01590 676754
⌘ monkeybrewhouse.co.uk ◷ 11.00–23.00 daily. You don't have to love beer to enjoy it here but it helps because it is brewed on-site. Will Bradshaw, who grew up in the New Forest, wanted to set up a free house that would cater to locals and offer an alternative to the pub chains that are sweeping across the area. So he purchased the pub and built a glass extension where diners can watch the brewing process from their tables. Choose from 12 beers, including pale ales, IPAs and classic English bitters. Its namesake comes from a former landlord in the early 1900s who kept monkeys at what was then the Crown Inn. Mains range from sharing boards to more ambitious plates, including seafood curry, duck confit and fish of the day. More history comes in the form of the Grade-II-listed 18th-century toll house adjacent to the pub, where tolls were collected in order to maintain the road. Live music every Sunday night, plus a monthly pub quiz.

16 LYMINGTON

🏠 **Warborne Farm** (page 223)

Yachting is the flavour of Lymington, but that's not readily apparent when you arrive at Lymington High Street. The harbour is tucked away down a hill at the eastern end of town and then strings along the Lymington River, which runs south and flows into the Solent. The predominantly Georgian buildings display a pleasing mix of brick and pastel-painted shopfronts and the slope down to the harbour reinforces a Slow feeling. The pavements routinely host groups of chatting residents, who pause amid their daily errands, usually with dogs in tow.

A bit like Ringwood, Lymington has a split personality of high-end boutiques catering to visitors and retirees with boats moored in the harbour mixed with budget-minded retail outlets. The frequency of business closures reflects a reality veiled beneath the fancy shops. Like so many towns in southern England, Lymington suffers from chain-store malaise. Independent shops come and go but beneath the surface, the village spirit fights back, especially on Saturday, when market stalls fill High Street (page 134). The **market** is central to Lymington's history, and to a certain degree, its identity. When Lymington was made a town by William de Redvers between 1190 and 1200, he granted the people a charter to hold a market. The wide High Street was designed to make room for the stalls, which ultimately led to the shops that line the street today.

"The pavements routinely host groups of chatting residents, who pause amid their daily errands, usually with dogs in tow."

You have to work a bit to find Lymington's character away from the harbour. The best start is at the very fine **St Barbe Museum & Art Gallery** (New Street, SO41 9BH ✆ 01590 676969 ☌ stbarbe-museum. org.uk). A real effort has been made here to welcome children; there are interactive displays, dressing-up costumes, mischievous knitted farm animals, and stepstools all around. Exhibits on the salt industry, boat building, smuggling, the Forest in wartime and ancient artefacts found around the Forest give a clear sense of the town's development. Lymington hasn't always been a tranquil sailing port; in addition to salt-making and boat building, one of the town's most flourishing industries was smuggling. Contraband usually consisted of tobacco,

---

1 Lymington Marina. **2** Quay Street, Lymington. **3** Seaside essentials for sale. ▶

New Forest
ICE CREAM

CRABBING GEAR
BUCKETS FROM £1.50 LINE £1.00
BAIT £1.50 NETS £1.50

LINES
£1.00

ROGER UTTING/D

alcohol, tea and silk because taxes were particularly high on these items. The illicit trade thrived all along this coast, prompting Daniel Defoe to write in 1720 that it was the 'reigning commerce of all this part of the English coast'. The New Forest lends itself to smuggling because of the flat, shallow coastland – and plenty of Forest to disappear into with your goods.

Residents often conjecture about the hidden tunnels that are rumoured to exist beneath Lymington High Street around the Angel Inn. Although it's easy to find reports on the internet from people who have seen them, most historians believe they are more likely to be drainage tunnels. 'But that doesn't mean contraband wasn't moved through them as well,' a local historian told me.

The one thing that is clear from newspaper reports (on display in the museum) is that smuggling rings could be violent.

Like the museum, the art gallery (in the same building) is welcoming to children. School groups regularly attend and there are activity trays readily accessible for individual visitors. Special text panels are made for the changing exhibitions to engage children; in summer, exhibitions are tailored to youngsters.

IF IT'S SATURDAY, IT MUST BE LYMINGTON

Lymington market ⊘ 08.00–17.00 Sat; some traders begin to pack up at 16.00

On an early spring morning, Lymington market is crammed with people who peruse the rows of timepieces displayed on tables and racks of clothing hung from frames of market stalls. Children jump up and down in excitement over toy stalls and dogs strain at leads in order to hoover any scraps of food.

The scene before me suggests a thriving market. And it is, in terms of a fun day out, but for the traders it might be another story – one that reflects a disappearing aspect of life in England. For Wayne Bellows, who has been a fruit and vegetable trader for his entire life, it has become an unviable career. 'The fruit and vegetable game has changed,' Wayne

told me, matter of factly. 'Supermarkets sell produce for cheaper than we can afford to. The Covid lockdown had a huge effect – we had a regular customer base that moved on during that period of closure.' He explained that he used to sell 200 boxes every Saturday; now it's down to ten.

There has been a market in Lymington since 1250 and Wayne's family has been part of it for over a hundred years. He started when he was five, standing beside his father and grandfather to sell produce to local people. Back then, the market was a more essential source of fruits and vegetables than it is today. His pride in the family business is

The busy and popular Old School Café highlights St Barbe's role as a community centre. The café serves light snacks and has an outdoor terrace in summer. Staff at the desk double as a tourist information service and there is a large stand displaying local brochures and maps.

The waterfront

At the bottom of the High Street, a cobbled pedestrian way curves down to **Lymington Quay**. Although lined mostly with souvenir and ice-cream shops (most of which are closed during winter months), this is the most appealing part of town. Children might enjoy swinging nets off the main pier in hopes of catching crabs, and it's a pleasure just to sit on the wall and watch boats come and go. A small fleet of fishing boats is still based at the quay, mostly catching fish and other seafood from the Solent. Oysters were once a mainstay of Lymington fishermen; shells periodically found during excavations in the High Street show that they were a staple from medieval times until the late 19th century. But oyster numbers declined so severely at the beginning of the 20th century that a regeneration project is now underway, involving oyster colonies suspended underneath pontoons at the Wightlink Ferry Terminal. The

palpable; he is joined today by his aunt and his daughter. But his sons have chosen not to carry on the market trade. It's a story that reflects a changing retail landscape. 'Outdoor markets thrive in Europe because they are cheaper and it's a way of life,' lamented Wayne. 'Here the supermarkets take priority.'

The market is busy but Wayne shook his head and said, 'it has all changed. The market used to be filled with 90ft-long stalls belonging to permanent traders. Now, it's largely casual, Saturday traders in smaller stalls.'

Today Lymington is one of the few markets in southern England that hasn't been privatised but is still run by the local council. That means pitch rental is cheaper and to the visitor, anyway, the market retains an old-time flavour. More than 90 stalls run the length of nearly all of Lymington High Street, from the top of the hill that comes up from the harbour, to the church. In the early days, the market was much smaller and focused on food, but has now expanded to include jewellery and other items.

According to Wayne, 'Saturday will be market day for a long time to come in Lymington, but what's for sale will reflect changing lifestyles.' And that's okay for visitors because as much as market day is about shopping, it's also about being part of Lymington life, even if just for a short time.

oysters have improved the water quality enough to encourage other endangered species, like the European eel, to return to these waters. Sheltered at the north end of the two-mile estuary leading to the Solent, Lymington Harbour is, like the Forest, a relatively small space shared by many interests. Fishing boats, pleasure craft and the Isle of Wight Ferry traverse these waters daily.

A short walk away from the port, towards Keyhaven along **Bath Road** (which is all land reclaimed from the river in the early 19th century), reveals a cross-section of Lymington history. Just past the town quay, the **Berthon Boat Company** produces pilot boats, used to guide large ships in and out of ports – as well as lifeboats and yachts. The company continues a long-established Lymington tradition that began with Thomas Inman, a yacht builder who came to the town in 1819 and introduced the idea of pleasure boating on the Lymington River. After about half a mile you arrive at **Bath Road Recreation Ground**, a wide-open grassy park that borders the Lymington River. The benches that line the waterway are a fine place for a picnic as you overlook the dense array of masts that stand as thick as a Forest woodland, while passing Isle of Wight ferries give the eerie impression of gliding on air. Every summer, for three days (usually in July), these grounds become a celebration of seafood and local produce with the Lymington Seafood Festival (⊘ lymingtonseafoodfestival.co.uk). It is a splendid array of food and drinks stalls with live music and is great fun.

"The oysters have improved the water quality enough to encourage other endangered species."

Further across the car park, just outside **the Royal Lymington Yacht Club**, stands one of the original gas lamps installed in the town in 1832, now a memorial and operated by electricity. Not long after this lamp was first installed, Lymington was one of the first towns in the south to convert to electric street lamps but, oddly, in 1933 the town switched back to gas until after World War II. Reportedly this was because of the high cost of electricity but might it have been because several town leaders held shares in the Lymington Gas and Coke Company?

A bit further west is one of Lymington's most special features, the **Sea Water Baths** (⊘ lymingtonseawaterbaths.org.uk), a huge outdoor, chlorine-treated saltwater swimming pool beside the Lymington Town Sailing Club. In peak summer season, the scene here is mayhem on sunny afternoons, as the pool hosts 656ft of inflatable obstacle course. There is also kayaking, water zorbs, paddle boards and, of course, plain old swimming. The town briefly flirted with the hope of becoming a spa under the auspices of the Lymington Bath and Improvement Company in the 1830s. The pool and bath house (now the Lymington Town Sailing Club) were built at a time when ocean bathing was believed to be unusually restorative. People did come for a while but Lymington's spa dream was not to be realised, as saltwater bathing went out of fashion. The Grade-II-listed, unheated pool is usually open from May to September but it closes on occasion for private parties so phone ahead. It's wise to wear plastic shoes as the bottom can have sharp shells or even nibbly crabs.

Lymington & Keyhaven Marshes Nature Reserve

SO41 8AJ ✎ 01590 674656 ⟲ hants.gov.uk or hiwwt.org.uk

Birdwatchers come from all over the UK and even further afield to enjoy the abundant flocks that reside in this glorious 500-acre reserve during winter (page 138). 'From December through February there are about 10,000 birds living here,' said Pete Durnell, manager of the site for Hampshire County Council. 'One of the things that makes the reserve special is that we are still very much part of the New Forest. In summer, commoners graze ponies and cattle here, which enables us to maintain the shore

"Birdwatchers come from all over the UK to enjoy the abundant flocks that reside in this glorious 500-acre reserve."

grasses at an optimum level for birds that return home each winter.' These include brent geese, wigeon, kingfishers, black-tailed godwits and the largest settlement of pintail ducks in Hampshire.

Diversity of habitat is another key feature of the reserve. 'Lagoons, reeds beds, saltmarshes and mudflats make an unusual combination that provides rich feeding ground for so many species.' Year-round residents include curlews, little egrets, redshanks and ringed plovers. The fenced-in lagoon provides a secure nesting spot for birds and the reserve is witnessing larger numbers of breeders. These saline lagoons that run between the Lymington River and Keyhaven are special for another reason. They provide a rare habitat for hard-to-see species, like lagoon shrimp and cockle, that can only live in water that has a salinity about halfway between salt and fresh water.

COASTAL BIRDING

I have always enjoyed walking and cycling along the Solent Way because it is a delightful trail without cars, has beautiful views of the Isle of Wight, and I like being surrounded by seabirds. But I had no idea of the intricacies of bird life here until I joined Marcus Ward of Wild New Forest (⌂ wildnewforest. co.uk) for a 'Discovery Walk' of **Lymington and Keyhaven Marshes Nature Reserve** (page 137).

This is one of the UK's top birdlife sites, both for observing and scientific study.

Although the human population here swells in summer, feathered creatures prefer winter so this area is jammed with waders from December to February. 'This is a pit stop for migrant birds,' said Marcus, as he scanned the sky with binoculars. 'In winter, many come from the Arctic on their way to warmer climates and rest here before tackling the Channel crossing. And in spring, this is the first landing point for birds coming the other way and heading further north to breed. There are very few places where birds travelling to and from Africa can stop and refresh themselves.'

On my visit, Marcus was pleased to spot avocet. 'Avocets are a conservation success story here,' he said with obvious delight, as we surveyed the tall wader sweeping its bill from side to side in search of tiny crustaceans. 'They established in East Anglia and have now spread to the southwest. About 30 pairs have successfully raised young here, which is a record high for Hampshire.'

Another success story are the little egrets that jauntily parade in the sand. Marcus told our small walking group that they had been nearly hunted to extinction in the UK by Victorians seeking decorative hat plumage but in the mid 1990s began breeding in this sheltered habitat. Their increased presence might also be due to climate change, explained Marcus, as warmer temperatures

This area, along with nearby Hurst Spit, is continually changing. In the 19th century, grasses began colonising the mudflats here, reaching their peak in the 1920s. Now as they begin to die back, marshes are returning to mudflats.

Birds aside, this is a memorable spot for a coastal walk. 'This is one of the few places along this coast that's accessible to the public – most of it is privately owned,' said Pete. That's thanks to a far-sighted purchase in 1979 by Hampshire County Council in recognition of fast-paced development in the area and loss of habitats. The stretch to Keyhaven is along a gravel track that is wheelchair- and pushchair-accessible. In contrast to a bracing walk along the coast further west at Milford, the paths at Keyhaven reveal the intricacies of mudflats and grasses, as well as providing a clear view of the Isle of Wight.

in this area enable them to expand their range from the Mediterranean.

While this is exciting news for local birdwatchers, the overall implications of climate change are concerning for Marcus and his fellow ornithologists. Marcus explained that salt marshes form where sheltered water allows sediment to build up, but this important conservation area is under severe threat due to rising sea levels and more intense storms. Solutions to the coastline's protection must consider diverse needs and will require significant external funding (page 146). Although the sea wall and flood embankments further inland are essential for protection of coastal communities, their presence combined with rising sea levels create a process called 'coastal squeeze', which in effect reduces the coastal habitat area by preventing the natural process of coastal habitats moving inland.

The salt marsh is now retreating by up to 20ft a year. 'Already, rising sea levels mean we've lost valuable breeding space,' Marcus said. 'This year we had only 5,000 pairs of black-headed gull – down from 14,000 at one time.'

Our group stood at the edge of the seawall, silently gazing at the busy activity below us and contemplating the potential transience of the scene. And then Marcus cocked his head as he heard a trill on the breeze. 'A Dartford warbler, one that's difficult to see but has a distinctive song.' Marcus lined it up in the telescope for us and, although it took me ages, I was finally rewarded with a clear view of an oh-so-small bird perched on a gorse branch. The world paused, and admiring this single bird's beauty and fragility suddenly seemed like the most important thing that would happen all day.

Wild New Forest offers regular public and bespoke private walks for all ages and abilities.

There's limited parking at the end of Lower Pennington Lane in Keyhaven, but otherwise it's easy to park in Lymington at Bath Road Car Park and walk the 600 yards to the edge of the reserve and a further three miles to Keyhaven Marshes.

FOOD & DRINK

Chequers Inn Ridgeway Ln, SO41 8AH ☎ 01590 673415 ⌂ chequersinnlymington.com ⊙ 11.30–23.00 Mon–Sat, noon–20.00 Sun. This 16th-century pub was around in the days when the Salt Exchequer Offices were nearby. It's a friendly, popular pub where dogs wander in and out and sailors share tales at the bar. Standard pub fare, but the atmosphere is jolly, especially in summer when barbecues and bar service are held in the courtyard.

The Elderflower 4–5 Quay St, SO41 3AS ☎ 01590 676908 ⌂ elderflowerrestaurant.co.uk. Foodies can rejoice: this is one of the finest restaurants in the entire New Forest. Chef/owner

SALT MAKING AT LYMINGTON

It's hard to believe as you walk in this tranquil setting that 200 years ago this area was a busy industrial centre as sluice gates opened and closed, wind pumps whirred and boiling houses steamed. Salt making was Lymington's most important industry for hundreds of years and there is evidence that salt may have been manufactured here in the Iron Age. The first record of it is in the Domesday Book of 1086, which lists six salterns at nearby Hordle. The industry peaked around 1760 when there were 163 pans working. In 1800, 4,000 tons of salt were produced and exported to the Channel Islands, Newfoundland and Scandinavia. Wealth from the industry is reflected in the Georgian mansions around Lymington High Street.

By today's standards salt making seems like an extraordinarily laborious process but ingenious in its method of harnessing nature. At high tide, seawater filled feeding ponds. Sluice gates drained water into evaporation pans where it stayed until wind and sun evaporated most of it. Wind pumps then pushed the remaining brine into holding tanks, from where it was fed into boiling houses, where fires under metal pans boiled away the last bit of water. The remaining salt crystals were then transferred to buckets and carried away.

The obvious question is, especially if you visit on a characteristically soggy English day, how could that method be practical in this climate? And the answer is that it wasn't. Lymington ultimately lost out to the more efficient production methods and the cheaper rock salt being produced in Cheshire, as well as extremely high taxes on salt. By 1850, production had ceased.

Andrew Du Bourg, the former head chef at the nearby five-star Chewton Glen Hotel, serves elegantly crafted dishes to a discerning clientele. The food is best described as British with an undertone of French. Tasting menus only: four courses at lunch and a choice of four, five, or seven courses, with or without wine pairings, at dinner. Service is professional and friendly; Andrew's wife Marjolaine sets a relaxed tone. Did someone say Michelin star? Hurry before they get one and prices go up!

Goodall's Strawberry Farm South Baddesley Rd, SO41 5SH ✆ 07967 344008 ✎ goodallsstrawberries.co.uk ⏱ generally May–Oct, see website for details. Strawberries have been grown on Goodall land in Lymington for a century. From 1 May to mid-July you can pick your own strawberries in open fields and polytunnels. Eight varieties grow here to extend the season. As the season progresses, broad beans, raspberries, cherries, blackcurrants, blueberries and sometimes potatoes are added to the pickings. In summer, the small farm shop sells local goods, including its own-label jams, marmalade and honeys, homemade Scotch eggs, pork pies and sausage rolls, and bread from Tatchbury Manor Farm. You can even sit in the shaded tea garden and enjoy a cream tea. A lot of fun, and lovely views of the harbour. In October, you can pick your own pumpkins and in December, the Christmas trees are in.

The Ship Inn The Quay, SO41 3AY ✆ 01590 676903 ⌂ theshiplymington.co.uk ⊙ 11.00–23.00 Mon–Sat, 11.00–22.30 Sun. Location, location, location – right on the water. If you're lucky enough to snag an outdoor, waterside table in summer, you'll have a view of yachts and children catching crabs at the wharf. Food is decent and the atmosphere is lively.

Solent Cellar 40 St Thomas St, SO41 ✆ 01590 674852 ⌂ thesolentcellar.co.uk. A truly stand-out independent wine shop with friendly and knowledgeable staff, a relaxed atmosphere and hand-selected wines from all over the world. You're likely to find unusual bottles from small, independent producers. There's always an opportunity to taste and in summer you can sit out in the terrace for a glass or two. Owners Simon and Heather are passionate about their personal service and will be happy to recommend food pairings. Be sure to see the clay pipes that were uncovered during renovations to the 17th-century building –they are framed in the back of the shop.

Stanwell House Boutique Hotel 14–15 High St, SO41 9AA ✆ 01590 677123 ⌂ stanwellhouse.com. Three restaurants with distinctly different atmospheres. The Salt Bar is the most lively and has a charming atmosphere, with tables tucked into every available corner. It's a small space and does not take reservations, so come early on weekends for its good, hearty comfort food. The Orangery is a light-filled conservatory space that serves as the hotel's morning café and evening cocktail bar, with light lunches and afternoon tea in between. Samphire is the most formal restaurant, lined with banquettes and marble tables. There is a large outdoor courtyard as well. All menus are predominantly seafood but there is plenty of choice for everyone.

The Tinker's Granddaughter 20 High St, SO41 9AD ⌂ thetinkersgranddaughter. com ⊙ Wed–Mon. A friendly, chilled, plant-based café , deli and store, which started life as a food truck. A very welcoming atmosphere and *the* place to come for vegan and gluten-free options.

17 MILFORD ON SEA

⌂ **Vinegar Hill B&B** (page 223)

Milford is busiest in summer when you can stroll along the beach or above on the clifftops where there are views of the Isle of Wight and the colourful beach huts below. When the summer glare fades and the ice-cream crowd returns home, Milford dons a charm of a bygone age, especially at Christmas when the village green is adorned in lights. In the late 19th century, Colonel Cornwallis-West of Newlands Manor, a grand estate north of the town, had ambitious plans to make Milford a fashionable seaside resort akin to Eastbourne. He added the 'on sea' to Milford's name and began to develop the Hordle Cliff area, between Milford and Barton-on-Sea. Unfortunately, due to a typhoid outbreak and lack of funds, his dream never came true. That might, however, have been to Milford's advantage. The absence of high-street chains, the strong sense of community and the slow atmosphere make Milford a delightful place to visit. David Rogers and his wife Lucy of Vinegar Hill Pottery (page 143), both of whom grew up in nearby Lymington, have lived in Milford for many years and watched it blossom from a largely retirement village to a buzzing family community. 'It's a fantastic place to live,' said Lucy.

Milford has some good food options for such a small town. **Verveine** (page 145), connected to the fishmonger of the same name, attracts foodies because of its no-nonsense approach to preparing fish simply and with fresh, local ingredients. The annual **Milford Festival**

WALKS ALONG THE COAST

Technically, it's possible to walk west for 14 miles from Milford all the way to Bournemouth (with a short ferry crossing at Christchurch Harbour) on the Bournemouth Coastal Path. Closer to home, the three-mile walk from Milford to Barton-on-Sea – a combination of hard path, grass and earth – can be an invigorating seaside experience, especially off-season when colder winds blow. The area by **Hordle Cliff Beach**, about halfway along, is ideal for pushchairs and wheelchairs and you are treated to unfettered views of the Isle of Wight and, on a clear day, west to Hengistbury Head, Christchurch Harbour and the Purbeck Hills. Summer has its own charms, even if predictable ones. Children race in and out of the waves and couples stroll hand-in-hand across the bumpy shingle.

I heartily recommend walking the length of **Hurst Spit**, even if you don't plan to visit the castle (page 146). You can walk the full

2½ miles from the village green or begin at the public car park at Sturt Pond for a roughly 1½-mile walk. A bird hide is tucked away behind the Lighthouse restaurant, before the start of the spit. The **Solent Way** (⊘ solentway.co.uk) a 60-mile footpath linking Milford with Emsworth Harbour, just beyond Portsmouth, begins at Hurst Spit. The walk along here to Lymington, via Keyhaven, is nine miles; in the shelter of the Isle of Wight, you won't experience the onslaught of ocean winds – instead, this journey offers quiet contemplation of marshes and abundant birdlife (page 138). If you don't want to walk back to Milford, you can take a bus from Lymington (⊘ morebus.co.uk). You can use the public car park at Sturt Pond; parking is free along Saltgrass Lane, but watch the tide, as this road is known to flood.

The website ⊘ visitmilfordonsea.co.uk lists local walks, including guided options.

(⊘ visitmilfordonsea.co.uk), usually in May, showcases the community's spirit with food and activity stalls on the village green and music at various venues.

In a nod to a bygone age, Milford has **Pleasure Grounds**, 14 acres of ancient woodland with trails that run along the Dane Stream, parallel to the coast. They are located at the western end of the village, conveniently next to the car park. You can walk through the Pleasure Grounds (enter from Park Lane, just after crossing the bridge) to New Valley Road and on into **Studland Common Nature Reserve** to follow further footpaths along the river. It's not as remote as the Forest by any stretch but if you're here and you're looking for a woodsy experience, this is a good place to have it. It's also a good combination with the clifftop walks of the area.

Vinegar Hill Pottery

SO41 0RZ ⊘ 01590 642979 ⊘ vinegarhillpottery.co.uk

David Rogers's hands smoothed the spinning clay into a perfect round shape as his pottery wheel rumbled and whirred. 'Our set-up just kind of evolved because all aspects work so well together,' he said, referring to the multi-faceted business of pottery studio, classroom and B&B that he and his wife, Lucy, run in Milford. Dave, an accomplished artist in his own right, decided to start teaching his craft to people who came to stay at their B&B. Or was it people who came to stay at the house became interested in taking pottery classes? Either way, it's a splendid mix and Dave still finds time to create his signature brilliant blue tableware and earthy casserole pots.

One- and three-day courses, limited to nine people, take place throughout the year and Dave will arrange special group events.

"The strong sense of community and the slow atmosphere make Milford a delightful place to visit."

The solar-powered, purpose-built studio boasts nine wheels so that each student has their own station. 'Many people tend to do evening courses when they study pottery but it's just not long enough,' said Dave, whose glowing reviews almost always cite his exemplary patience. 'But we add in the fun of some really good food. We break for coffee and cake in the morning and then, after guests have had a good turn at the wheel, we head over to the gallery for a relaxing lunch.' Potters are fortified with a three-course meal prepared by a local chef, eaten in the gallery, surrounded by Dave's creations for inspiration.

The three-day courses also include a turn at raku firing, an ancient Japanese technique in which glazed ceramics are taken from the kiln while still glowing hot and placed in sawdust, leading to a dramatic, fiery display.

FOOD & DRINK

Beach House Park Ln, SO41 0PT ✆ 01590 643044 ♘ beachhousemilfordonsea.co.uk. You'll feel as if you've stepped back in time when you enter Beach House, but this is a good place to come after walking the coast between Lymington and Barton-on-Sea or as a destination in summer for the terrace and large garden overlooking Christchurch Bay and the Isle of Wight. The two small dining rooms have a bland, hotel ambience but the views are worth it.

The Gun Inn Keyhaven Rd, SO41 0TP ✆ 01590 642391 ♘ theguninn.co.uk ○ noon–23.00 Wed–Sun. Charming, friendly Grade-II-listed, 18th-century pub just a mile east of Milford on Sea but also a pleasant walk from Lymington. The beautifully presented food is way above standard pub fare; menus change regularly, reflecting the emphasis on seasonal, local produce. The truffle mac and cheese is to die for. The huge garden seats 60 people beneath a cover and 60 more in open air. Dogs and children welcome. Hosts regular events like open-mic nights; check the website.

Mr Pink's Church Hill, SO41 0QH ✆ 01590 642930 ○ 11.30–1.45 & 17.00–20.00 Tue—Sat. How can you visit the seaside and not have fish and chips? Mr Pink's, something of an institution in Milford, is the place to do it. Sit on a bench on the village green to enjoy your meal or walk down to the beach.

Muffins Galore at Braxton Gardens Lymore Ln, SO41 0TX ✆ 01590 641501 ♘ braxtongardens.co.uk ○ 10.00–16.00 Wed–Sat. The café at this plant nursery tucked away off the A337 is a quirky place for a light lunch or afternoon tea. In summer, tables are set up in the small, manicured gardens and, if it's cold, the conservatory has a wood-burning stove. Delicious scones and cakes and a charming setting.

Ray's Italian Kitchen 11 High St, SO41 0QF ✆ 01590 645300 ♘ raysitaliankitchen.co.uk. Hearty, yummy pastas and pizzas with a friendly atmosphere.

Verveine High St, SO41 0QE ✆ 01590 642176 ♘ verveine.co.uk. Many restaurants tout use of local ingredients but it is the mantra at Verveine. Virtually every ingredient on the menu is sourced from within the New Forest. The menu is a simple blackboard of today's catch (usually plentiful) with a choice of four sauces and accompaniments that brilliantly play with your expectations. The small kitchen is just a few steps from the dining area and it's an informal, friendly experience. Good-value set lunches. Highly recommended.

◀ **1** Hurst Point Lighthouse, Milford on Sea. **2** Studland Common Nature Reserve. **3** Hurst Castle on Hurst Spit.

18 HURST CASTLE

SO41 0TP ✆ 01590 642500 ⌖ hurstcastle.co.uk ☺ Apr–Oct daily; English Heritage.

Getting to Henry VIII's fortress is as much fun as the castle itself. You can walk the two mile-long stretch of Hurst Spit from Keyhaven, the very small village one mile from Milford that is a base for boaters, or take a ferry. The most satisfying option is to walk out and get the ferry back, or vice versa. If you walk one way and ride the other, park in Keyhaven car park. The ferry landing is a short walk away and Hurst Spit is about a quarter of a mile further along Keyhaven Road. For a longer walk, park at the seafront in Milford to walk the full length of the spit.

WHEN LONGSHORE DOESN'T DRIFT

For a lesson in how protection of one stretch of land can negatively affect other areas, head to Hurst Spit. Sea walls and groynes installed in recent years at Milford to prevent cliff erosion have prevented by-products of erosion from travelling to the spit.

The 1½ mile-long spit, formed some 7,000 years ago when the Isle of Wight separated from the mainland, was getting pushed further landward by wave and tide action and was gradually disappearing. In 1989, a major storm shortened the spit by 9ft in one night, prompting ecologists to campaign for rebuilding the spit. A model was built in a wave tank to test the effects of wave action, tides and currents in order to determine the best preservation method. Rocks were brought in to build up the spit and to preserve this guardian of the western Solent.

Since then, the effects of climate change have worsened and brought flooding and severe storms at a quicker rate than experts expected. Some predictions suggest that sea levels could rise by above 3ft within the next hundred years.

Several expensive repairs have been made, leading to the realisation that a more permanent and sustainable solution must be found. Talks are underway among the Environment Agency, local councils and environmental groups to determine the best course of action. This could include a 'managed retreat' of some areas of the sea wall that would lead to the loss of some of the protected habitats. The salt marsh is more than a precious habitat; it is also an important resource against negative effects of climate change. Salt marshes are a natural flood defence by diffusing wave energy and reducing their height, which lessens damage to the shore. The marshes also absorb CO_2.

The challenge is managing the risk to local communities, while protecting the natural environment. Without the spit, the saltmarsh nature reserves would be devastated, the castle would become an island, Keyhaven and Lymington would be vulnerable to flooding (as witnessed in 1989), and the northwest part of the Isle of Wight would suffer severe erosion.

Walking towards Hurst Castle provides such a close view of the Needles and the Isle of Wight (it is only three-quarters of a mile away from the castle) that it seems as if you could walk straight on to the island. The stones on the sandbar produce a satisfying crunch with each step, although it can get tiring, so wear solid shoes. Waves either pound or lap the pebble beach, depending on the wind.

Henry VIII knew that he had angered Catholics in Europe when he divorced his first wife, Catherine of Aragon, and dissolved the monasteries, so he set about building a string of coastal defences at each end of the Solent. Calshot was the first, with construction beginning in 1539, and Hurst was the last to be completed in 1544.

This is the best castle in the area for young imaginations, and bodies, to run free. There are many large, vacant rooms, narrow staircases and dark, dank cellars to explore. The flip side of that freedom is that there is little information in the rooms. Children won't necessarily mind the absence of historical explanations; the two huge Victorian guns and many passageways to explore are diversion enough.

When you enter, turn left to see Henry VIII's portion of the circular castle, designed to defend against land or sea attack. The drab wings that extend from the original Tudor circular castle were added in the 1860s, when the only perceived threat was from the sea itself. That threat has increased in severity: in 2021, the Victorian East Wing collapsed and English Heritage spent £3 million trucking in 22,000 tonnes of shingle and rock to shore up the defences. But even with those repairs, the future of the castle is in doubt. Protecting the fortress from the sea is becoming more challenging as sea levels rise and storm surges ravage the protective wall. In 2022, Hurst Castle was placed on the World Monuments Watch list.

"The stones on the sandbar produce a satisfying crunch with each step, although it can get tiring, so wear solid shoes."

During both World Wars, the castle was garrisoned. An interesting remnant of life for the more recent troops is the recently restored **Garrison Theatre** in the West Wing, possibly the only surviving garrison theatre from World War II. English Heritage does a good job maintaining the military flavour; even the lavatories are modelled on the Garrison latrines of 1870.

When you climb to the top and see the views of Hurst Spit and the Isle of Wight, it becomes clear how difficult this land would have been to protect, but what an ideal vantage point the fortress had. Both rooftops display interesting plaques describing what the scene would have been like in different periods of history.

Inside the grounds of the West Wing, the café has outdoor tables sheltered from the wind. I'd recommend planning ahead and bringing a picnic so you can sit outside the castle walls and enjoy the view of the Solent or marshes of Keyhaven.

¶ FOOD & DRINK

The Lighthouse Marine House, Hurst Rd, SO41 0PY ✆ 01590 718040
⬧ thelighthousemilford.co.uk ◷ 09.00–late daily; reduced hours in winter. Extremely popular seafood restaurant situated at the cliff's edge, just outside of Milford village and at the start of Hurst Spit. Despite the great location, the restaurant doesn't have water views, but in summer there are some outdoor bar tables with slightly obstructed views. It has a lively, buzzy atmosphere, friendly staff and good food. Well situated for coastal walks, too.

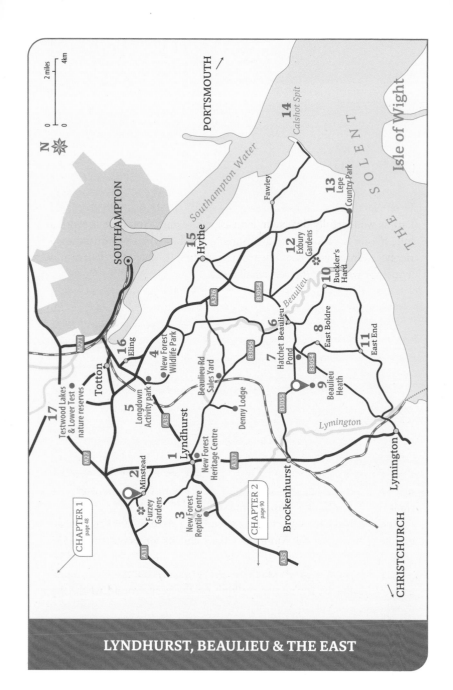

LYNDHURST, BEAULIEU & THE EAST

3
LYNDHURST, BEAULIEU & THE EAST

From 'capital' to coast, the eastern part of the New Forest National Park is wonderfully diverse in landscape and aura. You have to work a little harder here to escape the tourist crush but when you do, you are richly rewarded with distinctive communities, wildlife experiences and landscape within a relatively small area.

If you don't have much time, or are unfamiliar with the Forest, **Lyndhurst** – the Forest's unofficial capital – is an ideal starting point, especially if you want town facilities (think how often it rains) as well as nature walks. In the height of summer, it might be hard to find a local in this small town, and the engaging High Street may feel so crowded with souvenir shoppers that you forget you're in the New Forest at all, but there are some stunning walks in pristine landscape just minutes away. This proximity to open forest and the presence of the New Forest Heritage Centre make Lyndhurst well worth a visit.

Very nearby are some of the Forest's most beguiling places, such as **Swan Green**, **Bank**, **Emery Down** and **Minstead** with its enchanting **Furzey Gardens**. **Cycling** on the quiet lanes around here is perfectly feasible, although there is some traffic. The Forest cycle network has trails from Lyndhurst to Brockenhurst.

Much of this area comprises the **Beaulieu Estate**, a 7,000-acre estate privately owned by the Montagu family and its ancestors since 1538 when land belonging to **Beaulieu Abbey** passed into secular ownership. Wherever you are in Beaulieu, you're probably on land belonging to Lord Montagu. You're also walking on the very ground where the monks of Beaulieu Abbey once prospered.

While the dominance of the estate might not be apparent to the casual visitor, local business owners tell tales of strict regulations imposed by Lord Montagu, right down to the size of signs and their lettering. Aside from the hassles for locals, the restrictions help the area maintain its

NEW FOREST DESTINATION PARTNERSHIP

pristine appearance. The clock really does seem to have stopped here, especially on lazy days when cows lounge on the grass by the mill pool and donkeys nuzzle tourists at the edge of the Beaulieu Estuary.

Just two miles southeast of Beaulieu, is the historic settlement of **Buckler's Hard**. The museum here is well worth a visit in order to appreciate this hamlet's ship-building history, which gives the area a punchy legacy relative to its size. But even if you are not interested in the history, the pretty view from the hillside outside the museum overlooking the Beaulieu River justifies a visit.

Further east are some odd juxtapositions. Rugged beaches at **Lepe** and **Calshot** challenge the bland suburbs of Southampton up the road, while the bucolic village of Exbury is just moments away from unphotogenic sprawl. In the shadow of Fawley oil refinery, rare birds preen and parade and seem all the more thrilling because of their backdrop.

The rocky coastline of Calshot and Lepe gradually gives way to the tamed walkways of **Exbury Gardens**, which in turn differ dramatically from the open forest of East Boldre and Beaulieu Heath. **East End**, a hamlet about seven miles west of Exbury, has its own distinct landscape of sleepy country lanes bordered by distant ocean and fields. If you are torn between a love for Forest landscape and the sea, East End offers a balance.

World War II left its mark on Beaulieu and its coast. Remnants of the three runways built at Beaulieu Heath in 1942 are used today as bike trails and for launching model aircraft. Streets and bridges were widened to accommodate tanks (especially evident in the village of Pilley); private homes along the Beaulieu River and coast were requisitioned to serve as headquarters and training camps for members of the Special Operations Executive, a secret spy-training unit; and the Beaulieu River and Lepe became crowded with troops, landing craft and barges in preparation for D-day. Troops that trained at Exbury left there for Normandy; for many, Beaulieu River was their last view of England. Exhibits at Beaulieu Palace, Buckler's Hard, Lepe and Calshot provide excellent background and remind us that not all that long ago the Forest coast was overshadowed by war, a far cry from the blissfully peaceful atmosphere that pervades today.

◀ The countryside around Lyndhurst includes some of the Forest's most enchanting scenery, such as here at Swan Green.

LYNDHURST & SURROUNDING AREAS

Lyndhurst is on the doorstep of the wilder north Forest, not too far from the coast and handily placed for pottering around and sightseeing generally. Several animal-centred activities are nearby and the three highlighted in this section are informative and fun, especially the **New Forest Wildlife Park**, which is beautifully landscaped. The town's connection with royalty is evident at **King's House** and the view of **St Michael's and All Angels Church** from Bolton's Bench is quite special, while exhibits at the **New Forest Heritage Centre** open an excellent window on the Forest for both newcomers and old-timers.

This area certainly has money; if the Maserati and Ferrari dealership in the High Street isn't clue enough, Lyndhurst frequently pops up in 'most expensive town' surveys. Lime Wood, one of the priciest hotels in southern England, is just beyond the town centre. You could argue that these extravagances diminish the New Forest flavour of this area. But town pavements change abruptly to woodlands and heath around Lyndhurst. The ancient parish of **Denny Lodge**, just to the east, mostly comprises heathland with some 90 Bronze Age barrows. Lyndhurst Old Park, the large deer park created by Norman kings, was supplanted by 'New Park' up the road at Brockenhurst in 1484. You can still walk where bygone horsemen rode, across Park Pale, an earthen bank and internal ditch that enclosed the medieval deer park, and along the time-worn track of Beechen Lane, once a regular route for travellers between Denny Lodge and Lyndhurst.

1 LYNDHURST

🏠 Angels Farm Pottery (page 224), **Lime Wood Hotel** (page 224), **Penny Farthing Hotel** (page 224) 🏠 **Spot in the Woods** (page 224) ⚊ **Ashurst Caravan and Camping Site** (page 224)

> The people of Lyndhurst ought, I always think, to be the happiest and most contented in England, for they possess a wider park and nobler trees than even Royalty. You cannot leave the place without going through the Forest.
>
> John R Wise *The New Forest: Its History and Its Scenery*

Lyndhurst has been considered the capital of the Forest since William I designated it as such in 1079. In subsequent years, when kings and queens visited William's hunting ground, they stayed at the royal manor, now known as the King's House (which changes its name depending on the gender of the monarch). Although royalty has long departed, Lyndhurst still feels like the capital as the **King's House** is the local headquarters of Forestry England, and the **Court of Verderers** (page 156), which oversees commoning practices, is right next door. The court's monthly sessions are open to the public ten times per year. It's also possible the New Forest Heritage Centre (page 157), which serves as the town's unofficial tourist information centre and is situated in the middle of town, will arrange tours in the future.

The town's central location at the junction of two major thoroughfares, which have evolved from medieval tracks, also plays a role in its capital distinction. Southampton Road (A35), which runs between Southampton and Bournemouth, and Lyndhurst Road (A337), which goes from the M27 and Cadnam on to Lymington in the south (changing its name along the way), converge here. The long traffic queues that build up in the one-way system are a testament to the power of the Verderers who have vetoed any efforts to install a bypass. Congestion is particularly bad in summer when it can take more than 30 minutes to pass through town on the A337.

'A tourist honeypot' is how Forest management views Lyndhurst and it's easy to see why. The town has an impressive array of restaurants, cafés and gift shops. Within minutes you can be deep in the Forest, as John Wise so eloquently pointed out. Just a few steps from High Street, **Bolton's Bench** is a distinctive hill capped with a yew tree, leading out to the heathlands of White Moor. Another restful walk can be found in Pondhead Inclosure (page 158), an ancient forest protected from grazing animals. Although only one mile south of Lyndhurst, it is situated off the busy A337 which has no pavement so it's not safe to walk out there.

Lyndhurst comes in to its own at Christmas. Bolton's Bench is occasionally frosty white and I can't think of too many places that wear sparkly lights so well. That endless traffic queue seems to die down a bit and even if you do get stuck in it, it's worth it when you see High Street all dressed up for St Nicholas. Lyndhurst becomes a small town with a heightened feeling of anticipation and a rich sense of the past.

Along with the official buildings at the top of Lyndhurst High Street, the 19th-century **church of St Michael and All Angels** presides from its lofty position atop a prehistoric artificial mound. This is the third

GUARDIANS OF AN ANCIENT WAY OF LIFE

The walls of the ancient Court of Verderers in Lyndhurst are adorned with deer heads, including two skulls with interlocking antlers facing the same way – a remnant of two rutting bucks that became entangled and ultimately lay down to die. They serve as reminders of the New Forest's founding as William's royal hunting ground and the Verderers' original role to uphold Forest Law on behalf of the Crown.

On one wall hangs a small stirrup that also dates from the harsh days of Forest law. Dogs too large to fit through the 'Rufus stirrup' were deemed to be a threat to the King's deer and had their paws maimed so they couldn't chase them. Dogs small enough to pass through the stirrup were spared.

Nowadays, the venerable panel of Verderers safeguards commoners' rights rather than those of the Crown. No prosecutions take place in this chamber, although in past days those who broke Forest law were spared no mercy. Present-day sessions are really more like open forums with contentious issues left to private consultation among members.

Anything that will affect commoners' work, including a major event in the Forest, has to get past these ten overseers. They consider proposals for development or any action that will influence the Forest, ranging from the installation of power lines to the designation of cycle trails. Sessions are held on the third Wednesday of each month, during which time anyone can present a proposal.

Positions are unpaid, and presumably undertaken from sheer love of the Forest and the opportunity to influence its management. Five are elected by commoners and five are appointed by government organisations that are responsible for Forest management. Verderers often visit the Forest to investigate land under question but day-to-day field work is conducted by Agisters (page 18), who look after commoners' stock when they are out grazing on the Forest.

The term 'Verderer' derives from the French word, *vert*, for green, meaning that these agents were official keepers of the green. It's still an apt name as they have huge influence on retaining the character and borders of the Forest.

church to stand here, the present one succeeding Saxon and Georgian versions. The structure, designed by William White, was financed by subscriptions from local people who felt the existing Georgian house of worship was too small. However, when it was constructed between 1860 and 1870, some locals decried the many-coloured bricks as too garish – especially on such a visible point in town. By the altar is a fresco of wise and foolish virgins in which local people were depicted as biblical figures. It was painted by Lord Frederick Leighton who was excited to try out his new acrylic paints; its gold lettering sparkles when the sun shines on it. Alice Liddell, the inspiration for the Alice in *Alice in Wonderland*, lived nearby and is buried in the churchyard. Her grave sometimes displays red and white roses in a tribute to the royal gardeners in the book who painted white roses red. The church bell ringers practise on Thursday nights.

New Forest Heritage Centre

Main car park, SO43 7NY ✐ 02 80 283444 ⊘ newforestheritage.org.uk
⊙ 10.00–16.00 daily

This is an ideal place to begin a visit to the New Forest. An unassuming building in the centre of Lyndhurst, this is one of the few locations in the area where the many overseeing powers can put aside their differences to share a mutual love of the Forest. The New Forest Heritage Centre is run by an independent charity that was started in 1979 by a group that believed people should be educated about the Forest. 'We are a hub for both visitors and locals,' explained Angus Harley, director of the centre.

A visit to the small, free **museum** on the ground floor will enhance a visit to the Forest – even if you're not a first timer. The exhibitions underline that critical balance of tourism and Forest sustainability. There are displays on the history of the Forest; flora and fauna; New Forest ponies and how they maintain the landscape; a model of Beaulieu Road Sales Yard; and ongoing conservation efforts. Although it's not exactly cutting edge, its charm and simple approach are in keeping with Forest ethos.

Children are especially welcome; there are child-sized tables with crayons and activities to encourage little ones to engage with the landscape before heading out to the real thing. During school holidays, the centre holds fun, drop-in activity days for families at which children make crafts and examine elements of the Forest.

One unusual exhibit is the **New Forest Embroidery**, a 25ft-long tapestry designed by Belinda, Lady Montagu of Beaulieu in 1979 to commemorate the 900th anniversary of the creation of the New Forest. The colourful work depicts the most important historical events in the Forest set against a backdrop of flora and fauna. A digitised version that will enable visitors to interact with this magnificent piece is in the works.

The **gallery** next to the museum hosts changing exhibitions, including book signings, art exhibitions and videos that showcase the Forest in creative ways. There is an extensive range of books for sale, as well as crafts and gifts. The **café** adjacent to the shop and information area offers snacks and coffee.

This is also a good place to pick up tourist information. The reception area has leaflets on Forest attractions and cycling and hiking trails and the front desk is staffed by friendly locals who can help with basic itinerary suggestions. One of the best resources here is the **Christopher Tower Reference Library**. Its extensive collection includes classical works

COPPICING: NEOLITHIC WOODLAND MANAGEMENT

'My earliest memory is of my grandfather bringing me out to the Forest where he worked as a woodsman,' said Dave Dibden, 67, a modern-day coppicer. 'I was very small and he would place me on the back of his Irish wolfhound, from where I'd watch him work.'

Coppicing is cutting a tree at its base to promote growth of several different shoots rather than one stem. Almost immediately after making the cuts, new green shoots emerge which, after many years, will become trees. By continuing to make cuts in the stool (the base from which new growth occurs) a coppice generates a continuous supply of new wood. This ancient form of forest management provides both fuel and raw materials, as well as encouraging diverse habitats.

I was privileged to walk with Dave many years ago, when he had begun clearing and coppicing **Pondhead Inclosure**, a 193-acre historical woodland near Bolton's Bench in Lyndhurst. (The entrance is off Beechen Lane, south of Lyndhurst.) This is one of the only places in the Forest where you can see how the New Forest would look without the influence of grazing animals.

The fenced inclosure keeps out most animals (although deer have a remarkable ability to get in anywhere, it seems) so there is dense growth at ground level. In most parts of the Forest you don't have dense undergrowth and can see a clear graze line (the level up to which grazing animals can reach to feed). Pondhead is also one of the best places in Hampshire to see wild native bluebells (usually late April/May), which are becoming increasingly rare.

The land here had grown wild until 2004 when Dave was asked to manage it through coppicing. Using old maps, he worked for many years to restore this inclosure back to how it would have been in the 18th century. By hand, Dave and volunteers carved out generous trails through dense overgrowth of brambles and trees. 'When we started here, the old trails from the 1970s were completely overgrown – they were like dark tunnels.'

The workers began by clearing and coppicing a small area and fencing it off temporarily to prevent animals from grazing and to allow new growth to develop, which in turn provided habitats for important insects and butterflies. New patches of growth published from the 18th to the 20th centuries, as well as natural history books, travel guides, maps, art, postcards, photos and information on individual Forest towns, and a lot of material on the New Forest's military history. Anyone can visit the library but appointments must be booked in advance by phone or online.

The centre has a lot of exciting ventures in the pipeline. 'We are planning interactive exhibits of Forest stories from people who live

were nurtured while the old ones matured and began to host still more varied species by enabling small areas of suntraps and microclimates. 'The coppicing at Pondhead is still done in a seven-to-ten year rotation to promote different levels of habitats that accompany different levels of growth.'

Coppicing has been used since Neolithic times (about 4000BC). It was the most common form of woodland maintenance in Britain until the 1800s and, at one time, it was considered the *only* way. But in today's world of pesticides and quick fixes, this ancient art is taking on a new significance – a viable system that honours a rural tradition. Coppicing stops the Forest from becoming overgrown and dark, which is vital for butterflies and birds that rely on open light in order to thrive.

We stopped to examine an old bit of honeysuckle hanging from a tree branch. 'We can encourage the white admiral butterfly by leaving these old bits of honeysuckle. The caterpillar lays its eggs on the old bits because there are no berries and birds won't be attracted and therefore won't eat the caterpillar.' Suddenly Dave pointed ahead on

the path. A small butterfly, a pearl border fritillary, zig-zagged above the tiny flowers that lined the path. Dave was visibly pleased. 'They haven't been in this area since the 1960s. Because butterflies don't travel far, once you lose them, you really lose them. But they're coming back now that the magic light is allowed in.'

Dave uses all the wood that is cut away in his coppicing projects throughout the Forest to make crafts in the style of ancient woodsmen. He sells his hand-carved walking sticks, bird feeders and gardening materials at local fairs and to private clients (✆ 02380 872679 ⌂ coppice-products.co.uk).

The award-winning Pondhead Conservation Trust (⌂ pondheadconservation.org) now manages Pondhead, dedicated to restoring the ancient woodland of the inclosure. To access Pondhead Inclosure, there's limited parking in Beechen Lane off the A337 or a little further away at Park Pale, just east of Boltons Bench in Lyndhurst, from where you can enter from the backside through a gate, about 400yds and across Beaulieu Rd from the car park.

AN ANCIENT NEW FOREST TRADITION REVIVED: CHARCOAL BURNING

If you walk through Pondhead Inclosure (page 158) during summer, you are likely to smell the distinct aroma of wood smoke, reminiscent of medieval times when this smell would have been omnipresent. If you walk towards the source of that pungent air, you will find enthusiastic volunteer burners (the people who actually do the burning) tending their kiln. They seem to have stepped out of time.

Charcoal burning is one of the oldest New Forest industries, possibly dating back to the Bronze Age or even before. Charcoal was the fuel used to smelt tin and copper together to make bronze; later, during the Iron Age, charcoal burning was the primary heat source to produce iron.

The practice is traditionally associated with coppiced woods because the young tender shoots that are a by-product of coppicing were burned to produce charcoal. As fires burned for many days, charcoal burners lived in huts in the woods near their 'burns'. It was a lonely life but a not unusual one in the New Forest. In fact, one charcoal burner's story is prominent in New Forest legends. A man called Purkis is said to have found the body of King William II, also known as William Rufus, who was allegedly killed by an arrow shot by Sir Walter Tyrell in 1100 (page 66). Purkis was a charcoal burner who transported King William's body to Winchester where he was ultimately buried in the cathedral.

Charcoal burning continued until the late 19th century when it declined with the use of coal and coke. But the practice was revived again during both world wars, when charcoal was needed to make filters for gas masks. By the 1970s, all commercial charcoal industries were gone.

'We know that the last ones were in Pondhead because you can still see the old ring kiln in the pond,' explained Derek Tippetts, co-founder of the Pondhead Conservation Trust (pondheadconservation.org.uk) and long-time New Forest resident.

The extremely dedicated group works throughout winter to coppice trees and clear rides in order to let light into the forest floor and encourage diverse habitats. 'By the 1860s most of the rides in Pondhead were grown over but we've opened up 90% of the land,' he told me. 'With all the talk of forests promoting good mental health, we are excited to provide a peaceful place for people to walk.' Indeed, this is one of the most tranquil spots in the Forest, and one where traditional management techniques are visible.

The group stops conservation work in March in order to protect ground-nesting birds, at which point they turn their attention to charcoal burning. Wood harvested from the clearance is used both for traditional crafts, including deer fencing, and to produce charcoal which is sold via the website. It's a great alternative to the 90% of barbecue charcoal sold in the UK that is imported from developing countries where deforestation often takes place. The group is extremely proud of its environmentally friendly kiln that redirects greenhouse gases into the kiln's firebox and provides the sole source of heat for the remainder of the burn.

and have lived here,' Angus told me. 'Through these stories we can communicate the sensitive way the Forest needs to be maintained in order to preserve it for future generations.'

¶¶ FOOD & DRINK

The Forage 39 High St, SO43 7BE ✆ 02380 175710 ♘ the-forage.co.uk ☽ café 08.30–17.00 daily; restaurant 17.00–22.00 daily. A clean-lined café and restaurant with lots of outdoor seating in summer. The daytime menu includes traditional cooked breakfasts, brunch, burgers and sandwiches. After 17.00, the restaurant menu features a huge range of choice including pizza, pasta, salads and grills. Dog friendly.

The Fox and Hounds 22 High St, SO43 7BG ✆ 02380 282098 ♘ foxandhoundslyndhurst. co.uk. A light and airy interior with a menu of upscale pub fare that stands out among nearby pub choices.

Greenwood Tree 65 High St, SO43 7BE ✆ 02380 282463 ♘ thegreenwoodtreecafe. co.uk ☽ 08.30–17.00 daily. A large daytime café with reasonably priced breakfast food, sandwiches and cream teas. Cakes are baked on-site. There are also gluten-free and vegan menus, including flotted cream, a plant-based alternative to clotted cream.

Lime Wood Hotel Beaulieu Rd, SO43 7FZ ✆ 02380 287177 ♘ limewoodhotel.co.uk. This is a special-occasion spot with a price tag to match, but the setting, just 1½ miles east of Lyndhurst and yet in the heart of forest, is divine. Noted chef Angela Hartnett is at the helm of the restaurant at this luxury hotel and spa. Locally sourced ingredients are used in Italian dishes that mama would make, but better. Afternoon tea is served in the conservatory bar and lounge areas or outside in the spacious gardens in summer. Service can be uneven, which hurts at these prices – but it's nonetheless a memorable treat.

Mad Hatter Tearooms 10 High St, SO43 7BD✆ 07393 748273 ♘ madhatterlyndhurst. co.uk. ☽ 09.00–16.00 Mon & Thu–Sat, 10.00–16.00 Sun. *Alice in Wonderland*-themed café at the top end of High Street, near the church where Alice Liddell is buried. Some visitors come dressed in character. Breakfast, lunch and afternoon tea are served.

Oak Inn Bank, SO43 7FE ✆ 02380 282350 ♘ oakinnlyndhurst.co.uk. Just one mile outside of Lyndhurst, the Oak is one of the great New Forest pubs: although many come here to dine, it has managed to retain its old-fashioned pub feel. On a sunny day, the garden is an idyllic spot for lunch and the inside is cosy with a lively atmosphere on winter evenings. A great stop on cycle ride or walk. Booking advised.

Renoufs 23 High St, SO43 7BE ✆ 07473 074733 ♘ renoufswinebars.co.uk. ☽ 17.00–23.00 Mon–Fri, noon–23.00 Sat. If you've had enough of country charm and muddy pubs, Renoufs makes a welcome change. The cosy wine bar has 200 bottles to choose from and you can dine on various platters of cheese and charcuterie. It's part of a successful chain of wine bars and cheese shops in Dorset and Hampshire. Booking essential.

Waterloo Arms Pikes Hill SO43 7AS 023 8028 2113 waterlooarmsnewforest.co.uk.
One of the better pubs in the area, located in the tiny hamlet of Pikes Hill, half a mile north of
Lyndhurst. Standard pub fare, with a large menu of all those comforting classics like fish and
chips, lasagne and fish pie. Nice layout with a comfy bar area and plenty of tables to choose
from. The garden is spacious.

2 MINSTEAD

Acres Down Farm (page 224)

The delightful village of Minstead is about two miles north of Lyndhurst
but many miles away in atmosphere. It is a sleepy place with a green, a
large tree to sit beneath and watch comings and goings, an historic pub,
and a shop that illustrates village pride. What a fantastic place to slow
down. The thatched cottages and public walking trails through fields
make Minstead a delightful place to spend a half-day. But the prize
feature here is Furzey Gardens, less than a mile from the village green.
First established more than a hundred years ago, the gardens are well
worth a visit, especially with children.

Just up the hill behind the village green stands All Saints' Church,
where fans of Sherlock Holmes make pilgrimages to see the final resting
place of **Sir Arthur Conan Doyle** (page 164), who lived in the village in
the early 1930s. He has a plum position beneath a giant limb of an oak
tree at the far edge of the burial yard and there is usually a pipe placed
thoughtfully on the tombstone. A bench is waiting for you to have a
quiet read of one of Conan Doyle's stories of the master sleuth.

The church itself is a pleasing mishmash of different time periods. The
oldest relic is the **Saxon font**, which was lost during the Reformation,
perhaps buried for safekeeping, and then dug up in the Old Rectory
garden and placed back in the church in 1893. The Norman doorway
dates from 1200, while the 16th century saw the arrival of the oak pews
and three-tiered pulpit – with the top-level for preaching, the middle
for Bible readings and the bottom level where the clerk stood to say
the 'Amens' after prayers. The timbered upper gallery dates from 1700
and the bell tower is Georgian. Off the sanctuary is a private pew that
was built for the residents of nearby Malwood Castle who enjoyed all
the comforts of home including a fireplace and a private door through

---

1 All Saints' Church, Minstead. **2** An adder at New Forest Reptile Centre. **3** The headstone
of Sir Arthur Conan Doyle. **4** One of many hidden fairy doors at Furzey Gardens. ▶

DEREK TIPPETTS

DEREK TIPPETTS

DEREK TIPPETTS

JORDON SHARP/S

which their dinner could be delivered. The bell ringers usually practice on Thursday nights.

If you are hoping to stretch your creative muscles while you're in the Forest, it's worth checking what's on at **Minstead Study Centre** (School Ln, SO43 7GJ ℰ 02380 813437 ⊘ hants.gov.uk/minsteadstudycentre),

AT HOME WITH SIR ARTHUR CONAN DOYLE

The path which the young clerk had now to follow lay through a magnificent forest of the very heaviest timber, where the giant bowls of oak and of beech formed long aisles in every direction, shooting up their huge branches to build the majestic arches of Nature's own cathedral.
Sir Arthur Conan Doyle, *The White Company*, 1891

Probably Minstead's best-known resident was **Sir Arthur Conan Doyle**, who bought his second wife, Jean, a cottage here for her birthday. The house, Bignell Wood, has now been enlarged and modernised and is not visible from the road. Conan Doyle's affection for the area is evident from the words above describing Minstead Wood.

Conan Doyle was heavily involved in spiritualism, and is reputed to have hosted spiritualists' retreats at Bignell Wood, but his daughter, Jane, denied this in an interview before her death, saying that it was purely a place of relaxation. She reported that he was friendly towards the travellers that lived in the woods around the house and recalled him going off to visit them.

The success of Sherlock Holmes convinced Conan Doyle that he could quit practising medicine and be a full-time writer. But he preferred many of his other writings, according to Dr Roger Straughan, author of *An Elementary Connection*. Conan Doyle's many published works included historical fiction, verse, plays, short stories and books on spiritualism. The

first section of the 1891 novel, *The White Company*, takes place in the 14th-century New Forest. 'Well, I'll never beat that!' he is reported to have said when he completed it. He also penned a short story, *Spedegue's Dropper*, about a cricketer who practised bowling special high-pitched lobs in the New Forest by slinging a cord between two trees.

The spot under the tree in Minstead Churchyard was not the author's first resting place. At his death in 1930, he was buried (allegedly vertically) in the garden of his Sussex home in Crowborough but he was exhumed and moved to Minstead when Jean died, which was where she had wanted to be buried.

'He was the archetypal Englishman,' said Dr Straughan, during a speech at the New Forest Heritage Centre. 'It's appropriate that his final resting place is under an oak tree at Minstead, in the New Forest that he loved so well.' But Straughan pointed out that it's just as well that the writer lies 'a discreet distance from the church,' as he was at odds with the Church of England for most of his life.

situated a short distance from Minstead village. The centre, which mainly hosts environmental courses for large groups, also runs regular public workshops, usually on weekends, such as on baking, pruning, felting and making willow structures. The seven-acre site comprises ancient woodland, meadows and ponds, and self-catering accommodation of groups up to 40 people is available.

Furzey Gardens
School Ln, SO43 7GL ✆ 02380 812464 🖝 minstead.org.uk/furzey-gardens

The playful and fanciful layout of Furzey Gardens, less than a mile northwest of the village, will stay with you long after you have left. 'Although the garden attracts serious – and more casual – horticulturalists, it is children who really love it here. There is a special children's area where thatched round houses and playhouses are linked by tunnels and walkways, while the **Typhoon Tower**, a viewing platform with a thatched tower, has beautiful views over the Forest towards the Isle of Wight. Best of all, Simon Sinkinson, the thatcher responsible for the enchanting structures, also carved some 40 fairy doors, hidden among flowers and trees. Children delight in searching for the doors and potential fairies that may float behind them. As Pete White, the head gardener, and I sat on one of the many benches, we watched youngsters running on the wide lawn near the entrance. 'We have made the garden child-friendly and are now working to make everything more accessible to disabled people, which is a challenge on this hilly and often damp site.'

What distinguishes these enchanting gardens is that they are tended by 30 people with learning disabilities and some 20 volunteers as part of the work of the Minstead Trust, a charity that supports 200 vulnerable people. 'Working here gives people with learning disabilities a place where they fit in and can contribute, which is especially important because they often feel excluded from other walks of life, 'said Pete. 'The students like that they make a difference to the landscape and to visitors' experiences here. That then translates to greater confidence and independence.'

Pete, who has directed the work in the gardens for 22 of the 33 years for which he has worked for the charity, believes that the community spirit and joy of empowering the disenfranchised is conveyed to visitors. 'The underlying ethos of the entire project enables visitors to enjoy a spiritual sense when they are here,' Pete told me as we strolled along the narrow pathways that necklace across the sloping land. 'It's broad strokes here, not the fine details you might see in a more formal layout. We don't want to bludgeon nature into submission but gently draw it out.'

The gardens were originally planted in 1922 by Bertram Dalrymple, a native Scot who built Furzey House, now a Christian retreat next door. He brought in topsoil to replace the native gorse and clay substructure and then proceeded to plant exotic rhododendrons and azaleas that plant hunters of the day were bringing home from the Himalayas and Australasia. After Dalrymple's death, the land and buildings began to decline. In 1972, the property came on the market with approval granted to demolish the 16th-century thatched **Cobb Cottage** at the entrance. Fortunately, a trustee of what is now the Minstead Trust, which now runs the site, swooped up the land with the idea of restoring the cottage

A short walk around Minstead & Furzey Gardens

OS Explorer map OL22; start: Trusty Servant Inn, ♥ TG054440; 1.4 miles; easy.

This circular stroll of just over a mile takes you to all the key sites around Minstead. Begin at the Trusty Servant pub by the village green; roadside parking is possible on Church Close as well as in the village car park by the Trusty Servant.

1 With the Trusty Servant behind you, take the road along the right side of the village green, passing the war memorial at the end of it. Enter the churchyard through the gate, and follow the path to the right of the church entrance to exit the churchyard through a gate on the right, opposite the bell tower. This will take you on to a path with a hedge on your right and a wire fence on your left. After a short distance, go through a second gate and follow the path down the hill through woodland (the area to the left has been coppiced).

2 Leave the wood through a kissing gate and turn right towards the main road. Across the road and a bit to the left you'll see a sign towards Furzey Gardens. Cross the main road and turn right into (unmarked) School Lane. Walk up the hill, past Minstead Study Centre on the right.

3 Continue on past the first lane on the left (about 250yds) and walk a further 600yds to where roads converge in a triangle; here you will see a sign to Furzey Gardens. Take the left fork and walk about 200yds to the entrance of Furzey Gardens.

4 After visiting the gardens, retrace your steps, turning right when you leave the gardens, back to the triangle where you also bear right to retrace your steps back along School Lane. Walk back in the direction from which you came, past a gated drive on your left.

and the 1920s flowerbeds. The cottage, built from boat timbers from nearby Lymington boatyards, has now been restored to provide an authentic vision of how people would have lived. Although the garden is particularly lovely in spring when the azaleas bloom, the colourful season extends into Autumn with an assortment of about 200 maples.

As much as Pete values caring for people and flora, he also enjoys nurturing a landscape that contains so much history. 'We've dug up bits of Roman pottery that could be from the Roman site that was near here. We're also working on an extensive replanting scheme based on original records. We know when everything first went in and as original growth begins to fade we can regenerate by taking seeds and cuttings.'

At the garden entrance, there is a **café** with outdoor tables and an area where plants grown by students are for sale.

5 Around 200yds from the triangle, you'll see a small opening in the hedge on the left, with a stile and footpath signpost. Cross the stile and walk downhill through a field with a hedge on your left. Cross a wooden bridge over a small stream and climb over a wooden fence with a Hampshire County Council yellow arrow footpath symbol. Continue uphill through the next field with a hedge on your left.

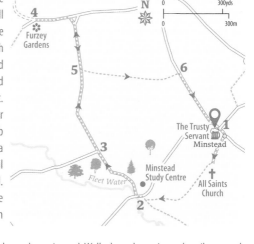

6 Cross the final stile and turn right on the main road. Walk along the main road until you reach the first house on the right. Opposite and across the road, next to a small outbuilding, is a small opening in the hedge leading to a path that runs parallel to the road but is safer to walk on. Cross the road and follow this path between hedges until it exits on to the verge, less than 100yds from Minstead Village. Continue on the road until you reach the Trusty Servant, on your right.

¶⃒ FOOD & DRINK

Minstead Community Shop ⌂ minstead.org.uk/village-community-shop ⊙ 10.00–
16.00 daily. Local people rallied when the village shop closed in 2018 – the first time in 250
years that Minstead found itself without one – and the Trusty Servant offered up its former
storeroom for a new location. Staffed and managed completely by volunteers, goods are
locally sourced and tea and coffee are served – which can be enjoyed at the picnic tables on
the pub terrace.

The Trusty Servant ✆ 02380 812137 ⌂ thetrustyservant.co.uk. Classic pub food in a
historical setting. Just on the edge of the village green, the pub building has been here since
the 1800s and the pub itself since 1903. Notice the sign which depicts a man with donkey's
ears, a pig's snout and stag's feet. The snout has padlocked lips to indicate discretion. A
similar painting of this odd creature hangs at Winchester College and it is believed that the
college once owned the land on which the pub now stands. In summer, the large garden
and terrace tables are almost always full and the small but cosy interior is a pleasant Sunday
lunch spot.

3 NEW FOREST REPTILE CENTRE

Holidays Hill, off the A35, 2 miles southwest of Lyndhurst ♀ SU271071 ⌂ forestryengland.
uk/new-forest-reptile-centre ⊙ varies seasonally; check website

It's best to visit this small but worthwhile reptile centre, just outside of
Lyndhurst and run by Forestry England, on a not-too-sunny, dry day
because the residents here hide when it's too hot *and* when it rains.
No matter the weather, patience is always required to see the reptiles,
there's a delightfully warm welcome and it's a great place to bring
children regardless.

Reptiles and amphibians particular to the New Forest, such as toads,
frogs and various types of snakes (including the rare smooth snake),
are housed in a series of outdoor enclosures. Much of this wildlife is
difficult to spot in the wild so the centre provides a wonderful chance
to catch a glimpse of these elusive animals. The Reptile Centre has also
successfully bred and reintroduced sand lizards, which were extinct in
the New Forest by 1970.

Besides the reptile enclosures, **walks** in the surrounding woods are
particularly lovely. This is an ideal place to compare the ancient and
conifer woodlands that make up the New Forest. The marked one-
mile **Discovery Trail** passes through a conifer woodland with very
tall Douglas firs, glades and a pond. Placards and wooden furniture
encourage visitors to engage with the environment. On the other side

of the centre, towards the A35, a stream meanders through an area of ancient woodland, comprising oaks and beeches.

One of the best features here are the nestbox **cameras,** and the cameras that move around the site, providing novel views of nests and the adder pod. There is also recorded footage of wildlife displayed on screens when the centre is open. If you come in the spring, you might get to see chicks being fed or squawking for food. In the hut where the videos are displayed, there is information about birds of prey and ground-nesting birds.

4 NEW FOREST WILDLIFE PARK

Deerleap Ln, Ashurst SO41 4UH ⌀ 02380 292408 ⌀ newforestwildlifepark.co.uk
⏲ spring & summer 10.00–17.30 daily; autumn & winter 10.00–16.30 daily

The collection of mammals and birds at this wildlife park is eclectic in the extreme. But it all makes sense when you consider that most of the animals here, like the deer, owls and foxes, live in the open Forest and others like the lynx, wild boar and wolves did so many, many years ago. Wild boar were hunted to extinction in the New Forest by the 17th century, but legend says that they bred with domestic Forest sows first. There are occasional wild boar sightings but Forestry officials say there are none.

"If you have never seen a giant otter before, you're in for a surprise: they are big."

As for the wallabies, they are a playful extra, though there are some living wild in the UK according to owner, Carol Heap. Carol and her husband Roger are dedicated to otter preservation so there are a lot of otters playing around. The Heaps were the first people to successfully breed the giant otter in this country, and there are plenty to observe here. If you have never seen a giant otter before, you're in for a surprise: they are big.

At the opposite end of the size spectrum are the Asian short-clawed otters, the smallest species of otter in the world. Jason Palmer, Curator of Collections, is the International Studbook keeper of this species and hopes that the park can successfully breed them. There is currently a group of ten of these little otters here on public display.

The park is one of the few centres in the country with a licence to look after rescued wild otters. Although they used to take in cubs, and may do so again in the future, Carol and Roger now focus their conservation efforts on species that 'need the extra boost', including wildcats, harvest mice and pine martens, a once-common carnivore in British forests. The Heaps work with the Vincent Wildlife Trust to reintroduce pine martens – which they breed – into the wild. Injured or abandoned deer, hedgehogs, foxes, owls and badgers are also looked after here.

Even if you're not a fan of wildlife parks, you may well enjoy this because its setting celebrates the Forest. Trails snake through woodland past enclosures, some of which are nestled deep in the trees. If you visit during term-time at a quiet time of day, you're likely to be completely alone for some soul-enriching viewing.

Deer and wallabies roam freely (not in the same section) so it's not unusual to find certain beasts on the same walkways as people. The deer are extremely tame – so much so that during my visit one snatched my map and consumed half of it before I had the wherewithal to snatch it back. Other creatures like the lynx and wolves can be harder to see. 'British wildlife is secretive and elusive, so it's difficult to enable visitors to see all the animals without stressing the animals out,' Jason told me. 'That's why we have frequent feedings and interactions throughout the day.' The keepers are adept at coaxing out shy animals and they are keen to share their knowledge.

There is a large adventure playground for children over six, padded with woodchips for safe landings, and a mini adventure playground near the entrance for younger kids. It's all done in a tasteful, understated way, better than many child-oriented attractions.

5 LONGDOWN ACTIVITY FARM

Deerleap Ln, Ashurst SO40 7EH ℐ 02380 292837 ♂ longdownfarm.co.uk
🕙 10.00–16.30 daily

It's hard to tell who is more important at Longdown Activity Farm: animals or children. The experience is all about introducing youngsters to farm life – and they love it. Interaction sessions, including bottle-feeding goat kids and calves or just holding baby rabbits and ducks, are held throughout the day. Even the most cynical will be charmed by the sight of children cradling guinea pigs and chickens, or, better yet, seeing the joy on adults' faces when they do the same. There is plenty of

---

1 New Forest ponies at Lyndhurst. 2 & 3 Longdown Activity Farm. 4 Herd of fallow deer near Lyndhurst. ▶

BRETT BLIGNAUT/S

LONGDOWN ACTIVITY FARM

LOU OSBORNE PHOTOGRAPHY

CHARLESY/S

FANCY TAKING A PONY HOME?

Beaulieu Road Sales Yard three miles south of Lyndhurst, by Beaulieu Road railway station on the B3056 & nfls.org.uk/the-sale-yard

Most of the year, the holding pens and auction ring at Beaulieu Road Sales Yard stand empty next to the Beaulieu Road railway station. But roughly five times each year the yard springs to life with sales of New Forest ponies and sometimes donkeys. All ponies sold at auction are registered either with New Forest Pony Breeding and Cattle Society or New Forest Commoners Defence Association, so buyers know they are getting the real thing. Most of the ponies sold at auction come directly from the Forest but others come from members in other parts of the country. New Forest ponies have undergone a recent surge of interest that has propped up their value considerably after an all-time low about ten years ago. It is unclear if those values will be maintained or if they were brought about by increased public interest in purchasing riding ponies during the pandemic.

New Forest ponies are capable of carrying adults but are also narrow enough to hold small children. 'The breed is good for riding because of their gentle nature and exposure to a variety of situations,' explained Jonathan Gerrelli, head Agister (page 18) who is involved in the management of commoners' stock while they are out grazing on the Forest.

There are strict criteria for animals to be registered as authentic New Forest ponies. There is no minimum height requirement but animals must be no taller than 58.25in. Official New Forest ponies can be any colour except piebald, skewbald or blue-eyed cream. Registered New Forest ponies that are sired and born on the open New Forest are termed as Forest bred.

Even if you have no interest in purchasing anything, it is definitely worth visiting the sales yard if you are in the area on the day of a sale. You can wander about freely anytime during the sale and look at the animals as they await their turn in the ring. The auction is a lively, sociable atmosphere as groups of commoners gather to talk about problems with their animals' health, Forest issues or just the weather. This is one of the best times for outsiders to fully appreciate that the New Forest is a working environment and not just a scenic place for a walk. Grab a perch in the spectators' seats around the auction area and watch the action. It's entertaining to try to guess what the prancing ponies will fetch on the open market – it's not always the show winners that achieve the best price.

fun here beyond the animals. A large playspace with swings, enclosed trampolines and playhouses gives kids a chance to run off steam while adults enjoy lunch at surrounding picnic tables. There is even a small crazy golf course and go karts for older kids. Tractor rides are hugely popular and run all year round. One of the most distinctive activities is the opportunity to look for freshly laid eggs and then carry them to the farm shop, located at the entrance. The shop, which stocks produce and meat from nearby farms, is a great place to buy supplies if you are in self-catering accommodation. Longdown makes extra effort for disabled visitors and children with special needs.

BEAULIEU ESTATE, BUCKLER'S HARD & EAST END

The village of Beaulieu and much of the surrounding area is virtually synonymous with the **Beaulieu Estate**, the largest private estate in the Forest. The 8,000-acre estate has been owned by the Montagu family since 1538, when Thomas Wriothsely, an ancestor of the current Lord Montagu, purchased 'the whole close of Beaulieu' from Henry VIII after the dissolution. The boundaries of the Estate originally mirrored the 10,000 acres of the Great Close of Beaulieu Abbey until the 1950s and 1960s when the southwestern portion around Sowley was sold.

I have a fondness for Beaulieu, although there's no getting away from the fact that it attracts big crowds in high season. Beneath the frenzy, the essence of the village shines through: on an early morning when mist rises above the mill pond with Palace House in the background you'd swear a medieval monk will appear on the lawn; on a busy Saturday afternoon when cows, oblivious (or not) to the long string of cars held hostage, insist on standing on the road markings leading to town; or during a quiet walk in the woods between Buckler's Hard and Beaulieu village when you hear only birds singing and see glimpses of the river through the trees.

For a bit of drama, windswept **Beaulieu Heath** is both historic and peaceful. It's a popular place to walk but even so, you can easily find yourself alone with the many ponies that tuck themselves into clumps of gorse. To the south, the Isle of Wight makes a pleasing backdrop but further east, the towers of the Fawley oil refinery are a reminder that the Forest borders serious industry. It's hard to walk or cycle along the remnants of the airfield here and not wonder what World War II pilots must have thought as they manoeuvred their planes on to the runways built during the war.

The peaceful country lanes around the Beaulieu coast offer superb **cycling**. My favourite routes are along the quiet roads of **East End**, from where you view the sea and expanses of fields. The public is granted rare access to the coast down Tanner's Lane which is off of Lymington Road, but it's a small stretch. The loop from Beaulieu past the sleepy hamlet of **Buckler's Hard** and on past the ancient site of St Leonard's is an excellent ride thanks to the relative lack of traffic. The B3054 is a lovely flat stretch through Beaulieu Heath but this also is a main route through the Forest, so is probably unsuitable for children. The cracked and sometimes bumpy tarmac cycling trails at Beaulieu Heath are reclaimed from a World War II airfield and an evocative place to ride.

6 BEAULIEU

⌂ Countryside Education Trust (page 224)

Abbey, Palace House and National Motor Museum ✆ 01590 612345 ⌂ beaulieu.co.uk

Beaulieu's history begins with the abbey. After Henry VIII's dissolution of the monasteries, the village population grew out of the settlement of workers who had provided services to the abbey and people who had sought sanctuary within its walls. Modern roads leading from Beaulieu developed from the ancient paths that monks used to stay in touch with their local and more distant landholdings. Today, estate-owned cottages, which are identifiable by their dark red doors and diamond logos, are rented to local people and former employees of the Estate.

"Modern roads leading from Beaulieu developed from the ancient paths that monks used."

Beaulieu's permanent population is about 840, but in summer the village swells with thousands of tourists who mostly come to visit the National Motor Museum, Abbey and Palace House. Lord Montagu's detractors cynically comment that the village of Beaulieu is nothing more than a money-making enterprise and that, according to one local resident, 'unless you bring income to the Estate, you can't live here'. Indeed, Lord Montagu's father admitted it is a 'corporate enterprise' in his book *Gilt and the Gingerbread*, but one that looked after its employees and grew from his deep love of the estate and sense of obligation to his title. That same sense of duty applies today. Ralph Montagu, the 4th Baron Montagu of Beaulieu, is dedicated to restoring the woodlands of the Beaulieu estate to their original condition. He has also worked to provide social housing in Beaulieu village so that locals are not priced out of the market – a contentious issue throughout this area. Whatever the inner workings, Beaulieu is a memorable place to visit and crammed with intriguing history that is kept alive by the throngs of tourists.

Beaulieu High Street is charming and it's no surprise that the village regularly appears in 'beautiful village' surveys. The ancient stone buildings of the former Abbey, along with the red-roofed houses, are mirrored in the waters of Beaulieu River and the Mill Pond located just at the top of the cobbled High Street. It's pleasant to meander along and visit the quaint shops selling gifts, chocolate and ice cream, all housed within brick buildings dating from the 17th, 18th and 19th centuries. Have a look for the three diamonds that symbolise the Montagu coat of arms on many buildings lining the road. At the southern end of the street, don't miss Patrick's Patch, a vegetable and flower garden open to the public where produce for Steff's Kitchen (page 188) is grown. It's an inspiring place to visit, especially for keen home gardeners.

One way to enjoy the largely private land of Beaulieu Estate is by joining one of the activities run by **New Forest Activities** (page 44), located just to the west of town on Hatchet Lane. The outdoor activity company runs activities including archery, treasure trails, combat games, canoeing and kayaking.

The Beaulieu Estate is also home to the **Countryside Education Trust** (CET; Palace Ln, SO42 7YG ✐ 01590 612401 ♂ cet.org.uk), a charity started in 1975 by Edward Lord Montagu. About 1,000 schoolchildren annually visit the trust to take part in residential programmes that are designed to connect children with the countryside, and other outreach initiatives, such as for toddlers and the elderly, are regularly run. Of interest to visitors are the CET's many community programmes (bookable through the website), which include falconry, birdwatching, forage and feast classes, and family days – all designed to foster a deeper understanding of the natural world. The CET is also home to the Fort Climate Centre, which hosts programmes and events on climate education, and hosts regular events and exhibitions on climate. I've taken part in several programmes sponsored by the CET and have always emerged enriched and inspired – just what the organisation hopes to achieve.

Beaulieu Abbey

Beaulieu Abbey is the foundation of this entire area. Legend proclaims that King John founded the Abbey after dreaming that the monks attacked him in retaliation for taxing them heavily. He began to fear the wrath of the religious community and in 1204 gave the Cistercians New Forest land to establish an abbey. John's pious son, Henry III and then later Edward I granted more land and by the end of the century there were some 200 men living and working within the abbey walls.

The location was perfect. Its proximity to the river meant that heavy stone from the Isle of Wight and Normandy, as well as marble from Purbeck, only had to be carried about 300yds to reach the construction site. Some 30 monks from the abbey of Citeaux in France travelled down Beaulieu River to the site just at the edge of the river to build their English domain, literally stone by stone.

Ironically, King John never witnessed the results of his good intentions because the buildings took 42 years to complete and he died before what would become the largest Cistercian abbey in England was finished. The land, already known as Bellus Locus Regis, meaning 'beautiful land of the king' in Latin, was then renamed Beaulieu by the French monks. Because the local Forest people didn't speak French, they pronounced Beau Lieu as 'Bewley', as it has been known ever since.

Only two original buildings remain. The monks' refectory is now **Beaulieu Parish Church** and the **Domus** is where the lay brothers, those who assisted the choir monks with manual tasks such as farming and building, lived. On the ground floor of the Domus, a dramatic video portrays the abbey's history alongside an exhibition describing the monks' daily lives.

"History lives on in the herb garden, with plants that the monks would have used for medicinal, veterinary and culinary purposes."

The **cloisters** is one of the less-visited areas of Beaulieu but it's well worth seeking it out. History lives on in the herb garden, with plants that the monks would have used for medicinal, veterinary and culinary purposes. As seen in the cloister today, they would have grown daffodil for antiseptic purposes, mint and thyme as digestive aids, lavender to cure 'pains of the head' and penny royal to alleviate toothache. But actually, this would have been a place for quiet contemplation rather than a garden. Herbs would have been grown in several locations elsewhere within the precinct.

It's easy to imagine a monk, swishing across the stone walkways, with simple sandals peeking out from beneath his brown flowing robes. But a monk would not have had time to chat, so it's lucky that when I

A DUCK'S-EYE VIEW OF THE BEAULIEU RIVER

New Forest Activities Hazel Copse Farm, Beaulieu SO42 7WA ✆ 01590 612377
🖰 newforestactivities.co.uk

It was raining lightly as I stepped into my kayak on the shores of the Beaulieu River. I was marginally enthused for this maritime adventure as heavier showers were predicted for later that day. Fortunately, however, New Forest Activities is well-stocked with wet-weather gear and I was given waterproof trousers along with my life preserver.

I was in a group of four. Steve, our instructor, patiently helped everyone get into their kayaks – even a slightly nervous man who couldn't swim and didn't even appear to like water much – and we began to paddle. Steve showed us how to twist the blade gently and how to use our torso for momentum so that we didn't get sore arms and we were off, literally skimming the water's surface to give us a duck's-eye view.

As we rounded one of the sharp bends in this tranquil river, we spotted a little egret that looked especially brilliant white on the dark day and I realised that the rain has its benefits. This was a more subtle pleasure: the gentle water drops patting on the smooth river water, the muted pinky-purples of shrubs and trees, and the distinct feeling that it was less about the kayaking than about being at one with the river.

Kayaks sit so low in the water that we could see how the saltflats rise up on top of mud piles. Behind them, the ancient oak woodland of the eastern shore furnished a green backdrop and Steve explained that the juxtaposition of these two habitats is extremely rare. The monks from Beaulieu Abbey kept salt pans in the river to gather salt for the purpose of preserving food.

We inspected odd green shoots sprouting from the top of the flats and Steve told us that this is the now highly sought-after samphire that garnishes fish dishes in fancy restaurants. It is the first flowering plant to colonise new saltmarsh and sells for quite a bit on the open market. Don't even think about collecting it here in this highly guarded river, though. Lord Montagu protects his fishing rights, which have been passed down since the monks' time, as fiercely as they did.

We paddled upriver towards Beaulieu and had terrific views of the very expensive properties that line the eastern shore. This is a clever way to get further upriver where larger craft can't go except at very high tide. As with all things on the Beaulieu Estate, comings and goings are carefully scrutinised and Lord Montagu's harbourmaster keeps a close watch on every boat that comes in and out of the river. You can't launch a canoe or kayak here, let alone moor for a few hours, without paying a fee.

It's an easy paddle and experienced kayakers might be bored but it's an ideal way to see one of the few privately owned rivers in the world close up. As we landed back on shore, even the non-nautical participant said he enjoyed the trip.

visited in peak summer, I met an archaeologist who is often on-site to talk to visitors about the history of the Abbey and what life was like for the monks.

The archaeologist told me that monks would have awakened well before dawn to attend one of seven masses of the day. They would have had one meal, usually a vegetable stew and a bit of bread, and – for monks who did especially good work – there might have been an extra piece of cheese or an egg, known as a pittance.

I smiled to realise this is where the expression 'earning your pittance' comes from. Meal times don't sound very exciting – the guide explained that the monks ate in silence except for one who stood in the pulpit and read from the Bible while the others ate.

Choir monks probably came from an educated family but unlike the lay brothers, they would have taken the strict vows of obedience, chastity and celibacy that were the foundation of the Cistercian order. Being a monk was one of the safest jobs in the country because the king couldn't enlist you to fight in battles. While many men became monks for religious reasons, others opted for this work because they received food and shelter in exchange for work and were, in effect, absolved from responsibilities of everyday life.

A man who became a monk might also bring status to a family if he became an abbot or prior, positions that might involve travel or even interactions with the king. Beaulieu was a relatively wealthy abbey in its time with further holdings in Oxfordshire, Berkshire and Devon. 'The abbot here was very senior and in good favour with the king,' explained the guide. 'Perhaps it's because it was bestowed by kings.'

"Being a monk was one of the safest jobs in the country because the king couldn't enlist you to fight in battles."

The popular conception of an abbey as perpetually quiet and sombre is false. When the king came to visit, he brought an entourage of hundreds of people so there was potentially excessive debauchery inside these walls at royal parties. This was also one of the few abbeys in England that offered permanent sanctuary, meaning that people in trouble with the law or just down on their luck would be offered refuge here.

---

1 Mill Pond. **2** Beaulieu Parish Church. **3** The clock tower at Beaulieu Abbey. **4** Beaulieu River. ▶

DEREK TIPPETTS

DAVID MERRETT

MICK HARPER,/S

BEAULIEU ENTERPRISES LTD

Monks' fortunes rose and fell but life on the whole was pretty good until the Reformation. When Henry VIII closed all the monasteries in England, he ordered all the buildings to be completely destroyed. The stone from Beaulieu was then used to construct the castles of Calshot, Hurst and Cowes on the Isle of Wight as defence points in case the French invaded. Monks became teachers or went to the Continent but the closures were rough on local people.

"Oddly, few people seem to venture out here so you might find yourself alone with the birds for a moment of contemplation."

'The Reformation had an enormous impact on Beaulieu townspeople as the closure of the Abbey left many people jobless,' explained my very knowledgeable guide. 'Outside the walls of the abbey were businesses like tanneries and wood masons who serviced the needs of the abbey. And because the monks looked after the sick and disenfranchised, these people had nowhere to go when the abbey was destroyed.'

It's lucky that anything survives at all. By the **Clock House** (page 183) and along **Mill Pond Walk**, down by the water, portions of the 12ft-high exterior wall that once surrounded the entire 58 acres of the abbey precinct still stand. (The Great Close was much larger, with about 8,500 acres incorporating the abbey's outposts.) The precinct walls would have enclosed all of the abbey's main buildings, including stables, guesthouses, a saddler and blacksmith's forge. Shoes were a main industry of the abbey because each monk received two pairs of shoes each year; he was given more if engaged in heavy outdoor work.

The abbey church

It would be easy to pass out of the abbey and miss the ruins behind the Domus, especially on a busy day. But it's only when you wander among the outlines in gravel of what was once the largest Cistercian church in England that you get a clear picture of this property's importance in British history.

An information board shows how the abbey church might have looked in the 1300s. The locations of the 68ft-high marble columns that supported the roof have been marked out with rubble piles. As you walk down the centre aisle towards the high altar, represented now by a box hedge, you begin to appreciate the scale of this immense structure. Oddly, few people seem to venture out here so you might find yourself alone with the birds for a moment of contemplation amid what can be a chaotically busy tourist attraction.

But don't stop there. Continue along the main road past the picnic area to where excavations in 1987–89 uncovered **Fulling Mill**. Once thought to be a wine press, this is where the monks improved cloth through beating, shrinking, thickening and cleaning.

Palace House

Palace House, once the gatehouse to the medieval abbey, was extensively remodelled in the 1800s into the elegant honey-coloured country house that it is today. The arched Gothic windows that the Victorians loved so well blend beautifully with the original medieval features. Most visitors head straight to the Motor Museum as this is the first stop after the ticket office. But if you want to see Palace House in relative quiet, it's best to go directly to the far end of the property. If you're lucky, you'll tour the house in relative solitude and get a genuine feeling for what it was like to live here during the Victorian era.

To get to the house and abbey from the ticket office is about a ten-minute walk, or you can take the longest **monorail** in the country, a visually jarring gimmick to transport visitors from one end of the estate to the other. It is oddly out of context here, but there is a nice view of the gardens from its elevated position. It is also a great reminder of the marketing genius of Edward, the 3rd Baron Montagu of Beaulieu and father

"Be sure to walk through the gardens at least one way though, to properly appreciate this tranquil setting."

of the current one, who created the monorail as an unusual way to transport visitors from the Motor Museum to Palace House. You can also ride a replica 1912 double-decker bus that goes back and forth from the abbey to the Motor Museum in summer. Be sure to walk through the gardens at least one way though, to properly appreciate this tranquil setting.

Palace House has been a Montagu family home since 1538, when Henry VIII's Dissolution of the Monasteries was completed. Lord Montagu's ancestor, Sir Thomas Wriothesley, later 1st Earl of Southampton, purchased the property – which had belonged to Beaulieu Abbey – from the king. With the purchase came full monastic rights that the current Lord Beaulieu still exercises today. Sir

ENTERPRISING MONKS OR RUTHLESS PREDATORS?

'Think of Beaulieu Abbey as the ancient Tesco or Walmart of its day,' said Richard Reeves, New Forest historian, with a twinkle in his eye. The image of monks living a pure life of prayer and helping the disenfranchised doesn't tell the whole story. Of course, they did practise altruistic deeds but there also was an element of hard core business about them. 'The monks gradually pushed the boundaries of their land and also helped themselves to the king's deer.' Richard explained that the monks allowed deer to wander onto their land but then devised traps in fencing that made it impossible for them to get back out.

Deer incidents like these, as well as territorial disputes with neighbours, are recorded in the cartulary, the collection of records for the abbey. As the monks gradually began occupying land outside the official delineation between the Great Close and the king's forest, Edward II officially recognised new boundaries for the monastery, for which the monks ultimately paid rent. But that didn't go down well with neighbours. In 1325, an organised demonstration of local residents destroyed the monastery's boundary wall and led to considerable animosity between monks and locals.

But this type of behaviour wasn't so unusual at this time. Although the monks guarded their rights and territorial boundaries closely, the Forest had a history of encroachment generally. There was a long-held tradition that if someone could build a structure with a roof overnight and have a fire going by morning than he was the rightful owner. After that, legal action was required to get someone off the property.

Whether or not the monks were a dominant enterprise is open to interpretation. But they clearly had a keen business sense. The few records that remain show that the brothers leased lands and operated a profitable venture, particularly with their wool production. The monks of Beaulieu Abbey were known for the high quality of their wool.

Although the Cistercian ideal was to achieve complete self-sufficiency, it is unrealistic to think the monks would have had all the manpower and skills they needed within their community. Records in late medieval times show that the monks leased lands, which gave them an income and a staff.

Thomas viewed the property more as a source of income than a home, choosing the 14th-century Great Gatehouse – now Palace House – for accommodation and as a hunting lodge.

In the 19th century, Lord Henry Scott (the current Lord Montagu's great grandfather) expanded the building to become a family residence. From the front garden, the difference in the stone used in medieval times and that of the Victorian addition is apparent.

The Clock House, located at the outer edge of the property towards Palace Lane, is one of the only remaining Abbey buildings and where monks administered aid to the poor who knocked on the outer gates. Today it has been reinvented with a modern extension dedicated to Soviet Russian art. The rotating exhibitions are chosen by Art Russe, a private collection of 20th-century works.

Ralph Douglas-Scott-Montagu, 4th Baron Montagu of Beaulieu, and member of the House of Lords, inherited Beaulieu in 2015, when his father, Edward passed away at the age of 88. Ralph grew up in the grand house and he curates the building so that visitors get a sense of the palace as a family home. He works from an office behind the public areas.

When Ralph's father, Edward, the 3rd Baron Montagu, himself inherited the estate in 1951, it was nearly insolvent. Like many English country houses, the post-war depression and changing social structures made maintaining a large estate extremely difficult, and, as elsewhere, Edward was aware he needed to open the house to the public in order to keep it in the family. But he also knew he couldn't compete with the enormous architectural masterpieces found throughout England. And so he made his father's motor car collection the selling point and dedicated his life to making Beaulieu viable.

"Palace House is not the grandest English stately home but its charm is that it is easy to imagine living here."

The current Lord Montagu's written recollections of growing up at Palace House as it became an attraction, appear throughout the house, making a visit feel like an intimate tour. The huge collection of family portraits provides an extensive history lesson that extends beyond the Montagu family. Unlike his father, who continued to live in a portion of Palace House, the current Lord Montagu lives in a family home elsewhere on the Beaulieu Estate, though private rooms are maintained for the family. The current private dining and drawing rooms upstairs were once chapels used by non-monastic guests who weren't allowed to worship in the abbey church. Unfortunately, there is no access to bedrooms.

Modern-day visitors are invited to step back in time while in Palace House, where museum guides are dressed as Victorian-era staff. When I arrived, I was greeted by Barkham, a housemaid here in 1889. She told me she is addressed only by her surname but the head housekeeper

BEAULIEU ENTERPRISES LTD

BEAULIEU ENTERPRISES LTD

BEAULIEU ENTERPRISES LTD

RONALD IAN SMILES/S

BEAULIEU ENTERPRISES LTD

would have been honoured with the title 'Mrs' in acknowledgement of her senior status. She remained in character the entire length of my visit and shared fabulous historic details about life for 'downstairs' staffers.

Palace House is not the grandest English stately home but its charm is that it is easy to imagine living here. In the dining room, pewter plates are laid on a table carved from a single elm tree, and a log fire burns in winter. Downstairs in the kitchen, the servants' bell indicator shows how family members called for their staff. The bells would continue ringing for a few minutes to ensure workers knew which room to go to. A menu printed on the kitchen blackboard changes daily to show what the family and staff might have eaten on that day in 1889.

The current Montagu family still enjoys Christmas dinner in the dining room that is open to visitors and, at the side of the fireplace, pencilled markings record the heights of Montagu children. The festive season is an especially good time to visit Beaulieu as well because the table is laid, Christmas trees abound and there is usually a festive fair with artisans selling goods.

The gardens are especially lovely in spring when some 15 species of daffodils carpet the moat and lawn outside the house. The **Victorian gardens** feature several garden styles of the Victorian age; some roses, which bloom throughout summer, date from the 1800s. Don't miss the topiary of the Mad Hatter's tea party. In the **kitchen garden**, a glass house which Henry, the 1st Lord Montagu built, contains a vine from that time. In October, pumpkins brighten the Victorian Vegetable Garden.

During school holidays, organised activities take place on the lawn by the mill pond, including Easter egg hunts, face painting and Victorian games like skittles. An aproned housemaid, dipping from Victorian character to present-day staffer, told me: 'It's wonderful to see that children are captivated by these simple garden games. They love the simplicity of tossing a ring over a pole and knocking down wooden pegs.' Distinctly non-Victorian school-holiday activities are held on the large open space between the house and Motor Museum, such as go-karting and assault courses. There is enough to do here with children to make it a really full day.

◀ 1 Palace House & Gardens. 2 Restored Victorian kitchen at Beaulieu. 3 The grand interior of Palace House. 4 A 1904 De Dion-Bouton at Beaulieu National Motor Museum. 5 Lord Montagu's falconer, Paul Manning.

A self-service restaurant near the main entrance by the Motor Museum has a few outdoor tables but on a sunny day it's better to bring a picnic and enjoy the gardens. Of several picnic areas, the nicest is just off the main pathway from the house, inside a large square garden boxed in by hedges and trees. On the main road by the church ruins, a large picnic area has tables and an enclosure useful for rainy days.

National Motor Museum, Beaulieu

I knew that the Motor Museum boasts a world-class collection of cars but it wasn't until I chatted with some of the knowledgeable staff that I saw the museum as a fascinating chronicle of motoring history, which helped me stop and think about how the automobile revolutionised the world.

Much of the museum is staffed by volunteers who are either stationed at the information desk or wandering among visitors. I stopped to chat with an enthusiastic volunteer and found myself whisked into a whirl of entertaining facts about cars and the important contributions of John, 2nd Lord Montagu of Beaulieu, to the motoring industry.

There are a few collection highlights but my favourite is the **1899 Daimler** in which John Montagu took the then Prince of Wales (later Edward VII) for a drive, thereby cementing their friendship but also forging the connection between Daimler and the Royal Family. Apparently, the Prince of Wales had so much fun that he ordered a similar car for himself, much to the chagrin of his minders.

"I stopped to chat with an enthusiastic volunteer and found myself whisked into a whirl of entertaining facts about cars."

It was also in this car that John, the MP for the New Forest from 1895–1905, drove from Beaulieu to the Palace of Westminster, making this the first car to drive into the House of Commons Yard. 'The speed limit at that time was 12 miles per hour,' my guide explained with a chuckle, 'but Lord Montagu wanted to make a point, so he drove faster than that as part of his campaign to raise awareness of the importance of motoring to improving society. In 1903 he helped pass a bill that raised the speed limit to 20 miles per hour and required all drivers to display registered number plates.'

Lord Montagu was a forward thinker who campaigned to improve Britain's roads after World War I. Apparently, he believed that motor cars would bring greater political, economic and social changes than

A JUMBLE OF TRANSPORT

The Motor Museum hosts numerous themed events throughout the year, including the Spring Autojumble and the Autumn International Autojumble, where motor enthusiasts buy and sell spare parts, memorabilia and even complete cars at hundreds of merchandise stands. The international event is a huge draw, attracting about 25,000 people. There are also numerous car rallies dedicated to specific manufacturers throughout the year. See 🖉 beaulieu.co.uk/events for more information.

the railways. John also campaigned for elevated roadways and for a motorway that would link London with Liverpool. He didn't live to see this dream to fruition because he died in 1929, before the first motorway was built in 1958. He was also an early supporter of the Channel Tunnel. 'He was so much more than a rich guy with a penchant to drive fast,' said my guide, whose interest in the motoring history and the second Lord Montagu was infectious. 'He started the first car magazine, *The Car Illustrated*, he instigated the law that raised the speed limit in the UK and he was a founding member of the RAC.'

Be sure not to miss the **1909 Rolls Royce Silver Ghost** (registration number R1909) that was Lord Montagu's pride and joy and is pictured in the portrait at the top of the stairs in Palace House. You might not realise that this car was reconstructed from a breakdown truck in Berwick-on-Tweed in Northumberland. The chassis was in excellent condition, so it just needed to be redesigned to make a stunning vehicle. Ask a staffer to see the photo that shows it in its original condition.

When I surveyed the monstrosity that is the steam-operated **1880 Grenville**, I had to laugh at how far car design has progressed. This car occasionally still gets taken out but it takes two hours to fire up and three people to operate it. It is believed to be the oldest self-propelled, passenger-carrying road vehicle that still works. There is a lot of just plain fun here, too. Cars used for advertising, like the butterball design of the Outspan Orange, are a treat to examine close-up. Also on-site is one of the six cars made for the *Chitty Chitty Bang Bang* film, as well as many famous racing cars and some land-speed record-breakers.

The World of Top Gear is one of the most popular exhibitions at Beaulieu. You can see some of the battered cars ruined by the original *Top Gear* team and visit the Enormodrome, which recreates the original TV studio.

AN EXCURSION INTO FALCONRY

I was nervous but I didn't want to admit it. I'd enrolled in a private introductory session in falconry with Paul Manning (01794 368487 amews.com), an experienced falconer and accredited trainer, based at Abbots Mews in the grounds of Palace House at Beaulieu. Paul holds the illustrious position of being Lord Montagu's falconer, the first one endorsed by the Montagu family for over 300 years.

When I arrived, Paul's falcons, hawks and one very large owl, sat patiently on their perches waiting for the session to begin. As I eyed the birds, some with steely gazes, I wondered, what had made me think I wanted to do this?

Paul is not keen on hotel-style afternoons of falconry in which patrons hold birds for a few minutes and then head off for afternoon tea. Instead he demands that participants on his course understand the discipline behind falconry. So the 3½-hour session began with a talk from Paul in which he described the evolution of falconry from an essential hunting technique thousands of years ago to the rise of birds as a status symbol in the 1500s, to the sport's gradual decline with the advent of guns and over-hunting of birds of prey.

I was absorbed by Paul's passion and expansive knowledge. Paul works regularly with young offenders and believes that the responsibility required to handle birds can make troubled youngsters see life differently. 'Falconry teaches humility because you have to serve the bird. It is life-enhancing to be around such an indomitable spirit.'

Paul described how he trained each of his birds, beginning with sitting motionless for

🍴 FOOD & DRINK

The Beaulieu Bakehouse High St (north end) 01590 611437 thebeaulieubakehouse.co.uk. The village's original bakery has been brought back to life in this pleasant café that serves breakfasts, light lunches and a pleasing array of cakes. The picnic tables outside in summer are a great place for families; kids can let off steam in the traffic-free passage.

Steff's Kitchen Fairweather's Garden Centre, High St, SO42 7YB 01590 612307 fairweathers.co.uk/steffs-kitchen. This café inside Fairweather's is a pleasant spot for lunch or tea, especially in warm weather. The outdoor terrace, always open, overlooks the nursery. Across the high street, **Steff's to go** has baked goods, sandwiches and drinks, and you can sit and eat in the outdoor terrace at Steff's Kitchen.

7 HATCHET POND

Although a relatively small pond, this is the largest body of water in the New Forest, and generally a busy place. The pond, just outside East Boldre at the junction of the B3054 and the B3055 at the edge of hours in a room while they learn to trust him. Then the endless days of gradual steps, to the time of letting the bird fly free and knowing it will return. Paul never goes away from home because even a few days away can erode the trust he has built. I felt a bit worried, knowing that if I jumped away when the bird flew towards me, I could ruin all of Paul's hard work in one afternoon.

Hence my anxiety when a few hours later I stood in a field watching Belle, a Harris Hawk with piercing eyes, poised on a tree limb, waiting for my signal to approach. Paul placed a piece of food into my gloved hand and told me to hide it quickly. I did so but not without a touch of squeamishness over what I thought might be a chicken foot.

I stood poised with arm outstretched. Belle swooped from a resting point across the field and in one magical dive, landed like a breath of air on my fist. She gobbled down the food before I even realised it was gone from my hand. When Paul handed me the next course – a larger piece of baby chick with fluff intact, I realised that, yes indeed, the appetiser had been a chicken foot.

By the end of the afternoon, I was handling chicken guts (albeit with my thick glove) and walking comfortably with Inajah, a lanner falcon, poised on my arm. Although I am not comfortable with hunting as an activity, I can see how a hunting expedition with Paul and his birds of prey would be exhilarating and timeless.

In addition to his public demonstrations at Beaulieu, Paul regularly runs half-day training sessions for small groups and four-day qualification courses.

Beaulieu Heath, was created in the 18th century to provide power for an iron mill. Ponies and cattle come to drink, donkeys arrive in hopes of raiding tourists' picnics, and photographers head here at sunset to capture the outlines of trees against the often brilliant purples and pinks that paint the sky behind Beaulieu Heath.

What most visitors don't realise is that the pond is also a Site of Special Scientific Interest for the more than 130 rare wetland species and many invertebrates that live here. Some of these species have been lost from other parts of the UK.

Unfortunately, the high visitor numbers to this beauty spot has led to pollution levels that threaten the pond and it has been designated as a Special Area for Conservation. Visitors can help by keeping dogs (and themselves) away from the water because swimming disturbs sediment and releases otherwise trapped chemicals. It is a lovely place to meander around at sunset or extend a stroll further into Beaulieu Heath.

Hatchet Pond also has some World War II history. On the north side, are rectangular, concrete outlines in the grass. These might possibly mark the outline of a long trough that was built to test amphibious tanks prior to operations. According to the diary of a former Forest keeper, the pool was filled with water and tanks would drive straight through and be tested for waterproofing, before journeying to open water. Once waterproofing was deemed secure, the tanks did further tests in Hatchet Pond.

"Even on the bleakest days, there is likely to be at least one tent with a fisherman determined to capture carp."

Researchers are still not completely certain that this structure existed here, but 1946 Verderers' records reference a 'considerable concrete structure that needs demolition'.

Hatchet Pond's other wartime contribution has been better documented. Video footage exists of amphibious vehicles equipped with flame throwers, known as Dragonflies, engaged in wartime exercises in Hatchet Pond. The dramatic footage shows these extraordinary armoured vehicles crossing Hatchet Pond, using their inflatable skirts that rapidly deflated in order emerge from the pond while firing flames. The firm, gentle slopes of certain parts of the pond made an ideal launching location – though it's almost unimaginable today in this place where donkeys stand around sheepishly eyeing children with ice creams from the local van.

Even on the bleakest days, there is likely to be at least one tent with a fisherman determined to capture carp – the record is reportedly a 31-pounder – and also bream, pike, eels and roach. Fishing is permitted from June to March. You need to have a fishing permit from Forestry England and an Environment Agency rod licence (which can be purchased online *&* forestryengland.uk). Day and week tickets are available from various points in the Forest, including East Boldre post office by Hatchet Pond and Roundhill Campsite (page 224) but season permits can only be purchased from Queen's House in Lyndhurst.

▍▍ FOOD & DRINK

Beaulieu Organic Farm Shop Hatchet SO42 7WA *&* 01590 612666
& beaulieuorganicfarmshop.co.uk. One of the first organic farm shops in the area, providing high-quality meats and organic vegetables. There are a few prepared snacks for picnics but this is an ideal place to come if you are in self-catering accommodation.

8 EAST BOLDRE

East Boldre is an intriguing place, defying the traditional English village that develops around a church and town hall. Like many other New Forest settlements, it is a linear development, about two miles long and only a quarter of a mile wide, without a true centre. East Boldre only became a parish in 1839 but there have been dwellings here long before that. It began as workers' settlements along the western boundary of the Beaulieu Estate sometime in the 1700s and was originally known as 'Beaulieu Rails', in reference to the wooden railings that topped the earth bank marking that boundary.

This is an example of an **encroachment community**, which this area is known for, when – in the 1800s – squatters hastily erected dwellings before the authorities could be bothered to enact legal proceedings of eviction. Although there are now many modern homes, you can still see some old thatched and cob cottages that date from this time. The crown land on the borders of Beaulieu and Boldre parishes was subject to exploitation by settlers trying to avoid taxes and affiliation

THE BEAULIEU LETTERS

Evidence of aviation history can be seen today in the form of letters spelling 'Beaulieu' that were carved into the heath at East Boldre sometime between 1910 and 1916. The Beaulieu letters were covered during World War II and gradually became overgrown with vegetation. In 2012, an enthusiastic group of volunteers exposed them and restored them to their chalky white glory.

The letters are 15ft high, making the whole word extend for 110ft. Debate continues as to their origin but many historians believe they served as a turning point for races up and down the heath by the civilian flying school. According to old maps, the turning point coincides with the position of the letters. Another theory proposes that it might have been a practical joke that aviation school

founder, J Amstrong-Drexel played on his colleague William McArdle (page 193) after the latter got lost on his way back from a flying show and landed in Fordingbridge.

The letters are obviously best seen from the air, but you can walk right up to them if you're willing to do a bit of sleuthing. If it has been raining, the ground will be wet – wellies are best. Park at Hatchet Moor car park and cross the road (B3054). On the other side of the road, take the well-trodden diagonal footpath to the right. When you reach the clearing, walk directly right for about 60yds, at which point you should be rewarded with the giant Beaulieu inscription. The letters are very close to the road, but the level of undergrowth and height of gorse here can vary according to season and Forestry burning.

DEREK TIPPETTS

MARK HEIGHES/S

with an official parish. Workers from Buckler's Hard and nearby farms, as well as from the iron works in Sowley and brickworks at Bailey's Hard (between Buckler's Hard and Beaulieu), took up residence here. They were in effect aided by the fact that this dormitory community benefitted employers at Beaulieu who avoided the poor tax levied by the parish and thus paid only wages. This led to inevitable disputes between the parishes of Beaulieu and Boldre as to which was responsible for caring for their poor parishioners. Eventually laws were formalised and, when East Boldre became its own parish, the community became more as it is now, with a post office, village hall, church and pub spread along East Boldre Road.

"East Boldre is an intriguing place, defying the traditional English village that develops around a church and town hall."

There is no indication today of the village's complicated social history but there are reminders of its impressive **aviation history**. The world's fifth flying school opened here in 1910; William McArdle, from Bournemouth, and American, J Armstrong-Drexel built two sheds and a rough runway here, despite being refused permission by the then Office of Woods. Just two years later, the school closed. But in 1915, the Royal Flying Corps (predecessor of the RAF) established a training school for pilots here called RFC Beaulieu. The present-day village hall was the officers' mess until the end of World War I when the airfield closed. The aircraft used in World War II were too large for this site, so the wartime airfield and accommodation quarters were established further west in Beaulieu Heath.

FOOD & DRINK

Turfcutter's Arms Main Rd, SO42 7WL ℘ 01590 612331 ℗ the-turfcutters-new-forest. co.uk. This old-fashioned pub is well situated if you're out walking, fishing or cycling and need sustenance. The plain wood floorboards and wall hangings of horses and riders are a welcome change from the slick décor of modern gastro pubs. At lunchtime, dogs sprawl beneath tables and hungry walkers tuck into their ploughman's. The standard pub fare is decent and the atmosphere is jolly with a lot of local flavour; one small room off the main area has a warm fire. The large garden with plenty of tables is ideal for families with small children or just a pleasant spot to enjoy lunch; there's sometimes local crafts sellers and possibly even a bouncy castle here in summer.

◄ **1** Heather in flower on Beaulieu Heath. **2** Hatchet Pond at sunset.

A Wartime Walk around Beaulieu Heath

❄ OS Explorer map OL22; start: Stockley Car Park, off the B3055 between Beaulieu and Brockenhurst ⚲ SU345019; 4 miles, including diversions; easy.

Beaulieu has some of the most fascinating World War II history in all of the New Forest. This walk passes through the former residential area for some 2,000 airmen and WAAF women; only a few buildings remain of a campus that once included a gymnasium, cafeteria, fire tender building, showers and toilets, post office, grocery and water tower. The route is fascinating for history lovers but also offers diverse terrain and scenery through working farms and the wild expanse of Beaulieu Heath, where there are visible reminders of war preparations. Note though that this is not a straightforward, circular route; there are a few detours and backtracking required in order to see the wartime remains. It can be very wet and muddy after rain; there is also some uneven ground.

1 From Stockley Car Park, face the Forest and head west on the gravel track that leads from the right side of car park, with the B3055 roughly parallel on your right. After about 800yds, you will come to the water tower that served the more than 2,000 airmen and the Women's Auxiliary Air Force (WAAF), who lived here during World War II. The structure dates from 1945 but was refurbished in 2014 and still serves Roundhill Campsite today. Just behind it is Bronze Age Pudding Barrow, distinctive, not only for its shape but because most of the barrows in this area were destroyed during the war efforts. Turn left from the track you arrived on and head south, following paved track with the main campsite on your right.

2 After about 120yds, you reach a three-way intersection of gravel tracks. You will see two vehicle barriers; ignore the one on the left and walk straight ahead, crossing the intersecting track to pass around the vehicle barrier located on the grass. Follow the grassy trail that runs beside a large farm field on your right with open forest on your left for about 600yds, to where the field ends in a line of trees. Just past this, you will see an aluminium shed on your right, on the opposite side of the fence. Turn into the woods towards the fence on the well-trod narrow paths. The first of two stone air-raid shelters is just behind the aluminium shed; the second is a bit further on. This was the area of the residential quarters of the WAAF.

3 Retrace your steps back to the vehicle barriers and turn left on to the tarmac road of Roundhill Campsite. Walk with the campsite on your right and a fenced field on your left; the latter was where airfield staff played football and rugby.

4 After about 600yds, pass another vehicle barrier and follow the road as it curves around to the left. (The main campsite road continues to the right.) Continue past a sign on the left marked 'Access to cottages'. At the first farm entrance, Dilton Corner, go through the pedestrian gate on the left, signposted 'Bridleway'. Walk a short distance until you reach the main farm entrance; here, make a sharp right to continue to follow the bridleway. Look on your right for two former airmen's huts, now overgrown with ivy. This was the site of the airfield's main residential quarters.

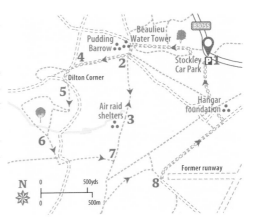

5 Follow the narrow path in between farm buildings (those on the right are behind a fence) and on past a fenced field that may have pigs. Cross a stream on a tarmac bridge (this can be very wet). The path curves around to the right, with a large field on your left, then eventually turns sharp left. Continue through the farm on a hilly, woodsy path. The bricks beneath the path date from World War II. Walk towards a large barn, on the left in the distance. The barn comes and goes from view as you follow the path as it curves around left. Soon you will see the barn clearly up ahead on the left.

6 Continue straight, past the barn on your left. Just past it is a vehicle track. Cross this and join a narrow footpath that runs to the right of two old, corrugated former Nissen huts, now used as barns. Follow the path around to the backside of the barns until you come to the main dirt road of the farm. Cross the road and continue through the heavy metal gate at the bridleway sign on to a farm track that runs between two fields. You'll need to undo the rope latch; be sure to re-affix it. Walk through the farm (you might pass directly through cow herds) until you reach its boundary fence and gate.

7 Exit the farm through the pedestrian gate, ignoring a second barrier on the adjoining track on the left. You are now on Beaulieu Heath. Walk straight ahead, across an ancient ditch, towards a wide grassy track in front of you. Turn right, keeping the bank and ditch (and farm) on your right. The wide grassy trail gradually curves left; follow it between gorse bushes. About 450yds from where you first entered the heath, you will come to a clear Y-junction where another path converges from your back left. Make a sharp left, almost turning back on yourself as you head on to this converging path. When the path curves around to the right, after about 600yds, look to your left to see a large Bronze Age barrow, and some other, smaller tumuli. ▶

A Wartime Walk around Beaulieu Heath (continued)

8 ◄ After a further 200yds, you'll reach another Y-junction; make a sharp left on to a wide gravel track here. This is the former taxi track for aeroplanes during World War II. Follow the track for about half a mile until you reach a T-junction. Take the left track and almost immediately on your right you will pass the concrete foundation for one of the hangars used by the Airborne Forces Experimental Establishment, a branch of the British Air Ministry, to store helicopters. Continue along this path; Stockley Car Park is about half a mile further on.

9 BEAULIEU HEATH

The great swathe of Beaulieu Heath can be an eerie place to explore. The flat terrain gives rise to big sky views but when you're out here alone and that seemingly perpetual wind blows, maybe with a few grey clouds thrown in, the atmosphere can feel a bit lonely, if not a tad ghostly. Ponies and cattle wander freely amid the scrub and there are views to the east of the Isle of Wight. Aside from the strong winds that build up momentum across the flat heath, cycling is exhilarating here, largely because of the open space and the sense of history as you traverse the trails created on the now-cracked tarmac of former World War II runways.

In addition to the cycle trails created on the smaller flying strips, the largest block of the three-runway airfield built here during World War II is used for model-aircraft flying. So if you are on or near the Heath and hear a distant whine, look up, because it's likely to be a model aircraft. Note that there are strict regulations to fly model planes: you must be a Civil Aviation Authority certified flyer and then obtain an annual permit from the **Beaulieu Model Flying Committee** (⊘ beaulieumodelflying.bmfa.org).

10 BUCKLER'S HARD

⌂ **Master Builder's House** (page 224)
⌔ 01590 616203 ⊘ bucklershard.co.uk

This tiny former port is overflowing with history from its inception in the 1720s to its heyday as a shipbuilding centre in the late 18th and early 19th centuries and through to its important role in preparations for World War II invasions. Buckler's Hard was built with two rows of workers' cottages lining the broad 'hard' that led down to the river, and this view remains remarkably unchanged. Eventually houses were built off the main street, including Slab Row, so-called because the bark hadn't even been taken off the wood used to construct the buildings. They were demolished in the mid 19th century as the shipbuilding era came to an end and the population declined.

The hamlet's name, which was originally 'Buckle's Hard', most likely derives from a local family, the Buckles, who had lived there for generations and used the site as a landing point for their boats. 'Hard' is the south coast term to describe a landing point in a river where the banks are especially soft. All you have to do is take the riverside walk from Beaulieu to see just how soft (page 200).

The hamlet originated in the early 18th century when John, 2nd Duke of Montagu, then owner of the Beaulieu Estate, envisioned the site as Montagu Town, a free port for the import and export of sugar from the West Indies. In the early 1720s, the duke laid out a smooth slope lined

A CRUISE ON THE BEAULIEU RIVER

At the bottom of Buckler's Hard hill, a small cruise boat docks for a 30-minute tour downriver towards the Solent (⌘ bucklershard.co.uk; tickets sold onboard). The Beaulieu River is unusual for two reasons: it is one of the only privately owned rivers in the world and it has a double tide, which means that the tide goes out very slowly and comes in very quickly so that in essence, they overlap for a bit.

The reasonably priced cruise, which runs throughout the day from Easter through October, is an ideal way to see much of the river's highlights. It takes you past opulent riverside houses that were requisitioned during World War II as bases for training spies, and you glimpse Gins, where the monks of Beaulieu kept their fishing boats. In addition to observing Exbury Gardens, which spreads along the eastern shore of Beaulieu River, you also get close-up views of the

saltmarshes and assortment of craft moored in the river. The guided tour points out the hand-dug oyster beds put in by the current Lord Montagu's great grandfather; oysters now grow wild here and Beaulieu is one of the few rivers clean enough to be licensed to harvest them. You'll also hear about salt production in the Beaulieu River and a few tales from World War II.

One of the best views, mid way through the cruise, is of the ancient barn at St Leonard's (page 202). Just as the boat begins to turn back towards Buckler's Hard, look up beyond the left side of the boat to see the tip of the triangle in the distance that forms the last remaining wall of this monastic ruin.

Private cruises from Buckler's Hard, more focused on wildlife, are available from Wild New Forest (page 45). The 2½-hour trips usually go at low tide for optimum wildlife viewing.

with cottages down to the river and built a quay in anticipation of his shipments. He organised an expensive and well-equipped expedition of seven ships to St Lucia, only to discover that the French had the same idea and were well-entrenched by the time the English got there. His envisioned Montagu Town lay dormant.

When hostilities between France and England heated up in the late 1730s, there was increased need for warships and the Navy hired private shipbuilders to meet the demand. With the infrastructure of the failed Montagu Town in place, the port was rejuvenated as Buckler's Hard. This is an ideal location for shipbuilding, not only because the gravel soil extends all the way down to the low-water mark but because of the abundance of surrounding trees. In 1744, the Navy Board sent Henry Adams to Buckler's Hard to supervise the building of the *Surprise*, the second ship to be built in the area. The first was the *Salisbury*, which was actually constructed further upriver just outside of Beaulieu village.

The **Buckler's Hard Museum,** located just after the main entrance to the hamlet, seems small but is packed with information that illustrates the breadth of historical roles played out here. This was the centre of shipbuilding during the Battle of Trafalgar and villagers have a strong sense of pride that Admiral Nelson's favourite ship, *Agamemnon*, was launched from this site. Buckler's Hard became a hub of wartime efforts again during World War II and the video describing this area's role is well worth watching. The Beaulieu River was a busy place as segments of 'Mulberry Harbours', the temporary concrete harbours used to offload cargo at Normandy, were constructed here. There also are exhibits dedicated to local sailors, including Sir Francis Chichester, who trialled his yacht, *Gipsy Moth IV*, in the Beaulieu River and the Solent before sailing it around the world in 1967.

"This tiny former port is overflowing with history from its inception in the 1720s to its heyday as a shipbuilding centre."

John Montagu, 2nd Baron Montagu, undoubtedly regretted sailing on the doomed ship, the *Persia*, in 1916. He was assumed drowned but the intriguing story of his rescue is an engaging story that is recounted here.

1 Georgian houses at Buckler's Hard. **2** St Paul's Church, East Boldre. **3** Shipwright's Cottage. **4** Exploring Britain's shipbuilding history at the Maritime Museum. ▶

INTREEGUE PHOTOGRAPHY/S

BEAULIEU ENTERPRISES LTD

GRASSROOTSGROUNDSWELL

BEAULIEU ENTERPRISES LTD

Back outside the museum, as you walk down High Street towards the water, don't miss **St Mary's Chapel**, which is tucked away on the left terrace. The chapel, officially known as Chapel of the Blessed Virgin Mary, is still privately owned by the Montagu family but regularly has services of worship and is usually open to visitors.

What's particularly fun here is the building's likely link to smuggling. In 2011, during renovations to walls above the chapel, workers noticed a void under the altar. Further investigations revealed a cellar containing broken wine and brandy bottles. The chapel was once a residential cottage, and so local experts believe it may have been a hub of smuggling. It's possible that goods could have been hidden here after being brought down the Beaulieu River from the Solent, possibly even by Henry Adams (page 198) himself. The cellar and some of the findings are visible through a viewing window inside the building.

"The chapel was once a residential cottage, and so local experts believe it may have been a hub of smuggling."

Next to the chapel is the **Shipwright's Cottage**, which has been furnished to show how shipwright Thomas Burlace and his family would have lived in the late 18th century. Climbing up the narrow stairs to the bedroom is a feat in itself and great fun for small children who delight in the creaking floorboards and cosy space at the top with minimal furnishings. It's interesting to see their reaction when they realise that the only entertainment would have been in the form of a Bible – no electronics here!

Entrance to Buckler's Hard is free but if you arrive by car, you need to pay the small parking fee. There is also an admission charge to the museum and for a river cruise.

A Walk from Beaulieu to Buckler's Hard

At the bottom of the hill near Buckler's Hard Marina is the beginning of the Riverside Walk to Beaulieu, a two-mile trail that is part of the Solent Way. There are two routes that run parallel to each other about 700yds apart: a straight path through the forest or one that diverts to follow the edge of the river. Either provides a very different walk and it's worth taking one up and one back.

Along the riverside walk, just past the marina at Keeping Marsh, is **a hide** for observing the many species of birds that live here during different times of the year. Depending on the season, you might see black-headed

LIVING IN HISTORY

As you wander along the sloping main street of Buckler's Hard, it's tempting to daydream about what it might be like to live here. The 18th-century cottages built originally as part of a free port for the importing and exporting of sugar, and later inhabited by shipbuilders, are now used by the Maritime Museum and the Master Builder's House hotel. Others are rented from the Beaulieu Estate by private tenants. Jane Yapp, Custodian of Buckler's Hard, lives in a cottage owned by the estate just behind the main street. I asked her what it's like having your home in a village that is essentially a living museum.

'It's magical. When the visitors leave and the gates are locked, we return to our own very special small community of about ten full-time residents,' Jane told me as we meandered down the central path, virtually devoid of visitors on an early spring day. 'Christmas Day, the only day the museum isn't open, is probably the most precious time, especially if there has been snow. The lights of the Christmas tree in the village twinkle, and the hotel guests and village residents have the whole place to themselves.'

She clearly appreciates living in a place that embodies so much history. 'It's incredible that such a small place has played such a big part in England's past. It's impossible not to think about all that's gone on here and the people who might have lived in my cottage long before me.'

Jane told me that past staff and their families who have lived in her cottage insist that they've heard thumps in the attic and seen apparitions, particularly a worried child in 18th-century clothing. Jane has heard unidentifiable sounds but won't go so far as to acknowledge sharing her home with ghosts. 'Who knows? With all that's gone on here before my time, I wouldn't rule out anything.'

gulls, Little Egrets and, if you have a very keen eye (and binoculars) possibly an osprey. This wildlife site developed when dredgings from building the marina were put here and birds flocked to the site. Work is underway to prevent the wetland from naturally converting back to woodland. The walk continues along the riverbank from here and can be muddy at times, although there are wooden walkways across the marshiest bits. Just before you reach the fields that ultimately lead to Beaulieu village, you can see a house with a tall chimney that was once part of the estate brickworks. This is where the *Salisbury*, the first ship to be built at Buckler's Hard was constructed.

The **path through the woods**, from where you can still catch glimpses of the river, makes a very pleasant contrast. Tall conifers line one side of the trail and on the other you catch glimpses of the river. I've walked here and found myself very close to deer without even breaking stride. They tend to eye walkers warily but stand still and watch people pass. Both paths have information boards describing the surroundings.

¶¶ FOOD & DRINK

The Captain's Table SO42 7XB bucklershard.co.uk. Located just outside the entrance to Buckler's Hard with a large outdoor seating area, this makes a good stopping point on a cycle or walk, as well as serving the Buckler's Hard site. A simple café, it serves mostly sandwiches and light meals. The cooked breakfast is popular with older locals. In the autumn, the café serves fresh apple juice made from apples from the small orchard by the car park.

Master Builder's House SO42 7XB 01590 616253 themasterbuilders.co.uk. As well as being a pleasant place to stay (page 224), the hotel has three places to eat, depending on the season. Throughout the year, the Yachtsman Bar serves an all-day menu with small plates and pub classics, including fish and chips. A splendid outdoor terrace (Crew Bar) with views of the Beaulieu River hosts a lunchtime barbecue on sunny summer days from July, on a first come, first served basis. A more formal choice is available at The Riverview, which is open every day for lunch and dinner with a small, seasonal menu as well as pub classics like fish and chips and burgers.

11 EAST END

 East End Arms (page 224)

East End is a hamlet southwest of Buckler's Hard, consisting of houses and a really fantastic pub – that's about it, and that's enough. This area combines the best of all worlds; you are close to the coast of Lymington to the southwest and to Lepe and Calshot to the east. Forest walks are only about one mile away and the attractions of Beaulieu only about four. It's perfect for cyclists too, because there are lots of country lanes to explore in the immediate vicinity and towards East Boldre.

One of the things you'll encounter on a walk or cycle ride are the imposing ruins of **St Leonard's Grange** situated on a small, rural road about half a mile southwest of Buckler's Hard. This is all that is left of what was once the largest barn, or *grangia*, at one of Beaulieu Abbey's farming outposts. It stands at the edge of the road, seemingly forgotten, with birds nesting in the medieval windows. If you look closely, you'll notice the bizarre barn within a barn that dates from the 16th century when farmers used materials from the crumbling monastic structure to build a second barn within it. You can't go in but a bench on the opposite side of the road facing the remains of what must have been a massive building makes the ideal spot to have a rest and contemplate the world of the monks.

Granges were managed by *conversi*, or lay brothers, a kind of 'monks' assistants', who attended far fewer services and carried out practical tasks. This enabled the choir monks to devote themselves to prayer, meditation and ministering to the poor. The lay brothers worked the land and sent grain and other produce to the abbey. The abbey in turn sent back bread, fish, salt and ever-important beer. Monks at the nearby holding of Bergerie handled the sheep and wool production for which Beaulieu Abbey was renowned. Wool produced at Bergerie was sent to the abbey's wool store in Southampton and exported to the continent, bringing the monks a generous profit.

▮▮ FOOD & DRINK

East End Arms East End SO41 5SY ℘ 01590 626223 ◈ eastendarms.co.uk. Dire Straits fans probably already know that John Illsley, the band's bass guitarist, owns this old-time pub in this very quiet corner of Hampshire. It's been getting progressively more slick as the years go by and is less pubby in the dining room than it used to be, but the bar still feels like a village watering hole. An ideal Sunday lunch spot but be forewarned: it's hugely popular, especially the garden in summer. It also has accommodation (page 224).

THE SOUTHAMPTON COAST: EXBURY, LEPE & ELING

The coastal land east of the mouth of the Beaulieu River is not part of the New Forest (although it is part of the national park) and is distinctly different in character and landscape. When I first came to this area, I avoided the stony beach here – despite a great love for the seashore – because of its proximity to urban Southampton, Fawley Power Station and the adjacent oil refinery.

How wrong I was. Although this coastline can't be compared to the glories of Dorset or Devon, or even those further along the Hampshire coast, it has its own appeal, not least because it is so close to urban sprawl. One day after visiting **Calshot Castle**, I walked on the rocky beach of **Calshot Spit** and discovered that if you face south out to sea and keep the towers of the power station and oil refinery at your back, you are rewarded with fine views of the Solent and the excitement of watching the very busy shipping activity of Southampton Water.

I also was unaware, as I think many are, of the important nature reserves tucked in behind the coast here. **Calshot Marshes**, although small, attracts rare waterfowl, while special habitats have been created to entice insects and birds at **Lepe Country Park**. The most rewarding **cycling** is the off-road trail within the park though you will have to ride on main roads if you are cycling from Beaulieu. Once you reach the hamlet at Lepe, though, you have the choice of several quiet lanes to get to Lepe Country Park.

"The juxtaposition of suburban sprawl outside the gates makes the intricacies of nature more distinctive."

The urban nature reserves at **Testwood** are rewarding in a similar way to the experience at Calshot. The juxtaposition of suburban sprawl outside the gates makes the intricacies of nature more distinctive.

Few people realise that the New Forest extends to the shore at **Eling**. The village is very different in feel to the Forest but the coastal grazing on nearby marshes is a reminder of where you are. In any case, spending a morning at the tidal mill and walking through the surrounding marshes is so delightfully Slow and historic that it fits in well.

12 EXBURY GARDENS

Exbury O45 1AZ ℃ 023 8089 1203 🗐 exbury.co.uk ☀ Apr–Oct

The New Forest isn't particularly noted for its grand gardens but Exbury, located just outside the Forest boundaries (but within the national park) enables this area to hold its own in the company of great gardens of England. 'One of the most special things about Exbury is its scale,' Tom Clarke, Exbury's head gardener, told me. 'Not only in terms of the plants themselves but the natural beauty of this corner of the New Forest where you have mature woodland but then you get glimpses of the Solent and Beaulieu River from within the gardens.'

It was easy to see what he meant. In one short morning, I wandered through the highly manicured **Sundial Garden** to the carefree **daffodil meadow** where the nodding yellow blossoms carpeted the field in front of a backdrop of the Beaulieu River. The contrast here is astounding, from the exotic colours of the azaleas and rhododendrons to the subtleties of rushes on a river walk.

---

1 Exbury House. **2** Exbury Gardens in early autumn. **3** Exbury Gardens Railway. **4** Middle Pond in full bloom. ▶

DAVID PETER ROBINSON/S

NEW FOREST DESTINATION PARTNERSHIP

HELEN HOTSON/S

NICHOLAS D DE ROTHSCHILD/S

I joined Tom on one of Exbury's guided tours that had been billed as a walk to view the early spring blooms of primroses and camellias but turned out to be so much more. Our small group of keen gardeners and dogs learned about the history of the house and titbits about the Rothschild family, who started the garden in 1912 and continue to maintain it today.

Exbury is known as a spring garden because of its celebrated collection of camellias, rhododendrons and azaleas, which peak in April and May. Roughly 70% of the 120,000 annual visitors come between mid-April and May, with another surge in October. Exbury has been voted one of the top ten sites for autumn colour in the UK by Visit England thanks to its waterside maples and prolific dogwoods.

There is no question that the flamboyant pinks, reds, oranges and yellows that flourish here in April are magnificent, particularly when you survey the circular **Azalea Bowl** from the Stone Bridge. But there is something to be said for visiting Exbury off-season. In the absence of dramatic showpieces and hordes of visitors, it's easier to appreciate the garden as a whole. Without the crowds, I am more aware of the

SURVIVAL THERAPY

Sunrise Bushcraft Summer Ln, Exbury SO45 1AG ℘ 01425 618622
⌀ sunrisebushcraft.com

I joined James White, founder of Sunrise Bushcraft, in a private woodland just outside the Forest near Ringwood for a one-day course in basic bushcraft survival. While it's unlikely you'd ever need survival skills in the New Forest, for me this was an opportunity to gain a deeper appreciation of how our ancestors might have lived in these woods. When I walk in remote parts of the Forest now, I think about those who walked here before people – people who knew how to use every plant and animal and where to take cover, before the days of picnic lunches and dedicated car parks. It was a stark wake-up to how out of touch I was with the natural world.

We began with fire-building skills – seven methods to be precise, all of which worked like a charm. Now I know to find graded kindling, from skinny twigs to thicker branches, and need not ever use kindling again. I also learnt to construct my own overnight accommodation from tree branches, leaves and compressed pine needles. I originally chose a lovely flat area beneath a beech tree to camp, figuring I'd be sheltered by the overhanging branches in case my structure wasn't rainproof. But James informed me that beech trees drop limbs regularly and that I might not survive the night. Good to know.

woodpeckers and birds and without the bright blossoms I notice how the paths are arranged and marvel at the foresight of Lionel Rothschild when he laid out his garden more than 90 years ago.

Lionel's vision was extraordinary, as was his determination to bring the garden to fruition in just 20 years. ' Lionel was not a man to take 'no' for an answer,' laughed Tom. 'He found a way to get it done.'

Lionel Nathan de Rothschild first moved to Exbury in 1912 with the purchase of Inchmery House, in an enviable clifftop location on the coast between Lepe and Exbury. He originally envisaged his garden in the grounds around the house but he couldn't secure planning permission for his design due to a public road near Lepe. When the Exbury Estate came up for sale, he purchased it and proceeded to create the grand gardens known today.

'Lionel set out to create a woodland garden on a grand scale in the golden age of woodlands gardening,' explained Tom. 'He designed a romanticised version of what a woodland garden should be, with cascades, open fields of flowers and hidden views of the river. He left the original oak trees and planted rhododendrons around them, and in that

We then walked through surrounding woods to identify edible and medicinal plants. With my penchant for the high-street chemist and local farm shop, I am unlikely to ever look for my medicines or dinner in the Forest, but touching, smelling and tasting woodland plants made me realise how distanced we humans have become from our environment. 'My goal isn't really to teach survival skills as much as it is to just get people out into the woods,' said James, who was born in the New Forest. 'People don't stop and live in the moment, they rush from thing to thing – they don't even breathe properly. Sitting around the campfire, listening to owls, your heart rate drops and you start to breathe, really breathe.'

James's words hit home when he handed me a block of wood and a knife and suggested that I carve a tent peg. I was flummoxed. I barely knew what a tent peg was, let alone had the skills to make my own. I felt silly as I awkwardly attempted to make crude incisions. But gradually I got the hang of it and was lulled into a peaceful state in which my focus was solely on etching the wood. The man perched on the log next to me hummed softly as he carved. 'Getting outside is important to maintain our sanity amid day-to-day stresses,' James told me later.

Sunrise Bushcraft offers weekend courses that are popular with families, and James can help find the right course for each group's budget and needs.

way got the best out of the site. He worked with nature, didn't move soil and didn't add follies or gazebos.'

Rothschild planted his garden in an age when plant hunters were bringing back new and exciting species from Asia and this might have spawned his obsession with hybridisation. He was determined to create rhododendrons that were hardier, more colourful and that flowered for longer. One of his great legacies, the fortune rhododendron, is large-leafed with huge yellow flowers that appear in mid-March. When this hybrid was first bred, it took 15 years to flower.

The microclimate at Exbury is ideal for growing exotic rhododendrons and azaleas but also presents challenges. 'Because we are in the shadow of the Isle of Wight, we get well below the national average of rainfall – in fact about half of what we really need,' said Tom. 'That, combined with the light, sandy soil of this area that doesn't hold water well, makes maintaining these exotic plants a challenge.'

"He was determined to create rhododendrons that were hardier, more colourful and that flowered for longer."

But it's not something that Tom is terribly worried about. 'Dry has always been an issue here. Lionel devised a very forward-thinking system for watering the garden that involved two water towers, 22 miles of underground pipes, and pumps to extract water from deep below the surface.' It's almost as if Lionel knew climate change and water shortages were coming. Although Exbury no longer uses the water tower, the gardens have never been reliant on the mains, so the garden is self-sustaining with its bore hole and reservoir.

Lionel's youngest son, Leopold, introduced the **Exbury Gardens Railway** in 2001, which draws a lot of visitors to Exbury. It not only reveals the passion and innovative thinking of Leopold, but it gives a view of the gardens that you don't get on foot as the train passes through areas without walking paths. The commentary is playful and the staff is welcoming – I've even brought my dog along for a ride. In October, Exbury runs a special Halloween 'Ghost' train and at Christmas, the Santa Steam Specials can be combined with a viewing of seasonal plants.

The entire estate comprises 200 acres of land that borders the Beaulieu River to the west and the Solent to the South. It is also worth visiting the small, linear village of **Exbury**, just south of the main entrance, built to provide housing for estate workers. Some garden staff still live here but most homes now are privately inhabited.

13 LEPE COUNTRY PARK

⋏ Lepe Beach Campsite (page 224)

Lepe SO45 1AD ✆ 02380 899108 ⌂ hants.gov.uk/thingstodo

About three miles south of Exbury Gardens on the coast of the Solent, lies the hamlet of Lepe and a bit further on, Lepe Country Park. There is more to do in this delightful coastal spot than just sit on the beach. Low tide gives scope to look for crabs and tiny sea creatures or bigger wildlife like cormorants and oystercatchers that patrol the mud looking for worms. You can walk out on the sandy spits but be aware of when the tide turns so you can get back to shore. People swim here but the currents can be strong and you have to cross shingle before you reach the water. At low tide, you'll notice the rows of timber groynes that stabilise the beach and help prevent cliff erosion and flooding.

In summer this becomes a giant playground but you'll be virtually alone if you visit early in the morning or outside of summer season. As you trudge along the bumpy shingle beach at Lepe and brace yourself against the inevitable wind, it's easy to imagine all the defence preparations made here from the time of Henry VIII right through to 1945; remnants of World War II demonstrate this area's importance in the lead-up to D-day (page 210).

Lepe was a departure point for troops, vehicles and supplies headed for France during World War II. Still in the water are concrete structures used in the construction of **Mulberry Harbours**, the prefabricated floating harbours towed to France as a means of re-supplying Allied troops. An excellent downloadable audio tour that chronicles Lepe's role in D-day, including interviews with soldiers who served, is available from the website.

Even on a windy day, you can tuck yourself up beneath the cliff, and enjoy the view of the Isle of Wight and one of the busiest shipping lanes in England. Above the beach, the grassy clifftop parkland is a particularly good vantage point for observing boats, especially during Cowes Regatta in mid August. Two barbecue areas with sea views are available for hire during the day, though they are popular so it's wise to book ahead (✆ 02380 899108).

Shelter from the often relentless wind can be found at **Lepe Point**, the clifftop area above the beach, which is a nature reserve. Behind the tall hedges that were planted to encourage wildflowers, small mammals and birds, you can walk in a flower garden that is usually at its best from June

OPERATION OVERLORD: LEPE'S ROLE IN D-DAY PREPARATION

On 6 June 1944, thousands of troops, many based on the New Forest coast, left Britain for the Normandy beaches. Temporary harbours, with sheltered water, piers and roadways, were towed across the English Channel to disembark troops, vehicles, weapons and supplies. These so-called **Mulberry Harbours** were constructed in the Beaulieu River and at Lepe and Marchwood. Some 176,000 men participated in Operation Overlord and 6,000 of those troops and their vehicles left from Lepe, and a number of physical reminders of Lepe's role in the preparation of this invasion can still be seen.

Today, Lepe Beach is a great place to watch sailboats and other pleasure craft. But on the approach to D-day, the view would have been of a huge flotilla of wartime ships. People who remember this time say that you almost could have walked from one shore to another across the decks of ships. In preparation, smaller vessels headed towards the Beaulieu River to wait for action. You can see the river entrance to the west of the beach, marked by red and green posts. Massive floating docks were assembled in the oyster beds of the river and towed out to join up with works at Lepe.

You can see a number of wartime markers by walking east on the beach for about half a mile from the car park. The most visible remnants are the tall wooden dolphins in the ocean, which formed part of the pier heads used to load ships. A bit further east is a D-day memorial and just inland and slightly

through summer. Also here is the Sensory Cottage Garden that hosts events during school holidays and is an interesting place to walk. There is a bird hide and boardwalk from where you might observe a variety of overwintering waders, ducks and geese. Bird Aware Solent (⏣ birdaware. org) runs occasional bird walks here. If you want a more formal trail than just walking along the beach, the **Lepe Loop** (downloadable from the website or on the NPA walking app) is a pleasant five-mile walk that covers coastline, fields and woods. The off-road cycle trail does pass along some small roadways but is a pleasant route through farmland and bridleways.

When you've exhausted yourself, you can return to the visitor centre and Lookout Café. The building is elevated 8ft above the sand in anticipation of what high-water level will be in 100 years' time. It's a reminder that storms are fierce here – the infamous Valentine's Day storm of 2014 took out the previous café. On a more optimistic note, the elevated position means there are great views. Food is simple and west of that is the brick base of a water tower, built to sustain the 700 construction workers stationed here to build the six Phoenix caissons, which were towed across the Channel and installed on the French coast. These enormous breakwaters were built against great odds: there was a shortage of materials and labour, and then of tugs to tow the completed piers. Because of the intense secrecy of the project, workers didn't even know what they were constructing. The caissons were launched sideways from this site and at low tide you can still see bits of the concrete ramps that were used.

It wasn't just construction activities that took place here. Near where you can see the environmental groynes extending off the coastline is where British and American troops practiced the Normandy landings. Troops were brought here from other parts of Britain to practice. At the top of the cliff above the beach, where pine trees provide shelter from the coastal winds, army encampments were hidden in the trees, where soldiers awaited instructions to leave for France. Troops were guarded carefully to ensure they didn't slip out and interact with locals and inadvertently give away the top-secret plans. The woods also sheltered amphibious vessels.

One of the most extraordinary elements of the wartime remains here is that none of them are protected. This means that at some point all of them will disappear or remain as fragmented bits of a distant war that no-one remembers first hand.

the wood-burning stove is a great place to warm up after a chilly beach walk. A digital information board displays a timeline of Lepe's history, from its role in the 1500s as a defensive point under Henry VIII, to becoming a fishing community and shipbuilding hub, and then its significant wartime role.

¶| FOOD & DRINK

The Lookout Lepe Country Park ⊙ Apr–Sep 09.00–17.00 daily; Oct–Mar 09.00–16.00. Straightforward café food, including children's options; dogs welcome. Great views of the Solent and Isle of Wight.

14 CALSHOT SPIT

🏠 **Luttrell's Tower** (page 224)

This mile-long stretch of shingle beach is a lovely place to walk, especially if you look out to sea, keeping the oil refinery towers behind you. You can walk all the way to Exbury (about seven miles), though you have to cut inland a few times, most notably after Luttrell's Tower where there is a private nature reserve and no public access. The huts at the western end of the beach have been here since the early 1900s when Calshot and Lepe were popular tourist destinations. Today, on the rare occasions when they come up for sale, they cost about £35,000.

Rocky **Calshot Beach** is popular with sailboard enthusiasts, sailors and kitesurfers, all of whom tend to be experienced because wind is generated both from the mainland and the Isle of Wight. It's a popular place to swim in summer although at low tide you have to walk out a fair way to find deep enough water. You can rent paddleboards and kayaks here, though you need to reserve ahead (✆ 02380 894000 ⌖ 24-7boardsports.com); international qualifications are needed in order to hire kitesurfing and windsurfing gear.

On the other side of the spit, towards the power station, is **Calshot Marshes** nature reserve, part of the Hythe to Calshot Site of Special Scientific Interest. Birds here don't seem to mind the industrial activity – according to Natural England the site has more than 10,000 waterfowl in winter, with more than 1% of the national winter population of wigeon, teal, ringed plover, black-tailed godwit and redshank residing here. The site is especially proud of its significant winter population of dark-bellied brent geese. The best time to visit is from winter until the spring migration period. Summertime residents are fewer but you are still likely to observe sedge warbler, reed warbler and lesser whitethroat.

"The site is especially proud of its significant winter population of dark-bellied brent geese."

This large, flat expanse of marshland bordered by the hangars of Calshot and the Fawley Refinery is not the prettiest nature reserve you'll ever visit but there's something oddly inspirational and life affirming in the waterfowl who nest in winter and late spring, seemingly oblivious to the industrial site bordering their refuge.

Calshot Castle
✆ 02380 892023; English Heritage

You'd be forgiven for thinking that Calshot Castle has disappeared as you drive along narrow Calshot Spit and only see ocean. But keep going and Henry VIII's tower is indeed there, tucked away behind the more recent Sunderland Hangar, built in 1917.

The Tudor fort has been modernised during its four centuries but remains today much as Henry designed it: a central three-storey keep surrounded by a courtyard, curtain wall and moat. This is a splendid castle for children; it's not usually crowded and its relatively small size makes it a wonderful space for play-acting. A walk all the way around the moat drives home just how small and yet how well-fortified this structure is. Calshot, like other forts built at this time, represents a change in English castle building, with its rounded walls designed to repel 16th-century cannon artillery, newly developed at that time.

The entrance is across a 19th-century bridge that replaced the original, which could be raised. On the first floor, the barracks have been furnished as they would have been in the late 19th century when matchboard panelling was installed over the stone walls. The room was only used in peacetime during exercises by the Royal Garrison Artillery. Although it was heated by a stove that connected to the original Tudor flue, it's easy to imagine how cold it might have been when the sea wind whipped around the round tower. The panel behind the stove opens to reveal the original Tudor fireplace and stone walls.

The stairs leading to the roof are steep and uneven. The effort of the climb is rewarded by a sweeping view of the Solent, the Isle of Wight beyond, and the colourful beach huts that line Calshot Beach and the vast Fawley Oil Refinery on the other side.

Despite never experiencing gunfire, Calshot is filled with wartime history. For over 400 years the castle remained a fully manned artillery base. In World War I, Calshot Naval Air Station opened and the site was used as a training base for pilots. During World War II, the RAF purchased Calshot Spit and closed the beach huts. The hangars at Calshot housed and repaired Sunderland flying boats, which were widely used during World War II. As recently as 2011, 87 World War II bombs washed up together on the beach and were detonated in controlled explosions.

Calshot Activities Centre
✆ 02380 892077 ⌖ hants.gov.uk/thingstodo/outdoorcentres
When the Royal Air Force station closed at Calshot, it left some empty hangars on prime coastal land. The largest, Sunderland Hangar, now contains an impressive sports centre run by Hampshire County Council that offers residential and non-residential courses in sailing, windsurfing, kayaking and canoeing.

HELEN HOTSON/S

DEREK TIPPETTS

PENNY HICKS/S

HELEN HOTSON/S

NEW FOREST DESTINATION PARTNERSHIP

DEREK TIPPETTS

It's a bit strange to come inside from the windy seafront and see people gingerly making their way down the dry ski slope that takes up a healthy portion of this huge indoor space. The other popular pursuit here is rock climbing, with all levels of tuition offered, and the chance to negotiate the bumps and hand-holds on one of the biggest climbing walls in the area. You can also take courses from beginner level upwards at the velodrome as well as sailing, windsurfing, canoeing, kayaking and powerboating, and boats can be launched for a fee. Most of the facilities are accessible only through joining a course or session but, if you can prove your experience, it's possible to book private group sessions for rock climbing and archery. During winter, there are open group recreational sessions on the indoor ski-slope, as well as ringo experiences (riding the slopes in an inflatable ring) – guaranteed to bring a smile, and no experience needed.

¶¶ FOOD & DRINK

The Café Calshot Activities Centre ✆ 02380 624729 ⟁ hants.gov.uk/thingstodo/ outdoorcentres ⟳ 09.30–17.30 daily. Sandwiches, snacks and coffee. The large windows overlook Southampton Water but the choice seating is outdoors in sunny weather. There is a soft-play area next door.

15 HYTHE

Just outside the boundaries of the New Forest, on the western shore of Southampton Water, is the village of Hythe. Its pedestrianised shopping area has an old-time village feeling and is spared a string of cloned high street shops. There is not much to do other than wander along the waterfront, have a coffee or ice cream and, for a little dip into Victorian times, ride the ferry. But isn't that an optimal Slow morning?

The **Hythe ferry** (⟁hytheferry.co.uk) operates regularly all day (less often in winter) across Southampton Water, between Hythe and Southampton Quay. The ferry service has been struggling for years so it is essential to check the website for updates. There is little on the other side (unless you want to have a very un-Slow shopping experience at the Southampton malls, for which you can take a bus from near the ferry landing) but the 25-minute round-trip is a refreshing way to appreciate

◀ **1** Beaulieu Millennium Beacon. **2** Colourful beach huts on the Solent at Calshot. **3** Eling Tide Mill. **4** Calshot Castle. **5** Windsurfing at Lepe. **6** D-day pier remains at Lepe Beach.

the importance of Southampton as a port city. The ferry passes the home berths of the big cruise ships, *Queen Victoria*, *Queen Mary 2* and *Queen Elizabeth*.

It's thought the Hythe ferry might date from AD400 when the Saxon word 'Hithe', meaning 'good landing place', was used to name the town. The pier, the seventh largest in the country, opened in 1881 and the **pier train** began running in 1922. The world's oldest continuously operating pier train, it was built during World War I and originally used in the Avonmouth mustard gas factory near Bristol. As the train rocks and shudders along the pier to the ferry, you can't help but feel as if you're travelling back in time. Be sure to ride one way and walk the other; the pier has interesting historical placards that you miss if you ride the train both ways. For a small fee, you can just walk on the pier without taking the ferry.

¶¶ FOOD & DRINK

Restaurant choices are limited in Hythe. If the weather is fine, the best option is to get fish and chips or a sandwich from one of the shops and sit on the grass in **Prospect Place**, a manicured, flowered, waterfront park just beyond the town centre. Alternatively, a short walk from the Hythe waterfront is **Hythe Marina**, a modern development that has pleasant views of the marina and Southampton Water beyond. The **Boathouse Restaurant** (29 Shamrock Wy, SO45 6DY ✐ 02380 844066 ⬙ boathousehythe.co.uk) a convivial café, is popular for its large glass windows and terrace overlooking the marina.

16 ELING

Ten miles west of Southampton across the River Test lies the charming village of Eling. In a quaint (or annoying, depending on your perspective) nod to the past, a small toll is collected for every car that passes from Totton to Eling over Bartley Water, the small waterway that divides the two towns. The Eling Tide Mill's free car park is on the Eling side of the bridge, about six miles north of Hythe, so you don't have to pay the fee if you approach from this direction.

Eling's history pre-dates the Bronze Age and is linked with shipbuilding. By analysing fragments of charcoal and pollen grains found at nearby Testwood Lakes, archaeologists have determined that Stone Age people lived among willow trees and that the current virtually treeless landscape was created by humans over 4,000 years ago. Its ultimate Slow attraction harnesses the power of the tide: the **Eling Tide**

Mill ($\mathscr{O}$ 02380 869575 $\mathscr{O}$ elingexperience.co.uk; $\bigcirc$ Apr–Sep 10.00–17.00 Wed–Sun; Oct–Mar 11.00–16.00 Sat & Sun) is one of the few tide mills in the world still producing flour on a regular basis. A mill has been on this site for over 900 years; the present building, constructed in the 1700s, fell into disrepair in the 1940s but was restored by New Forest District Council and volunteers in 1975.

Try to visit when the mill is grinding, though this can be unpredictable because operations depend on the tide being in just the right place during opening hours. The mill pond needs to be full and the water on the other side needs to be just low enough to enable the wheel to turn; check the website or call in advance to check how it's running when you want to visit. Guided tours are available for groups of ten or more.

If you are lucky enough to stand beneath the low ceilings of the restored mill and watch the massive stone wheels turning with the force of the water, you'll appreciate the effort that went into food production in days gone by. Flour is ground as it would have been done hundreds of years ago, with grains straight between the millstones. The mill produces two flours, one of which, Flour of the Forest, holds a New Forest Marque because it is milled from grain grown a few miles away in the New Forest. You can buy the freshly ground flour in the on-site shop and at Sunnyfields Farm Shop in Totton (page 218).

Across the street from the mill, the **Visitor Centre** tells the story of 900 years of mill history and Eling as a centre of milling. There is also an explanation of how flour develops from wheat and fun, interactive displays that demonstrate how the mill works. The on-site café serves sandwiches and cakes – some of which are baked with flour from the mill.

"Benches provide the perfect spot to sit and watch the rhythmic, mechanised unloading of ships."

Just by the toll house is an entrance to the **riverside walk**, developed by local councils and volunteers, a pleasant two-mile stroll along a creekside path on boardwalks over the marsh. The route takes you past the millpond where you might see nesting swans, and across the road to Goatee Beach where you have a view over the local SSSI and also a contrasting look towards Southampton's container port. Benches provide the perfect spot to sit and watch the rhythmic, mechanised unloading of ships. Then it's on to St Mary's Church and back to **Eling Toll Bridge**.

🍴 FOOD & DRINK

Sunnyfields Farm Jacobs Gutter Ln, Totton SO40 9FX ⬡ sunnyfields.co.uk. Don't be put off by the somewhat industrial approach to Sunnyfields Farm Shop. It's a working farm and a busy one with lots of vehicles, equipment and sometimes mud. But the expansive farm shop stocks a great selection of vegetables, meat and environmentally friendly products, including sustainable refill items. Food is available from the on-site kitchen, butchery and bakery, and on Thursdays there is a fish van. The shop also stocks frozen meals from Cook, the socially and environmentally conscious packaged meal company. Sunnyfields hosts seasonal events and are best known for Pumpkin Time, an annual October pumpkin pick. Kids love pushing wheelbarrows around to select pumpkins to take home.

17 TESTWOOD LAKES & LOWER TEST NATURE RESERVES

Testwood Lakes Nature Reserve Brunel Rd, Totton SO40 3YD ✆ 02380 667929 ⬡ hiwwt. org.uk. ⊙ Car park summer 08.00–17.00 daily; winter 08.00–16.00 daily; **Lower Test Nature Reserve** Stirling Cres, Totton SO40 3BR ✆ 02380 667919; ⬡ hiwwt.org.uk

Testwood Lakes and Lower Test are two nature reserves managed by the Hampshire & Isle of Wight Wildlife Trust, located just one mile apart but with very different personalities. The Lakes is a more structured environment with bird hides and walks close to the education centre, while the Lower Test has more remote trails through the reserve.

"Imposing electrical pylons bisect the marshland yet cows graze and birds swoop over the flowers at their bases in summer."

Testwood Lakes Nature Reserve is part of Southern Water's reservoir to supply the Isle of Wight and other local areas. The 150-acre reserve is a mix of lakes, grassland and woodland with surfaced paths and bird hides. It's very popular with birdwatchers, local dog walkers and families; you can enjoy a pleasant short walk around Testwood Lake and Little Testwood Lake on your own or join one of the many organised sessions (see website) that engage youngsters in learning about birds, dragonflies, butterflies and bees. Note that some paths regularly flood in winter, and dogs are not permitted in all areas. Little Testwood Lake is a coarse fishery with rudd, roach, chubb, tench and bream. Day tickets are available from The Army Surplus Shop in Totton (43 Rumbridge Street). There's a busy education centre that hosts school and adult groups, and which is sometimes open to the public; check website for details.

BRACKEN CONTROL

Bracken is one of the most prolific plants in the Forest and can serve as protection for mushrooms, bluebells and wild gladioli. Although not harmful in itself, if left uncontrolled it will crowd out other important species, including heather and grasses.

The National Trust controls bracken using several methods. 'Sometimes spraying is the only effective means, but we are looking for an organic product that doesn't damage the surrounding area,' explained Dylan Everett, New Forest Operations Manager. 'Cutting is effective but needs to be done when ground-nesting birds are not present. Rolling with a machine is good because it bruises the stems and bleeds the sap so that in subsequent years, crops are lower and less thick, allowing other species to thrive. Where possible, we harvest the bracken, bale it, and try our best to reuse it as compost. In the past, commoners used every resource in the Forest and we want to do the same.'

Lower Test Nature Reserve has a much wilder atmosphere, and is predominantly frequented by birdwatching groups and serious nature observers. The 400-acre designated Site of Specific Scientific Interest (SSSI) supports about 500 species of vascular plants, which is about a quarter of the British total. A very good **self-guided trail** can be downloaded from the website. This five-mile walk covers a variety of terrain including country lanes, wooded paths, fields, marshland and, unavoidably, an industrial estate. The River Test snakes directly through the centre of the reserve and, as you walk through the large reed bed, created where the river begins to mix with the sea, you are very likely to find yourself alone with birds that might include, depending on the time of year, reed and sedge warblers, sand martins, swallows and – if you're lucky – ospreys and marsh harriers. It's an odd but strangely satisfying juxtaposition of two very busy worlds: in the background is the ever-present hum of the M27 but at your feet are chirping birds and grasses that gently swish in the breeze. Imposing electrical pylons bisect the marshland yet cows graze and birds swoop over the flowers at their bases in summer. It's pleasing to see this flourishing hidden world amid a landscape that might easily have been dismissed as an industrial void. And the reserve's urban location gives it a highly unusual distinction: this is one of the only places in southern England where you have the gradual transition from saltmarsh to brackenish grassland to neutral. At most seaside sites, there is a sea wall obstructing that gradual transition.

Several words of caution: because the Lower Test is tidal, footpaths and boardwalks can flood. After heavy rains, wear proper wet-weather boots or waders if you want to assure dry feet. Although part of the self-guided walk passes through Calmore Industrial Estate, which provides a harsh contrast to the peace of the wetlands, it is only a short section and very soon you're back in a field.

Lower Test does have a few **organised walks** during the year, usually in spring and summer, and a bird walk in winter. There is parking for a few cars in Testwood Lane by the Salmon Leap pub or at Old Redbridges, a lay-by on the A36 between Totton and Southampton. Use these car parks to visit the hide in the south of the reserve. You can also park at Testwood Lakes and walk along picturesque Mill Lane to access the reserve, which takes about 20 minutes; this is part of the self-guided walk available from the website.

Adventures in Britain

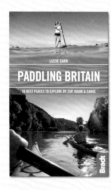

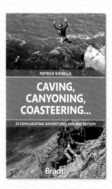

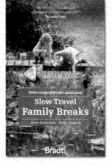

Bradt GUIDES

TRAVEL TAKEN SERIOUSLY

bradtguides.com/shop

BradtGuides   @BradtGuides   @bradtguides

ACCOMMODATION

The accommodation listed in this section is just a sampling of the many available offerings. This is not a comprehensive list; there are many delightful options that I have not included and where I would happily stay. I've chosen to list those that I feel reflect the Slow philosophy in some way, whether it's through commitment to the environment, a particularly lovely or convenient setting or a proprietor especially dedicated to their guests.

Because the New Forest is relatively small, there is some geographical overlap. So a lodging establishment or campsite can be just about the same distance from a town that's listed in a different chapter. With that in mind, peruse all three chapters when you are choosing a place to stay; don't assume that these are rigid location guidelines.

The accommodation featured in this section are listed in the guide chapters under the heading for the nearest town of village. Hotels and B&Bs are indicated by 🏠, self-catering by 🏡 and campsites by ⛺. For more information and longer reviews, go to ⟁ bradtguides.com/newforest.

1 THE NORTH & WEST

Hotels
The Bell Inn Roger Penny Wy, Brook SO43 7HE ⟁ 02380 812214 ⟁ bellinn-newforest.co.uk. The closest hotel to the north region of the Forest, although equally suited to the Lyndhurst area. Standard, fairly small modernised rooms housed within an 18th-century coaching inn.

B&Bs
The Three Lions Stuckton, nr Fordingbridge SP6 2HF ⟁ 01425 652489 ⟁ thethreelionsrestaurant.co.uk. Six fairly standard rooms grouped around a pleasant courtyard with outdoor seating. Three of the six rooms have hot tubs in a small private courtyard.

Self-catering
New Forest Shepherd's Huts The Royal Oak, Fritham SO43 7HJ ⟁ 07464 545428 ⟁ newforestshepherdshuts.co.uk. Three huts on the grounds of one of the Forest's best-loved pubs.

Newton Farmhouse Southampton Rd, Whiteparish SP5 2QL ⟁ 01794 884416 ⟁ newtonfarmhouse.com. A spacious, self-contained holiday cottage with full kitchen and two small studios with shared entrance and kitchenettes. Ideal location for those who want to explore both Salisbury and the New Forest.

Sandy Balls Godshill SP6 2JZ ⟁ 0844 693 2949 ⟁ sandyballs.co.uk. Family holiday centre located in a particularly beautiful part of the Forest. On-site cycle hire for guests.

Undercastle Cottage Woodgreen 🖉 01747 828170 ⌂ hideaways.co.uk (property number H211). Idyllic thatched cottage on banks of River Avon.

Camping

Harry's Field Abbotswell Rd, Frogham SP6 2JA 🖉 07476 988855 ⌂ newforestcampsite.com ☉ May bank hol w/e & mid-Jul–Aug w/e. Small family-run campsite with a convivial atmosphere in a flat field with shower block.

2 THE SOUTHWEST BROCKENHURST & THE LYMINGTON COAST

Hotels

Cottage Lodge Sway Rd, Brockenhurst SO42 7SH 🖉 01590 622296 ⌂ cottagelodge. co.uk. Quirky, low-key hotel run by charming, experienced hosts, within walking distance from Brockenhurst station. Eco-friendly measures abound; some of the 16 bedrooms have hand-carved furniture. Family rooms available.

The Manor at Sway Station Rd , Sway SO41 6BA 🖉 01590 682 754 ⌂ themanoratsway. com. Renovated Edwardian house with beautiful gardens, an easy walk from Sway station.

The Old Mill Silver St, Hordle SO41 6DJ 🖉 01590 683073 ⌂ theoldmillnewforest. co.uk An 18th-century mill house with beautiful gardens and a creek-side location, three miles from Lymington.

The Pig Beaulieu Rd, Brockenhurst SO42 7QL 🖉 01590 622354 ⌂ thepighotel.com. Chic, relaxed hotel just outside of Brockenhurst. The first in what has now become a litter of Pigs across the southwest. Great setting, wonderful bar and comfortable rooms.

B&B

Vinegar Hill B&B Vinegar Hill, Milford on Sea SO41 0RZ 🖉 01590 642979

⌂ vinegarhillpottery.co.uk. Good, old-fashioned B&B attached to a pottery studio (page 143), run by a delightful couple.

Self-catering

Upper Kingston Farm Cottages Upper Kingston, Ringwood BH24 3BX 🖉 01425 474466 ⌂ upperkingstonfarmcottages.co.uk. A working farm with clean, spacious self-catering accommodation, two miles from Ringwood.

Warborne Farm Warborne Ln, Boldre SO41 5QD ⌂ warbornefarm.co.uk. Just a mile from Lymington, this is an incredibly special spot offering eco-friendly comfort on a working farm. Highly recommended and brilliant for children.

Wilf's Cabin Burley BH24 4HT 🖉 01425 403735 ⌂ burleyrailscottage.co.uk. Extremely unusual opportunity to stay inside an inclosure within the Forest. Warm hospitality and your horse can stay too. Delightful proprietors.

Camping & glamping

Aldridge Hill Campsite Rhinefield Rd, Brockenhurst SO42 7QD 🖉 01590 623152 ⌂ campinginthenewforest.com ☉ Summer only. A particularly pretty Forest campsite just two miles from the centre of Brockenhurst. No toilets, showers or electricity.

Fernwood Glamping Ringwood BH24 3JN 🖉 07730 586601 ⌂ fernwood-ringwood. co.uk. A stand-out in the glamping scene, partly because of hostess, Rachel. Immaculate shepherd's hut and caravan with every detail considered. Highly recommended.

Long Meadow Campsite New Park, Brockenhurst SO42 7QH 🖉 01590 622489 ⌂ longmeadowcampsite.com ☉ Mar–Oct. Large field in a central location with lots of space to run around and all facilities. Glamping bell tents available.

Red Shoot Camping Park Linwood BH24 3QT 🖉 01425 473789 ⌂ redshoot-campingpark. com. Very family orientated, busy campsite with a shop, electrical hook-ups and a pub right next door.

Roundhill Caravan & Camping Site Beaulieu
Rd, Brockenhurst SO42 7QL ✆ 01590 624344
⌖ campinginthenewforest.com ☺ Apr–Sep.
Lovely location east of Brockenhurst with good
family biking on doorstep. No toilets or showers.

3 LYNDHURST, BEAULIEU & THE EAST

Hotels

Lime Wood Hotel Beaulieu Rd, Lyndhurst SO43
7FZ ✆ 02380 287177 ⌖ limewoodhotel.co.uk.
One of the top destination hotels in the area. This
former Georgian country home is the ultimate in
luxury for its spa, cuisine and plush furnishings.
Located just 1½ miles from Lyndhurst with easy
access to open Forest.

Master Builder's House Buckler's Hard SO42
7XB ✆ 01590 616253 ⌖ hillbrookehotels.
co.uk. Part of the former ship-building village of
Buckler's Hard, on the Beaulieu River. The main
hotel was the home of the master shipbuilder,
Henry Adams and has characterful rooms. The
modern extension has standard rooms but you
still get the fun of having the hamlet to yourself
when daytime visitors go home.

Spot in the Woods 174 Woodlands Rd,
Woodlands SO40 7GL ✆ 02380 293784
⌖ spotinthewoods.co.uk. Low-key hotel in the
east/central Forest that feels like home.

B&Bs

Angels Farm Pottery Pinkney Ln, Lyndhurst
SO43 7FE ✆ 02380 284079 ⌖ angelsfarm.co.uk.
A charming B&B with pottery studio, just outside
of Lyndhurst.

East End Arms Main Rd, East End SO41 5SY
✆ 01590 626223 ⌖ eastendarms.co.uk.

Standard hotel rooms above a delightful pub
in a beautiful location three miles east of
Lymington and about five miles southwest of
Buckler's Hard.

Penny Farthing Hotel Romsey Rd,
Lyndhurst SO43 7AA ✆ 02380 284422
⌖ pennyfarthinghotel.co.uk. No nonsense B&B
and self-catering rooms in Lyndhurst.

Self-catering

Countryside Education Trust Palace Ln,
Beaulieu SO42 7YG ⌖ cet.org.uk. An opportunity
to stay on a working farm just outside of
Beaulieu. Ideal for groups, particularly families
travelling together, with four family rooms
with bunk beds and a commercial-size kitchen.
Shared bathrooms for each wing.

Luttrell's Tower Eaglehurst, Fawley SO41 1AA
⌖ landmarktrust.org.uk. Quirky lodging for four
in a tower that overlooks the Solent.

Camping & glamping

Acres Down Farm Minstead SO43 7GE
✆ 023808 13693 ⌖ acresdownfarm.co.uk. Basic
camping facilities on a commoner's farm, three
miles west of Lyndhurst.

Ashurst Caravan and Camping Site
Lyndhurst Rd, SO40 7AR ✆ 01590 631641
⌖ campinginthenewforest.com ☺ Apr–Sep. A
large campsite with showers and toilet blocks,
close to Ashurst train station.

Lepe Beach Campsite Lepe Rd, SO45 1AD
✆ 0330 1000 842 ⌖ eazycamp.co.uk ☺ May
half-term & early Jul–Aug. One of the very
few campsites in the New Forest area with a
water view. Basic tent-only campsite; bell tents
available. Toilets and showers, and campfires are
allowed. No electricity.

NOTES

INDEX

Entries in **bold** refer to major entries; those in *italics* refer to maps.

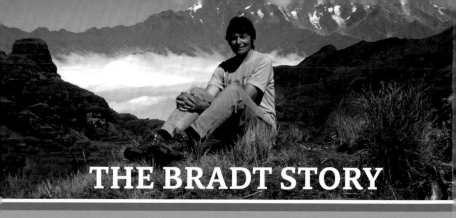

THE BRADT STORY

In the beginning
It all began in 1974 on an Amazon river barge. During an 18-month trip through South America, two adventurous young backpackers – Hilary Bradt and her then husband, George – decided to write about the hiking trails they had discovered through the Andes. *Backpacking Along Ancient Ways in Peru and Bolivia* included the very first descriptions of the Inca Trail. It was the start of a colourful journey to becoming one of the best-loved travel publishers in the world; you can read the full story on our website (bradtguides.com/ourstory).

Getting there first
Hilary quickly gained a reputation for being a true travel pioneer, and in the 1980s she started to focus on guides to places overlooked by other publishers. The Bradt Guides list became a roll call of guidebook 'firsts'. We published the first guide to Madagascar, followed by Mauritius, Czechoslovakia and Vietnam. The 1990s saw the beginning of our extensive coverage of Africa: Tanzania, Uganda, South Africa, and Eritrea. Later, post-conflict guides became a feature: Rwanda, Mozambique, Angola, and Sierra Leone, as well as the first standalone guides to the Baltic States following the fall of the Iron Curtain, and the first post-war guides to Bosnia, Kosovo and Albania.

Comprehensive – and with a conscience
Today, we are the world's largest independently owned travel publisher, with more than 200 titles. However, our ethos remains unchanged. Hilary is still keenly involved, and **we still get there first**: two-thirds of Bradt guides have no direct competition.

But we don't just get there first. Our guides are also known for being **more comprehensive** than any other series. We avoid templates and tick-lists. Each guide is a one-of-a-kind expression of an expert author's interests, knowledge and enthusiasm for telling it how it really is.

And a commitment to wildlife, conservation and respect for local communities has always been at the heart of our books. Bradt Guides was **championing sustainable travel** before any other guidebook publisher. We even have a series dedicated to Slow Travel in the UK, award-winning books that explore the country with a passion and depth you'll find nowhere else.

Thank you!
We can only do what we do because of the support of readers like you – people who value less-obvious experiences, less-visited places and a more thoughtful approach to travel. Those who, like us, take travel seriously.

Bradt GUIDES

TRAVEL TAKEN SERIOUSLY